DAVID BUSCH'S CANON® EOS REBEL® XS/1000D

GUIDE TO DIGITAL SLR PHOTOGRAPHY

David D. Busch

Course Technology PTR

A part of Cengage Learning

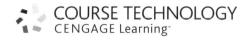

COURSE TECHNOLOGY
CENGAGE Learning™

Australia, Brazil, Japan, Korea, Mexico, Singapore, Spain, United Kingdom, United States

COURSE TECHNOLOGY
CENGAGE Learning™

**David Busch's Canon® EOS Rebel®
XS/1000D Guide to Digital SLR
Photography**
David D. Busch

**Publisher and General Manager, Course
Technology PTR:**
Stacy L. Hiquet

Associate Director of Marketing:
Sarah Panella

Manager of Editorial Services:
Heather Talbot

Marketing Manager:
Jordan Casey

Executive Editor:
Kevin Harreld

Project Editor:
Jenny Davidson

Technical Reviewer:
Michael D. Sullivan

PTR Editorial Services Coordinator:
Jen Blaney

Interior Layout Tech:
Bill Hartman

Cover Designer:
Mike Tanamachi

Indexer:
Katherine Stimson

Proofreader:
Sara Gullion

For product information and technology assistance, contact us at
Cengage Learning Customer & Sales Support Center, 1-800-354-9706

For permission to use material from this text or product,
submit all requests online at **cengage.com/permissions**.
Further permissions questions can be emailed to
permissionrequest@cengage.com

Canon and EOS Rebel XS/1000D are registered trademarks of Canon, Inc.
in the United States and/or other countries. All other trademarks are the
property of their respective owners.

Library of Congress Control Number: 2008939961

ISBN-13: 978-1-59863-903-2

ISBN-10: 1-59863-903-X

Course Technology, a part of Cengage Learning
20 Channel Center Street
Boston, MA 02210
USA

Cengage Learning is a leading provider of customized learning solutions
with office locations around the globe, including Singapore, the United
Kingdom, Australia, Mexico, Brazil, and Japan. Locate your local office at:
international.cengage.com/region

Cengage Learning products are represented in Canada by Nelson
Education, Ltd.

For your lifelong learning solutions, visit **courseptr.com**

Visit our corporate website at **cengage.com**

Printed in the United States of America
1 2 3 4 5 6 7 11 10 09

For Cathy

Acknowledgments

Once again, thanks to the folks at Course Technology PTR, who have pioneered publishing digital imaging books in full color at a price anyone can afford. Special thanks to executive editor Kevin Harreld, who always gives me the freedom to let my imagination run free with a topic, as well as my veteran production team including project editor Jenny Davidson and technical editor Mike Sullivan. Also thanks to Bill Hartman, layout; Katherine Stimson, indexing; Sara Gullion, proofreading; Mike Tanamachi, cover design; and my agent, Carole McClendon, who has the amazing ability to keep both publishers and authors happy.

About the Author

With more than a million books in print, **David D. Busch** is one of the best-selling authors of books on digital photography and imaging technology, and the originator of popular series like *David Busch's Pro Secrets* and *David Busch's Quick Snap Guides.* He has written seven hugely successful guidebooks for Canon digital SLR models, including the all-time #1 best-seller for the Canon EOS 40D, additional user guides for other camera models, as well as many popular books devoted to dSLRs, including *Mastering Digital SLR Photography, Second Edition* and *Digital SLR Pro Secrets.* As a roving photojournalist for more than 20 years, he illustrated his books, magazine articles, and newspaper reports with award-winning images. He's operated his own commercial studio, suffocated in formal dress while shooting weddings-for-hire, and shot sports for a daily newspaper and upstate New York college. His photos have been published in magazines as diverse as *Scientific American* and *Petersen's PhotoGraphic*, and his articles have appeared in *Popular Photography & Imaging, The Rangefinder, The Professional Photographer*, and hundreds of other publications. He's also reviewed dozens of digital cameras for CNet and *Computer Shopper.*

When About.com named its top five books on Beginning Digital Photography, debuting at the #1 and #2 slots were Busch's *Digital Photography All-In-One Desk Reference for Dummies* and *Mastering Digital Photography.* During the past year, he's had as many as five of his books listed in the Top 20 of Amazon.com's Digital Photography Bestseller list—simultaneously! Busch's 100-plus other books published since 1983 include best-sellers like *David Busch's Quick Snap Guide to Digital SLR Lenses.*

Busch is a member of the Cleveland Photographic Society (www.clevelandphoto.org), which has operated continuously since 1887. Visit his website at http://www.dslrguides.com.

Contents

Chapter 3
Setting Up Your Canon EOS Rebel XS   45

Chapter 4
Getting the Right Exposure   97

Chapter 5
Advanced Techniques for Your Canon EOS
Rebel XS   125

Chapter 6
Working with Lenses   167

Chapter 7
Making Light Work for You   199

Chapter 8
Downloading and Editing Your Images   227

Chapter 9
Canon EOS Rebel XS: Troubleshooting and Prevention   251

Glossary   275

Index   287

Preface

You don't want good pictures from your new Canon EOS Rebel XS—you demand *outstanding* photos. After all, the Rebel XS is the most advanced low-cost, entry-level camera that Canon has ever introduced. It boasts more than 10 megapixels of resolution, blazing fast automatic focus, and cool new features like the real-time preview system called Live View. But your gateway to pixel proficiency is dragged down by the slim little book included in the box as a manual. You know everything you need to know is in there, somewhere, but you don't know where to start. In addition, the camera manual doesn't offer much information on photography or digital photography. Nor are you interested in spending hours or days studying a comprehensive book on digital SLR photography that doesn't necessarily apply directly to your XS.

What you need is a guide that explains the purpose and function of the XS's basic controls, how you should use them, and *why*. Ideally, there should be information about file formats, resolution, aperture/priority exposure, and special autofocus modes available, but you'd prefer to read about those topics only after you've had the chance to go out and take a few hundred great pictures with your new camera. Why isn't there a book that summarizes the most important information in its first two or three chapters, with lots of illustrations showing what your results will look like when you use this setting or that?

Now there is such a book. If you want a quick introduction to the XS's focus controls, flash synchronization options, how to choose lenses, or which exposure modes are best, this book is for you. If you can't decide on what basic settings to use with your camera because you can't figure out how changing ISO or white balance or focus defaults will affect your pictures, you need this guide.

Introduction

Canon has done it again! It's packaged up many of the most alluring features of its advanced digital SLRs and stuffed them into a compact, highly affordable body called the EOS Rebel XS (known as the EOS 1000D in some countries). Your new camera is loaded with capabilities that few would have expected to find in an "entry-level" dSLR. Indeed, the XS retains the ease of use that smoothes the transition for those new to digital photography. For those just dipping their toes into the digital pond, the experience is warm and inviting. The Rebel XS/1000D isn't a snapshot camera—it's a point-and-shoot (if you want to use it in that mode) for the thinking photographer.

Nor will you easily outgrow this camera. It has 10 megapixels of resolution, autofocus that's improved over its predecessor Digital Rebel XTi, and many customization options. Canon must love fledgling photographers, because it seems to work extra hard to give them incredible value for their money.

But once you've confirmed that you made a wise purchase, the question comes up, *how do I use this thing?* All those cool features can be mind-numbing to learn, if all you have as a guide is the manual furnished with the camera. Help is on the way. I sincerely believe that this book is your best bet for learning how to use your new camera, and for learning how to use it well.

If you're a Canon EOS Rebel XS owner who's looking to learn more about how to use this great camera, you've probably already explored your options. There are DVDs and online tutorials—but who can learn how to use a camera by sitting in front of a television or computer screen? Do you want to watch a movie or click on HTML links, or do you want to go out and take photos with your camera? Videos are fun, but not the best answer.

There's always the manual furnished with the XS. It's compact and filled with information, but there's really very little about *why* you should use particular settings or features, and its organization may make it difficult to find what you need. Multiple cross-references may send you flipping back and forth between two or three sections of the book to find what you want to know. The basic manual is also hobbled by black-and-white line drawings and tiny monochrome pictures that aren't very good examples of what you can do.

Also available are third-party guides to the XS, like this one. I haven't been happy with some of these guidebooks, which is why I wrote this one. The existing books range from skimpy and illustrated by black-and-white photos to lushly illustrated in full color but too generic to do much good. Photography instruction is useful, but it needs to be related directly to the Canon EOS Rebel XS as much as possible.

I've tried to make *David Busch's Canon EOS Rebel XS/1000D Guide to Digital SLR Photography* different from your other XS learn-up options. The roadmap sections use larger, color pictures to show you where all the buttons and dials are, and the explanations of what they do are longer and more comprehensive. I've tried to avoid overly general advice, including the two-page checklists on how to take a "sports picture" or a "portrait picture" or a "travel picture." Instead, you'll find tips and techniques for using all the features of your Canon EOS Rebel XS to take *any kind of picture* you want. If you want to know where you should stand to take a picture of a quarterback dropping back to unleash a pass, there are plenty of books that will tell you that. This one concentrates on teaching you how to select the best autofocus mode, shutter speed, f/stop, or flash capability to take, say, a great sports picture under any conditions.

David Busch's Canon EOS Rebel XS/1000D Guide to Digital SLR Photography is aimed at both Canon and dSLR veterans as well as newcomers to digital photography and digital SLRs. Both groups can be overwhelmed by the options the XS offers, while underwhelmed by the explanations they receive in their user's manual. The manuals are great if you already know what you don't know, and you can find an answer somewhere in a booklet arranged by menu listings and written by a camera vendor employee who last threw together instructions on how to operate a camcorder.

What's Different about the Rebel XS— and This Book?

What makes the EOS Rebel XS so cool is that it has virtually all of the features of its slightly more expensive cousin, the Rebel XSi/450D. For a little less money than you'd pay for the XSi, you can buy a fully featured camera, giving up only some of the capabilities of the older model. I know there are many of you who have purchased both the XSi and XS, with one camera used as a main camera and the second as a backup or, perhaps, sharing both cameras within a family.

So, in a nutshell, here are the basic differences between the two:

- **Slightly lower resolution.** XS has 10.2 megapixels of resolution, rather than 12.2 megapixels, like the XSi.

- **No IR remote.** The Rebel XS lacks the XSi's infrared sensor on the handgrip, and so you must use an optional plug-in remote control instead.

- **No eyepiece "sensor."** The XS does not have a Proximity Sensor just below the viewfinder eyepiece. On the XSi, this sensor serves to turn the back-panel LCD on or off when you bring the camera to your eye, or remove it from your eye.

- **Seven focus zones.** The XS has 7 focus zones to capture autofocus information, rather than 9 points, as found on the XSi.

- **No spot metering.** XS does not have Spot metering mode to zero in on a very small area of the frame for measuring exposure. Its Partial mode operates in much the same way, though, but with a slightly larger measuring area.

- **Imperceptibly slower burst mode.** The Rebel XS's top continuous "burst" mode is 3.0 frames per second, rather than 3.5, as found on the XSi.

- **No highlight boost.** XS does not have Highlight Tone Priority mode, which, on the XSi, helps improve detail in the brightest portion of the image when shooting scenes with very high contrast.

- **Less viewfinder magnification.** XS viewfinder magnification is .81X life size, rather than .87X, giving you a slightly reduced size view.

- **Smaller LCD.** The Rebel XS has a large 2.5-inch back panel LCD, instead of a huge, 3-inch screen.

- **Less weight.** The XS is a tad lighter at 1.1 lb, roughly 1.6 ounces lighter than the Rebel XSi. The other dimensions of the cameras are identical. The XSi does have textured rubber on some gripping surfaces, while the XS is clad entirely in tough polycarbonate.

You can see that, given all the great features that the Rebel XSi and XS share, the differences are slight. This similarity created an interesting situation when I was finishing up my most recent Rebel guidebook, *David Busch's Canon EOS Rebel XSi/450D Guide to Digital SLR Photography*. I had just wound up that book, but it hadn't yet been prepared for the printer when the XS was announced. I could see from the specifications that the XS was, in most respects, identical to the XSi. Should I revise my Rebel XSi book to include the features of the XS, and end up with a single book devoted to both cameras?

The decision was made not to do that. Even when two cameras are very similar, a guidebook designed to do double-duty is necessarily filled with distracting advice along the lines of, "If you have *this* version, do this, but if you have *that* version, do this other thing." Plus, it's always nice for a new owner to have a book that refers only to the product that he or she owns. I know that I certainly wasted a lot of time trying to figure out the "up-convert" feature of my new DVD player, because the manual didn't point out that my particular model didn't offer that capability.

So, you Canon EOS Rebel XS owners get your own book, devoted solely to your own camera. (But for the sake of those who own both, or who are curious, I will point out, from time to time a feature or two found on the Rebel XSi, but not the XS, just for perspective.)

Even so, I do have one warning: if you own the XSi *and* the XS, you do not need to buy both of my books. Much of the material, especially pertaining to shared features, is the same in both. I've freshened this book up with many new illustrations, and have upgraded many descriptions to take advantage of things I've learned since I wrote the original book for the Rebel XSi. But the cameras are so similar that the same basic descriptions of features, and how to use them, works for both. This approach does mean that you don't have to sort through dual XSi/XS text: this book is expressly for *you*.

Of course, once you've read this book and are ready to learn more, I hope you pick up one of my other guides to digital SLR photography. Four of them are offered by Course Technology PTR, each approaching the topic from a different perspective. They include:

Quick Snap Guide to Digital SLR Photography

Consider this a prequel to the book you're holding in your hands. It might make a good gift for a spouse or friend who may be using your XS, but who lacks even basic knowledge about digital photography, digital SLR photography, and Canon EOS photography. It serves as an introduction that summarizes the basic features of digital SLR cameras in general (not just the XS), and what settings to use and when, such as continuous autofocus/single autofocus, aperture/shutter priority, EV settings, and so forth. The guide also includes recipes for shooting the most common kinds of pictures, with step-by-step instructions for capturing effective sports photos, portraits, landscapes, and other types of images.

David Busch's Quick Snap Guide to Using Digital SLR Lenses

A bit overwhelmed by the features and controls of digital SLR lenses, and not quite sure when to use each type? This book explains lenses, their use, and lens technology in easy-to-access two- and four-page spreads, each devoted to a different topic, such as depth-of-field, lens aberrations, or using zoom lenses. If you have a friend or significant other who is less versed in photography, but who wants to borrow and use your Canon EOS Rebel XS from time to time, this book can save you a ton of explanation.

David Busch's Quick Snap Guide to Lighting

This book tells you everything you need to know about using light to create the kind of images you'll be proud of. It's not Canon-specific, and doesn't include any details on using any of the three Canon dedicated flash units, but the information you'll find applies to any digital SLR photography.

Mastering Digital SLR Photography, Second Edition

This book is an introduction to digital SLR photography, with nuts-and-bolts explanations of the technology, more in-depth coverage of settings, and whole chapters on the most common types of photography. While not specific to the Rebel XS, this book can show you how to get more from its capabilities.

Digital SLR Pro Secrets

This is my more advanced guide to dSLR photography with greater depth and detail about the topics you're most interested in. If you've already mastered the basics in *Mastering Digital SLR Photography*, this book will take you to the next level.

Why the Canon EOS Rebel XS Needs Special Coverage

There are many general digital photography books on the market. Why do I concentrate on books about specific digital SLRs like the Rebel XS? One reason is that I feel dSLRs are the wave of the future for serious photographers, and those who join the ranks of digital photographers with single lens reflex cameras deserve books tailored to their equipment.

When I started writing digital photography books in 1995, digital SLRs cost $30,000 and few people other than certain professionals could justify them. Most of my readers a dozen years ago were stuck using the point-and-shoot low-resolution digital cameras of the time—even if they were advanced photographers. I myself took tons of digital pictures with an Epson digital camera with 1024 × 768 (less than 1 megapixel!) resolution, and which cost $500.

As recently as 2003 (before the original Digital Rebel was introduced), the lowest-cost dSLRs were priced at $3,000 or more. Today, anyone with around $600 can afford one of these basic cameras, and around $800 buys you a sophisticated model like the Canon EOS Rebel XS (with lens). The digital SLR is no longer the exclusive bailiwick of the professional, the wealthy, or the serious photography addict willing to scrimp and save to acquire a dream camera. Digital SLRs have become the favored camera for anyone who wants to go beyond point-and-shoot capabilities. And Canon cameras have enjoyed a dominating position among digital SLRs because of Canon's innovation in introducing affordable cameras with interesting features and outstanding performance (particularly in the area of high ISO image quality). It doesn't hurt that Canon also provides both full-frame and smaller format digital cameras and a clear migration path between them (if you stick to the Canon EF lenses that are compatible with both).

You've selected your camera of choice, and you belong in the Canon camp if you fall into one of the following categories:

- Individuals who want to get better pictures, or perhaps transform their growing interest in photography into a full-fledged hobby or artistic outlet with a Canon XS and advanced techniques.

- Those who want to produce more professional-looking images for their personal or business website, and feel that the Rebel XS will give them more control and capabilities.

- Small business owners with more advanced graphics capabilities who want to use the Rebel XS to document or promote their business.

- Corporate workers who may or may not have photographic skills in their job descriptions, but who work regularly with graphics and need to learn how to use digital images taken with a Canon EOS Rebel XS for reports, presentations, or other applications.

- Professional webmasters with strong skills in programming (including Java, JavaScript, HTML, Perl, etc.) but little background in photography, but who realize that the XS can be used for sophisticated photography.

- Graphic artists and others who already may be adept in image editing with Photoshop or another program, and who may already be using a film SLR (Canon or otherwise), but who need to learn more about digital photography and the special capabilities of the XS dSLR.

Who Am I?

After spending years as the world's most successful unknown author, I've become slightly less obscure in the past few years, thanks to a horde of camera guidebooks and other photographically oriented tomes. You may have seen my photography articles in *Popular Photography & Imaging* magazine. I've also written about 2,000 articles for magazines like *Petersen's PhotoGraphic* (which is now defunct through no fault of my own), plus *The Rangefinder, Professional Photographer*, and dozens of other photographic publications. But, first, and foremost, I'm a photojournalist and made my living in the field until I began devoting most of my time to writing books.

Although I love writing, I'm happiest when I'm out taking pictures, which is why I invariably spend several days each week photographing landscapes, people, close-up subjects, and other things. I spend a month or two each year traveling to events, such as Native American "powwows", Civil War re-enactments, county fairs, ballet, and sports (baseball, basketball, football, and soccer are favorites). A few months ago, I took 14 days for a solo visit to Europe, strictly to shoot photographs of the people, landscapes, and monuments that I've grown to love. I can offer you my personal advice on how to take photos under a variety of conditions because I've had to meet those challenges myself on an ongoing basis.

Like all my digital photography books, this one was written by someone with an incurable photography bug. My first Canon SLR was a Pellix back in the 1960s, and I've used a variety of newer models since then. I've worked as a sports photographer for an Ohio newspaper and for an upstate New York college. I've operated my own commercial studio and photo lab, cranking out product shots on demand and then printing a few hundred glossy 8 × 10s on a tight deadline for a press kit. I've served as a photo-posing instructor for a modeling agency. People have actually paid me to shoot their weddings and immortalize them with portraits. I even prepared press kits and articles on photography as a PR consultant for a large Rochester, N.Y., company, which shall remain nameless. My trials and travails with imaging and computer technology have made their way into print in book form an alarming number of times, including a few dozen on scanners and photography.

Like you, I love photography for its own merits, and I view technology as just another tool to help me get the images I see in my mind's eye. But, also like you, I had to master this technology before I could apply it to my work. This book is the result of what I've learned, and I hope it will help you master your Rebel XS digital SLR, too.

As I write this, I'm currently in the throes of upgrading my website, which you can find at www.dslrguides.com, adding tutorials and information about my other books. There's a lot of information about several Canon models right now, but I'll be adding more tips and recommendations (including a list of equipment and accessories that I can't live without) in the next few months. I hope you'll stop by for a visit.

Setting Up Your Canon EOS Rebel XS

I once read a camera guide that began with the author advising the Gentle Reader to resist the temptation to go out and take pictures until the proper amount of time had been spent Setting Up The Camera, apparently to avoid wasting electrons on shots that were doomed to failure if the arcane operational knowledge that was forthcoming wasn't first absorbed. What universe was he from?

Relax! I fully expect that you took several hundred or a thousand (or two) photos before you ever cracked the cover of this book—for several reasons. First, and foremost, the Rebel XS is incredibly easy to use, even for the absolute beginner. Even the newest digital camera owner can rotate the Mode dial to the green Auto position and go out and begin taking great pictures. Getting to that point by charging the battery, mounting a lens, and inserting a Secure Digital memory card isn't exactly rocket science, either. Canon has cleverly marked the On/Off switch with large ON and OFF labels, and the Basic Mode scene icons will provide a major clue for anyone interested in photographing something resembling a human profile, a mountain, a flower, a person leaning forward in racing stride, or a starlit scene.

So, budding photographers are likely to muddle their way through getting the camera revved up and working well enough to take a bunch of pictures without the universe collapsing. Eventually, though, many turn to this book when they realize that they can do an even better job with a little guidance.

Second, I know that many of you will be owners of the XS's predecessors, the Rebel XSi, or Digital Rebel XT/XTi cameras. Although Canon removed "Digital" from the Rebel product name, most of the basic operations of this new camera are quite similar to that of the older models. So, veteran Rebel owners can venture out, shoot first, and ask questions later.

Finally, I realize that most of you didn't buy this book at the same time you purchased your Rebel XS. As much as I'd like to picture thousands of avid photographers marching out of their camera stores with a Rebel box under one arm, and my book in hand, I know that's not going to happen *all* the time. A large number of you had your camera for a week, or two, or a month, became comfortable with it, and sought out this book in order to learn more. So, a chapter on "setup" seems like too little, too late, doesn't it?

In practice, though, it's not a bad idea, once you've taken a few orientation pictures with your XS, to go back and review the basic operations of the camera from the beginning, if only to see if you've missed something. This chapter is my opportunity to review the setup procedures for the camera for those among you who are already veteran users, and to help ease the more timid (and those who have never worked with a digital SLR before) into the basic pre-flight checklist that needs to be completed before you really spread your wings and take off. For the uninitiated, as easy as it is to use initially, the Rebel XS *does* have lots of dials and buttons and settings that might not make sense at first, but will surely become second nature after you've had a chance to review the instructions in this chapter.

But don't fret about wading through a manual to find out what you must know to take those first few tentative snaps. I'm going to help you hit the ground running with this chapter (or keep on running if you've already jumped right in). If you *haven't* had the opportunity to use your Rebel yet, I'll help you set up your camera and begin shooting in minutes. You won't find a lot of detail in this chapter. Indeed, I'm going to tell you just what you absolutely *must* understand, accompanied by some interesting tidbits that will help you become acclimated. I'll go into more depth and even repeat some of what I explain here in later chapters, so you don't have to memorize everything you see. Just relax, follow a few easy steps, and then go out and begin taking your best shots—ever.

Contents of the Table

You probably spread out on a table or desk the contents of the handsome box that transported the Canon EOS Rebel XS from its birthplace in Japan. The box is filled with stuff, including connecting cords, booklets, CDs, and lots of paperwork. The first thing you should do (or the *next* thing you should do, if you've already been taking pictures with your camera), is to double-check the contents of the box to make sure nothing was left out, or accidentally removed by the retailer. Someone might have checked out the camera for you as a quality assurance method, or a curious store employee might have rooted through the box to see what this cool new camera actually looks like. In either case, it's entirely possible that something went astray, and it's good to know that *now,* when you can easily bring any missing pieces to the attention of the store that sold you the camera. Otherwise, a month down the road you're going to decide to see what the output of your Rebel XS looks like on your TV screen, and discover that the video cable you *thought* you had has gone AWOL at some unknown time.

So, check the box at your earliest convenience, and make sure you have (at least) the following:

- **Canon EOS Rebel XS camera.** This is hard to miss. The camera is the main reason you laid out the big bucks, and it is tucked away inside a nifty bubble-wrap envelope you should save for protection in case the XS needs to be sent in for repair.

- **Rubber eyecup.** This slide-on soft-rubber eyecup should be attached to the viewfinder when you receive the camera. It helps you squeeze your eye tightly against the window, excluding extraneous light, and also protects your eyeglasses (if you wear them) from scratching.

- **Body cap.** The twist-off body cap keeps dust from entering the camera when no lens is mounted. Even with automatic sensor cleaning built into the XS, you'll want to keep the amount of dust to a minimum. The body cap belongs in your camera bag if you contemplate the need to travel with the lens removed.

- **Lens (if purchased).** Your Rebel XS probably came in a kit with the Canon Zoom Lens EF-S 18-55mm f/3.5-56 IS lens. Or, you may have purchased it with another lens. The lens will come with a lens cap on the front, and a rear lens cap aft.

- **Battery pack LP-E5 (with cover).** The power source for your Rebel XS is packaged separately. It should be charged as soon as possible (as described next) and inserted in the camera. Save the protective cover. If you transport a battery outside the camera, it's a good idea to reattach the cover to prevent the electrical contacts from shorting out.

- **Battery charger LC-E5 or LC-E5E.** One of these two battery chargers will be included.

- **Wide strap EW-100DB III.** Canon provides you with a suitable neck strap, emblazoned with Canon advertising. While I am justifiably proud of owning a fine Canon camera, I prefer a low-key, more versatile strap from Optech (www.optech.com) or UpStrap (www.upstrap.com).

- **Interface Cable IFC-200U.** This is a USB cable that can be used to link your Rebel XS to a computer, and it is especially useful when you need to transfer pictures but don't have a card reader handy.

- **Video Cable VC-100.** Use this cable to view your camera's LCD output on a larger television screen, monitor, or other device with a yellow RCA composite input jack.

- **EOS Digital Solution Disk CD.** The disk contains useful software that will be discussed in more detail in Chapter 9.

- **Software Instruction manual CD.** While the software itself is easy to use, if you need more help you'll find it in the PDF manuals included on this CD.

- **Printed instruction manuals.** These include the 195-page Instruction Manual, the Pocket Guide quick-start manual, and the CD-ROM Guide, which details the bundled software.

Initial Setup

The initial setup of your Canon EOS Rebel XS is fast and easy. Basically, you just need to charge the battery, attach a lens, and insert a memory card. I'll address each of these steps separately, but if you already feel you can manage these setup tasks without further instructions, feel free to skip this section entirely. You should at least skim its contents, however, because I'm going to list a few options that you might not be aware of.

Battery Included

Your Canon EOS Rebel XS is a sophisticated hunk of machinery and electronics, but it needs a charged battery to function, so rejuvenating the LP-E5 lithium-ion battery pack furnished with the camera should be your first step. A fully charged power source should be good for approximately 600 shots under normal temperature conditions, based on standard tests defined by the Camera & Imaging Products Association (CIPA) document DC-002. If half your pictures use the built-in flash, you can expect about 500 shots before it's time for a recharge. While those figures sound like a lot of shooting, things like picture review, playing with menus, and using the image stabilization features of your lens can use up more power than you might expect. If your pictures are important to you, always take along one spare, fully charged battery.

And remember that all rechargeable batteries undergo some degree of self-discharge just sitting idle in the camera or in the original packaging. Lithium-ion power packs of this type typically lose a few percent of their charge every day, even when the camera isn't turned on. Li-ion cells lose their power through a chemical reaction that continues when the camera is switched off. So, it's very likely that the battery purchased with your camera, even if charged at the factory, has begun to poop out after the long sea voyage on a banana boat (or, more likely, a trip by jet plane followed by a sojourn in a warehouse), so you'll want to revive it before going out for some serious shooting.

Power Options

Several battery chargers and power sources are available for the Canon EOS Rebel XS. The compact LC-E5, shown in Figure 1.1, plugs directly into a wall socket and is commonly furnished with the camera. Canon also provides the LC-E5E, which is similar, but has a cord. Purchasing one of the optional charging devices offers more than some additional features: You gain a spare that can keep your camera running until you can replace your primary power rejuvenator. Here's a list of your power options:

- **LC-E5.** The standard charger for the XS, this one is the most convenient, because of its compact size and built-in wall plug prongs that connect directly into your power strip or wall socket and requires no cord. This charger, as well as the LC-E5E, has a switching power module that is fully compatible with 100V to 240V 50/60 Hz AC power, so you can use it outside the U.S. with no problems. When I travel to Europe, for example, I take my charger and an adapter to convert the plug shape for the European sockets. No voltage converter is needed.

- **LC-E5E.** This is similar to the LC-E5, and also charges a single battery, but requires a cord. That can be advantageous in certain situations. For example, if your power outlet is behind a desk or in some other semi-inaccessible location, the cord can be plugged in and routed so the charger itself sits on your desk or another more convenient spot. The cord itself is a standard one that works with many different chargers and devices (including the power supply for my laptop), so I purchased several of them and leave them plugged into the wall in various locations. I can connect my XS's charger, my laptop computer's charger, and several other electronic components to one of these cords without needing to crawl around behind the furniture. The cord itself draws no power when it's not plugged into a charger.

- **AC Adapter Kit ACK-E5.** This device consists of Compact Power Adapter CA-PS700 and DC Couple DR-E5, and allows you to operate your Rebel XS directly from AC power, with no battery required. Studio photographers need this capability because they often snap off hundreds of pictures for hours on end and

Figure 1.1

The orange status light indicates that the battery is being charged.

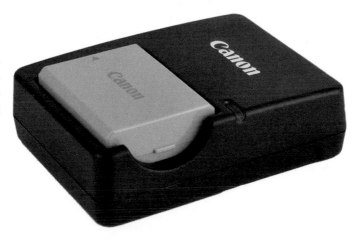

want constant, reliable power. The camera is probably plugged into a flash sync cord (or radio device), and the studio flash are plugged into power packs or AC power, so the extra tether to this adapter is no big deal in that environment. You also might want to use the AC adapter when viewing images on a TV connected to your XS, or when shooting remote or time-lapse photos.

■ **Car Battery Charger CBC-E5.** This is a charger that can juice up your battery when connected to your auto's 12V power source. The vehicle battery option allows you to keep shooting when in remote locations that lack AC power.

■ **Battery Grip BG-E5.** This accessory holds two LP-E5 batteries (another reason to own a spare, or two). It can also be equipped with six AA cells with the BGM-E5A battery holder. You can potentially increase your shooting capacity to 1,200 shots, while adding an additional shutter release, Main dial, AE lock/FE lock, and AF point selection controls for vertically oriented shooting.

Charging the Battery

When the battery is inserted into the LC-E5 charger properly (it's impossible to insert it incorrectly), a Charge light begins glowing orange-red. When the battery completes the charge, the lamp turns green, approximately two hours later. When the battery is charged, flip the lever on the bottom of the camera and slide the battery in. (See Figure 1.2.) To remove the battery, you must press a white lever, which prevents the pack from slipping out when the door is opened. (See Figure 1.3.)

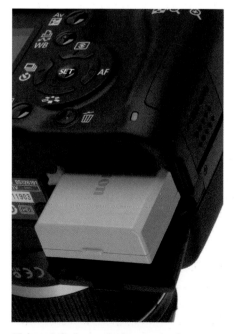

Figure 1.2 Insert the battery in the camera; it only fits one way.

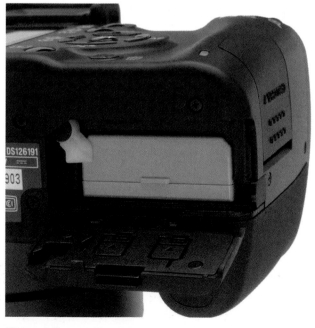

Figure 1.3 Press the white tab to release the battery when you want to remove it.

Final Steps

Your Canon EOS Rebel XS is almost ready to fire up and shoot. You'll need to select and mount a lens, adjust the viewfinder for your vision, and insert a memory card. Each of these steps is easy, and if you've used any Canon EOS camera in the past, you already know exactly what to do. I'm going to provide a little extra detail for those of you who are new to the Canon or digital SLR worlds.

Mounting the Lens

As you'll see, my recommended lens mounting procedure emphasizes protecting your equipment from accidental damage, and minimizing the intrusion of dust. If your XS has no lens attached, select the lens you want to use and loosen (but do not remove) the rear lens cap. I generally place the lens I am planning to mount vertically in a slot in my camera bag, where it's protected from mishaps, but ready to pick up quickly. By loosening the rear lens cap, you'll be able to lift it off the back of the lens at the last instant, so the rear element of the lens is covered until then.

After that, remove the body cap by rotating the cap towards the shutter release button. You should always mount the body cap when there is no lens on the camera, because it helps keep dust out of the interior of the camera, where it can settle on the mirror, focusing screen, the interior mirror box, and potentially find its way past the shutter onto the sensor. (While the XS's sensor cleaning mechanism works fine, the less dust it has to contend with, the better.) The body cap also protects the vulnerable mirror from damage caused by intruding objects (including your fingers, if you're not cautious).

Once the body cap has been removed, remove the rear lens cap from the lens, set it aside, and then mount the lens on the camera by matching the alignment indicator on the lens barrel (red for EF lenses and white for EF-S lenses) with the red or white dot on the camera's lens mount. (See Figure 1.4.) Rotate the lens away from the shutter release until it seats securely. (You can find out more about the difference between EF and EF-S lenses in Chapter 6.) Set the focus mode switch on the lens to AF (autofocus). If the lens hood is bayoneted on the lens in the reversed position (which makes the lens/hood combination more compact for transport), twist it off and remount with the "petals" facing outward. (See Figure 1.5.) A lens hood protects the front of the lens from accidental bumps, stray fingerprints, and reduces flare caused by extraneous light arriving at the front element of the lens from outside the picture area.

Adjusting Diopter Correction.

Those of us with less than perfect eyesight can often benefit from a little optical correction in the viewfinder. Your contact lenses or glasses may provide all the correction you need, but if you are a glasses wearer and want to use the Rebel XS without your glasses, you can take advantage of the camera's built-in diopter adjustment, which can be varied from –3 to +1 correction. Press the shutter release halfway to illuminate the

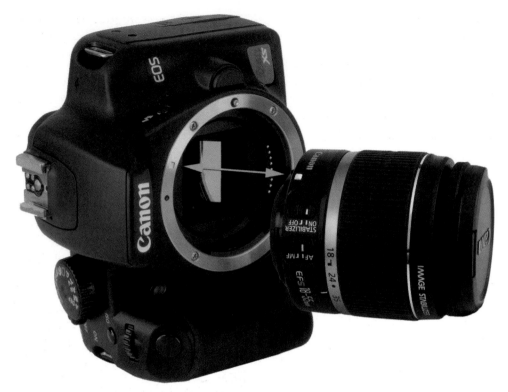

Figure 1.4
Match the white dot on EF-S lenses with the white dot on the camera mount to properly align the lens with the bayonet mount. For EF lenses, use the red dots.

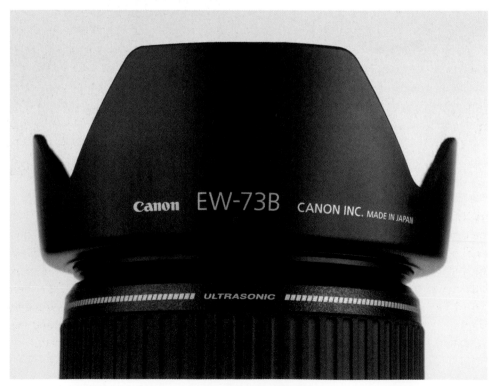

Figure 1.5
A lens hood protects the lens from extraneous light and accidental bumps.

indicators in the viewfinder, then rotate the adjacent diopter adjustment wheel (see Figure 1.6) while looking through the window until the indicators appear sharp.

If the available correction is insufficient, Canon offers 10 different Dioptric Adjustment Lens Series E correction lenses for the viewfinder window. If more than one person uses your XS, and each requires a different diopter setting, you can save a little time by noting the number of clicks and direction (clockwise to increase the diopter power; counterclockwise to decrease the diopter value) required to change from one user to the other. There are 18 detents in all.

Figure 1.6
Viewfinder diopter correction from −3 to +1 can be dialed in.

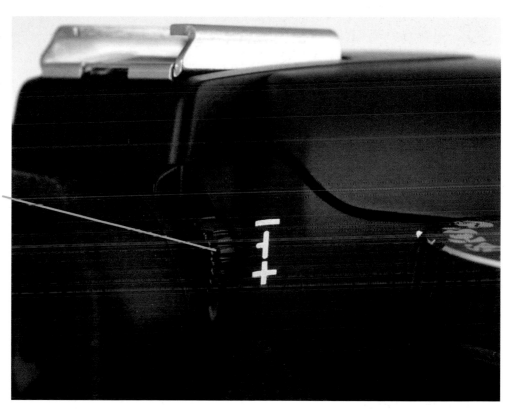

Diopter correction knob

Inserting a Memory Card

You can't take photos without a memory card inserted in your Rebel XS (although there is a Shoot w/o Card entry in Shooting Menu 1 that enables/disables shutter release functions when a memory card is absent—you'll learn about that in Chapter 3). So, your final step will be to insert a memory card. Slide the door on the right side of the body toward the back of the camera to release the cover, and then open it. (You should only remove the memory card when the camera is switched off, but the XS will remind you if the door is opened while the camera is still writing photos to the memory card.)

Insert the memory card with the label facing the back of the camera, as shown in Figure 1.7, oriented so the edge with the gold contacts goes into the slot first. Close the door, and your preflight checklist is done! (I'm going to assume you remember to remove the lens cap when you're ready to take a picture!) When you want to remove the memory card later, just press the memory card edge, and it will pop right out.

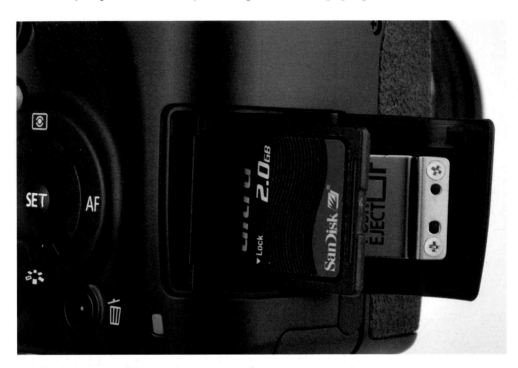

Figure 1.7
The memory card is inserted with the label facing the back of the camera.

Turn on the Power

Rotate the On/Off switch on top of the camera to the On position. Automatic sensor cleaning takes place (unless you specifically disable this action) as the XS powers up. The camera will remain on or in a standby mode until you manually turn it off. After 30 seconds of idling, the XS goes into the standby mode to save battery power. Just tap the shutter release button to bring it back to life. The automatic sensor cleaning operation does not occur when exiting standby mode.

When the camera powers up, you may be asked to set the date and time. The procedure is fairly self-explanatory (although I'll explain it in detail in Chapter 3). You can use the left/right cross keys to navigate among the month, year, and date format and the up/down keys to enter the correct settings. When finished, press the right cross key until you highlight OK, then press Set to confirm the date.

Once the Rebel XS is satisfied that it knows what time it is, the Shooting Settings display, shown in Figure 1.8, should appear on the LCD. It shows the basic settings of the camera, including current shutter speed and lens opening, shooting mode, ISO sensitivity, and other parameters. I'll explain these features as well as the Shooting Settings display itself, in later chapters of this book (especially in Chapter 4, which deals with exposure).

> **Tip**
>
> There is also a Shooting Information display available with several screens of information *about a particular photo* that you have taken. (Just press the DISP button when the image is presented for your review.) I'll explain the contents of that screen, too, later on.

Figure 1.8
The Shooting Settings display shows the current picture-taking settings of the Rebel XS.

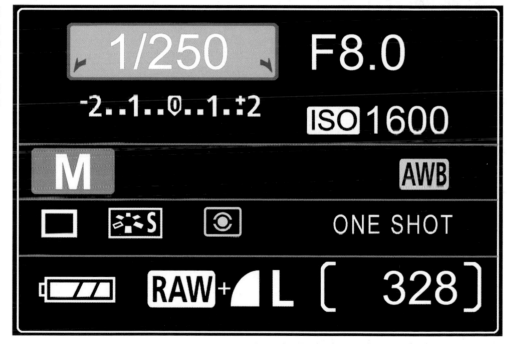

Selecting a Shooting Mode

You can choose a shooting method from the Mode dial located on the top right of the Canon EOS Rebel XS. (See Figure 1.9.) There are seven Basic Zone shooting modes, in which the camera makes virtually all the decisions for you (except when to press the shutter), and five Creative Zone modes, which allow you to provide input over the exposure and settings the camera uses. You'll find a complete description of both Basic Zone and Creative Zone modes in Chapter 4.

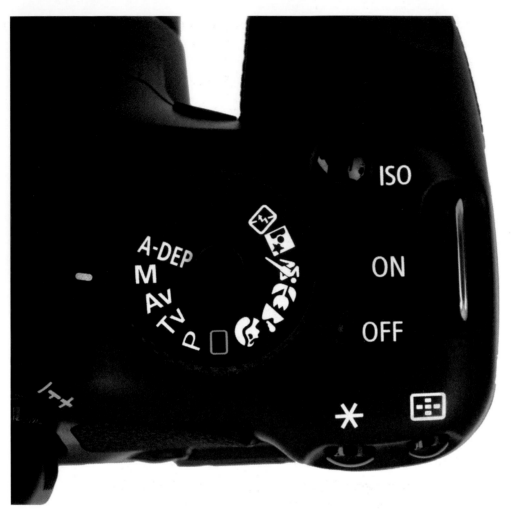

Figure 1.9
The Mode dial includes both Basic Zone and Creative Zone settings.

Turn your camera on by flipping the power switch to On. Next, you need to select which shooting mode to use. If you're very new to digital photography, you might want to set the camera to Auto (the green frame on the Mode dial) or P (Program mode) and start snapping away. Either mode will make all the appropriate settings for you for many shooting situations. If you have a specific type of picture you want to shoot, you can try out one of the other Basic Zone modes indicated on the Mode dial with appropriate icons, as shown in Figure 1.9:

- **Auto.** In this mode, the XS makes all the exposure decisions for you, and will pop up the flash if necessary under low-light conditions.

- **Portrait.** Use this mode when you're taking a portrait of a subject standing relatively close to the camera and want to de-emphasize the background, maximize sharpness, and produce flattering skin tones. The flash will pop up, if needed.

- **Landscape.** Select this mode when you want extra sharpness and rich colors of distant scenes. The flash does not pop up in this mode.

- **Close Up.** This mode is helpful when you are shooting close-up pictures of a subject from about one foot away or less. The flash will pop up, if needed.

- **Sports.** Use this mode to freeze fast-moving subjects. The flash doesn't pop up automatically in this mode.

- **Night Portrait.** Choose this mode when you want to illuminate a subject in the foreground with flash, but still allow the background to be exposed properly by the available light. Be prepared to use a tripod or an image stabilized (IS) lens to reduce the effects of camera shake. (You'll find more about IS and camera shake in Chapter 6.) The flash will pop up, if needed.

- **Flash Off.** This is the mode to use in museums and other locations where flash is forbidden or inappropriate. It otherwise operates exactly like the Auto setting but disables the pop-up internal flash unit.

If you have more photographic experience, you might want to opt for one of the Creative Zone modes, also shown in Figure 1.10. These, too, are described in more detail in Chapter 4. These modes let you apply a little more creativity to your camera's settings.

Figure 1.10
The Creative Zone modes (left side of dial as shown) let the photographer control how exposures are made, to increase creative options. The Basic Zone settings (right side of the dial) make all the exposure decisions for you.

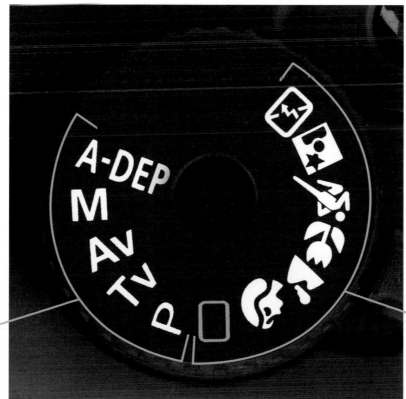

Creative Zone   *Basic Zone*

These modes are indicated on the Mode dial by letters A-DEP, M, Av, Tv, and P. The flash does not pop up automatically in any of the Creative Zone modes, but you can choose to use it by pressing the Flash button located above the Lens Release button.

- **A-DEP (Automatic depth-of-field).** Choose this mode if you want to allow the XS to select an f/stop that will maximize depth-of-field for the subjects in the frame as it adjusts focus and selects an appropriate shutter speed.

- **M (Manual).** Select when you want full control over the shutter speed and lens opening, either for creative effects or because you are using a studio flash or other flash unit not compatible with the XS's automatic flash metering.

- **Av (Aperture Priority).** Choose when you want to use a particular lens opening, especially to control sharpness or how much of your image is in focus. The XS will select the appropriate shutter speed for you. Av stands for *aperture value.*

- **Tv (Shutter Priority).** This mode (Tv stands for *time value*) is useful when you want to use a particular shutter speed to stop action or produce creative blur effects. The XS will select the appropriate f/stop for you.

- **P (Program).** This mode allows the XS to select the basic exposure settings, but you can still override the camera's choices to fine-tune your image.

Choosing a Metering Mode

You might want to select a particular metering mode for your first shots, although the default Evaluative metering (which is set automatically when you choose a Basic Zone mode) is probably the best choice as you get to know your camera. To change metering modes, press the Metering Mode button. (It's the "up" button on the keypad that surrounds the Set button, while using one of the Creative Zone modes. The four directional buttons for up/down/left/right are known as the cross keys.) When the button is pressed, a screen pops up on the LCD offering three choices (this is one fewer than the Rebel XSi, which had a fourth choice, Spot, which metered an even smaller portion of the screen than the Partial choice available with the Rebel XS). Keep pressing the Metering Mode button until the choice you want is highlighted. Then press the Set button to confirm your choice. The options are shown in Figure 1.11:

- **Evaluative metering.** The standard metering mode; the XS attempts to intelligently classify your image and choose the best exposure based on readings from 35 different zones in the frame, with emphasis on the autofocus points.

- **Partial metering.** Exposure is based on a central spot, roughly nine percent of the image area.

- **Center-Weighted Averaging metering.** The XS meters the entire scene, but gives the most emphasis to the central area of the frame.

You'll find a detailed description of each of these modes in Chapter 4.

Figure 1.11
Metering
modes (top to
bottom)
Evaluative,
Partial, Center-
Weighted.

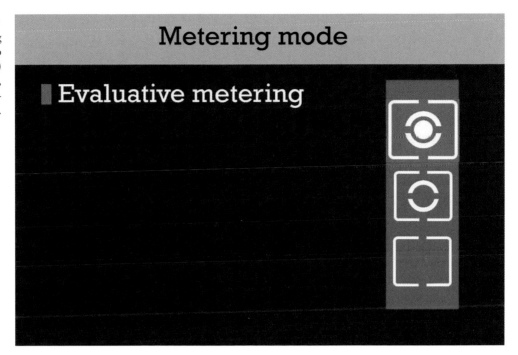

Choosing a Focus Mode

You can easily switch between automatic and manual focus by moving the AF/MF switch on the lens mounted on your camera. However, if you're using a Creative Zone shooting mode, you'll still need to choose an appropriate focus mode. (You can read more on selecting focus parameters in Chapter 5.) If you're using a Basic Zone mode, the focus method is set for you automatically.

To set the focus mode, press the AF button (it's the right cross key) on the back of the camera repeatedly until the focus mode you want is selected (see Figure 1.12). Then press Set to confirm your focus mode. The three choices are as follows:

■ **One Shot.** This mode, sometimes called *Single Autofocus*, locks in a focus point when the shutter button is pressed down halfway, and the focus confirmation light glows in the viewfinder. The focus will remain locked until you release the button or take the picture. If the camera is unable to achieve sharp focus, the focus confirmation light will blink. This mode is best when your subject is relatively motionless. Portrait, Night Portrait, and Landscape Basic Zone modes use this focus method exclusively.

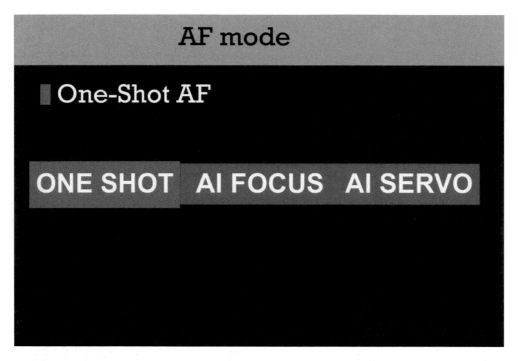

Figure 1.12
Set Autofocus mode.

- **AI Servo.** This mode, sometimes called *Continuous Autofocus*, sets focus when you partially depress the shutter button, but continues to monitor the frame and refocuses if the camera or subject is moved. This is a useful mode for photographing sports and moving subjects. The Sports Basic Zone mode uses this focus method exclusively.

- **AI Focus.** In this mode, the XS switches between One Shot and AI Servo as appropriate. That is, it locks in a focus point when you partially depress the shutter button (One Shot mode), but switches automatically to AI Servo if the subject begins to move. This mode is handy when photographing a subject, such as a child at quiet play, which might move unexpectedly. The Flash Off Basic Zone mode uses this focus method.

Selecting a Focus Point

The Canon EOS Rebel XS uses seven different focus points to calculate correct focus. In A-DEP, or any of the Basic Zone shooting modes, the focus point is selected automatically by the camera. In the other Creative Zone modes, you can allow the camera to select the focus point automatically, or you can specify which focus point should be used.

There are several methods to set the focus point manually. You can press the AF Point Selection button on the back of the camera (it's in the upper-right corner), and choose a zone from the AF Point Selection screen that pops up. (See Figure 1.13.) Press the Set button to toggle between automatic focus point selection (the camera does it for you) or manual focus point selection (you need to specify the point yourself). In Manual selection mode, the multi-controller's cross keys are used to highlight the point you want to use. Press the AF Point Selection button again (or just tap the shutter release button) to confirm your choice and exit.

Figure 1.13
Select a focus point and selection mode from the AF point selection screen.

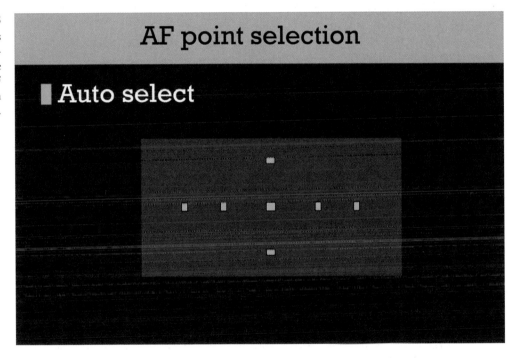

Or, you can look through the viewfinder, press the AF Point Selection button, and use the left/right/up/down cross keys to move the focus point to the zone you want to use. Press the Set button, and the center focus point becomes active, as shown in Figure 1.14.

You can also choose a focus point by pressing the AF Point Selection button and then rotating the Main dial. The focus point will cycle among the edge points counterclockwise (if you turn the Main dial to the left) or clockwise (if you spin the Main dial to the right), ending/starting with the center focus point/all seven focus points. When all seven points are illuminated, the Auto Select indicator is illuminated.

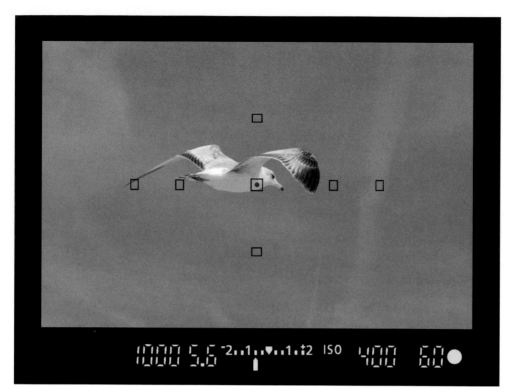

Figure 1.14
Or choose the
focus point
while looking
through the
viewfinder.

Other Settings

There are a few other settings you can make if you're feeling ambitious, but don't feel ashamed if you postpone using these features until you've racked up a little more experience with your Rebel XS.

Adjusting White Balance and ISO

If you like, you can custom-tailor your white balance (color balance) and ISO sensitivity settings. To start out, it's best to set white balance (WB) to Auto, and ISO to ISO 100 or ISO 200 for daylight photos, and ISO 400 for pictures in dimmer light. You'll find complete recommendations for both these settings in Chapter 4. You can adjust either one now by pressing the WB button located to the right of the LCD (for white balance) or the ISO button (between the Main dial and Mode dial) and using the cross keys to navigate until the setting you want appears on the LCD.

If you've been playing with your camera's settings, or your XS has been used by someone else, you can restore the factory defaults by selecting Clear Settings from the Setup Menu 3. Just press the Menu button (located at the upper-left corner of the back of the camera), press the right cross key until the yellow wrench icon with a vertical row of three dots is highlighted, then press the down cross key to select Clear Settings. A screen will pop up asking whether you'd like to Clear all camera settings, or Clear all Custom Func. (C. Fn.). Choose the one you'd like to reset, and press the Set button. I'll explain *why* you might want to reset your camera in more detail (for those who are now wondering why) in Chapter 3.

Using the Self-Timer

If you want to set a short delay before your picture is taken, you can use the self-timer. Press the Drive/left cross key button and then press the right cross key to select from either the 10-second self-timer, 2-second self-timer, or Self-timer: Continuous, which allows you to press the up/down cross keys to specify a number of shots to be taken (from 2 to 10) once the timer runs its course. (See Figure 1.15.) Press the Set button to confirm your choice, and a self-timer icon will appear on the Shooting Settings display on the back of the Rebel XS. Press the shutter release to lock focus and start the timer. The self-timer lamp will blink and the beeper will sound (unless you've silenced it in the menus) until the final two seconds, when the lamp remains on and the beeper beeps more rapidly.

Note: The XS differs from the Rebel XSi in that with the XSi, the 10-second self-timer can also be used with the optional RC-1and RC-5 infrared remote controls, which the XS does not support.

Figure 1.15
The Drive modes include (left to right) Single Shot, Continuous, 10-second delay, 2-second delay, and Self-timer: Continuous (which takes multiple shots when the self-timer's delay has elapsed).

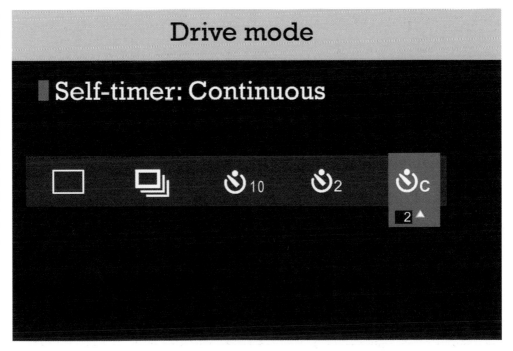

Canon recommends slipping off the eyepiece cup and replacing it with the viewfinder cap, in order to keep extraneous light from reaching the exposure meter through the viewfinder "back door." I usually just shade the viewfinder window with my hand (if I'm using the self-timer to reduce camera shake for a long exposure) or drape something over the back of the camera (if I'm scurrying to get into the picture myself).

Reviewing the Images You've Taken

The Canon EOS Rebel XS has a broad range of playback and image review options, including the ability to jump ahead 10 or 100 images at a time. I'll cover them in more detail in Chapter 3. For now, you'll want to learn just the basics. Here is all you really need to know at this time, as shown in Figure 1.16:

- Press the Playback button (marked with a blue right-pointing triangle) to display the most recent image on the LCD.

- Press the left cross key to view a previous image.

- Press the right cross key to view the next image.

- Press the DISP button repeatedly to cycle among overlays of basic image information, more detailed shooting information, or advanced information.

- Press the Magnify button repeatedly to zoom in on the image displayed; the Reduce Image button zooms back out. Press the Playback button to exit magnified display.

- Use the multi-controller cross keys to scroll around within a magnified image. An inset box shows the relationship of the magnified image to the entire frame.

- The Reduce Image button in full-frame view switches from single image to display of four or six reduced-size thumbnails. To change from a larger number of thumbnails to a smaller number (from nine to four to single image, for example), press the Zoom in button until the display you want appears.

- When viewing a single image, press the up/down cross keys to select a "jump" mode of either one image, 10 images, or 100 images. Once a jump increment has been selected, you can leap forward or back that number of pictures by rotating the Main dial. Turn it counterclockwise to review images from most recent to oldest, or clockwise to start with the first image on the memory card and cycle forward to the newest, using the jump size you've selected.

You'll find more information on viewing thumbnail indexes of images, jumping forward and backward 10 or 100 images at a time, automated playback, and other options in Chapter 3.

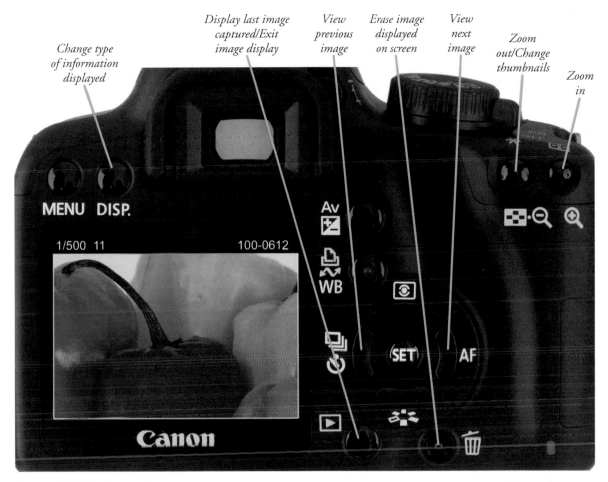

Figure 1.16 Review your images.

Transferring Photos to Your Computer

The final step in your picture-taking session will be to transfer the photos you've taken to your computer for printing, further review, or image editing. Your XS allows you to print directly to PictBridge-compatible printers and to create print orders right in the camera, plus you can select which images to transfer to your computer. I'll outline those options in Chapter 3.

For now, you'll probably want to transfer your images either by using a cable transfer from the camera to the computer or by removing the memory card from the XS and transferring the images with a card reader. The latter option is usually the best, because it's usually much faster and doesn't deplete the battery of your camera. However, you can use a cable transfer when you have the cable and a computer, but no card reader (perhaps you're using the computer of a friend or colleague, or at an Internet café).

To transfer images from the camera to a Mac or PC computer using the USB cable:

1. Turn the camera off.

2. Pry back the rubber cover that protects the Rebel XS's USB port, and plug the USB cable furnished with the camera into the USB port. (See Figure 1.17.)

3. Connect the other end of the USB cable to a USB port on your computer.

4. Turn the camera on. Your installed software usually detects the camera and offers to transfer the pictures, or the camera appears on your desktop as a mass storage device, enabling you to drag and drop the files to your computer.

To transfer images from a memory card to the computer using a card reader, as shown in Figure 1.18:

1. Turn the camera off.

2. Slide open the memory card door, and press on the card, which causes it to pop up so it can be removed from the slot.

3. Insert the memory card into your memory card reader. Your installed software detects the files on the card and offers to transfer them. The card can also appear as a mass storage device on your desktop, which you can open, and then drag and drop the files to your computer.

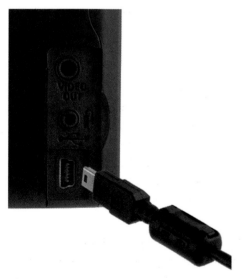

Figure 1.17 Images can be transferred to your computer using a USB cable.

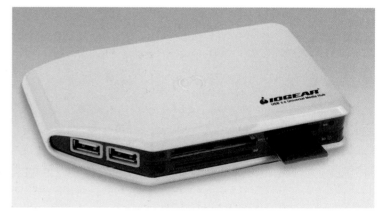

Figure 1.18 A card reader is one way to transfer photos.

2

Canon EOS Rebel XS/1000D Roadmap

One thing that always surprises new owners of the Canon EOS Rebel XS is that the camera has a total of 496 buttons, dials, switches, levers, latches, and knobs bristling from its surface. Okay, I lied. Actually, the real number is closer to two-dozen controls and adjustments, but that's still a lot of components to master, especially when you consider that many of these controls serve double-duty to give you access to multiple functions.

Traditionally, there have been two ways of providing a roadmap to guide you through this maze of features. One approach uses two or three tiny 2 × 3-inch black-and-white line drawings or photos impaled with dozens of callouts labeled with cross-references to the actual pages in the book that tell you what these components do. You'll find this tactic used in the pocket-sized manual Canon provides with the Rebel XS, and most of the other third-party guidebooks as well. Deciphering one of these miniature camera layouts is a lot like being presented with a world globe when what you really want to know is how to find the capital of Belgium.

I originated a more useful approach in my field guides, providing you, instead of a satellite view, a street-level map that includes close-up full-color photos of the camera from several angles (see Figure 2.1), with a smaller number of labels clearly pointing to each individual feature. And, I don't force you to flip back and forth among dozens of pages to find out what a particular component does. Each photo is accompanied by a brief description that summarizes the control, so you can begin using it right away.

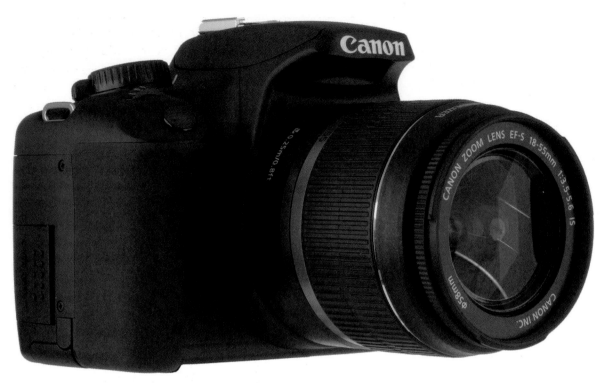

Figure 2.1

Only when a particular feature deserves a lengthy explanation do I direct you to a more detailed write-up later in the book.

So, if you're wondering what the depth-of-field preview does, I'll tell you up front, rather than have you flip to Page 1,282. This book is not a scavenger hunt. But after I explain how to use the ISO button to change the sensitivity of the XS, I *will* provide a cross-reference to a longer explanation later in the book that clarifies noise reduction, ISO, and its effects on exposure. I think this kind of organization works best for a camera as sophisticated as the Rebel XS.

By the time you finish this chapter, you'll have a basic understanding of every control and what it does. I'm not going to delve into menu functions here—you'll find a discussion of your setup, shooting, and playback menu options in Chapter 3. Everything here is devoted to the button pusher and dial twirler in you.

Front View

When we picture a given camera, we always imagine the front view. That's the view that your subjects see as you snap away, and the aspect that's shown in product publicity and on the box. The frontal angle is, for all intents and purposes, the "face" of a camera like the Rebel XS. But, not surprisingly, most of the "business" of operating the camera happens *behind* it, where the photographer resides. The front of the XS actually has very few controls and features to worry about. Four of them are readily visible in Figure 2.2:

- **Shutter release.** Angled on top of the handgrip is the shutter release button. Press this button down halfway to lock exposure and focus (in One Shot mode and AI Focus with non-moving subjects). The XS assumes that when you tap or depress the shutter release, you are ready to take a picture, so the release can be tapped to activate the exposure meter or to exit from most menus.

- **Main dial.** This dial is used to change shooting settings. When settings are available in pairs (such as shutter speed/aperture), this dial will be used to make one type

Figure 2.2

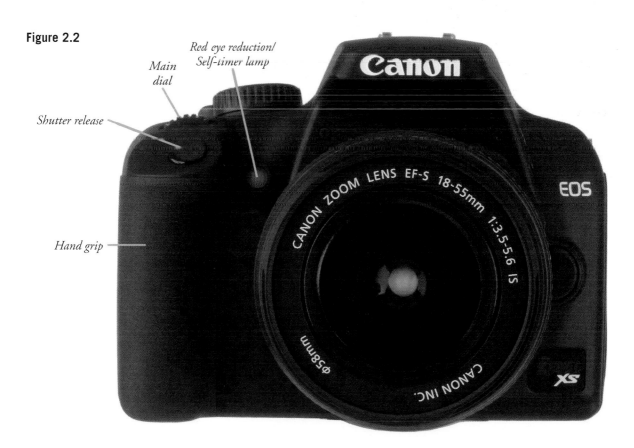

Main dial

Red eye reduction/
Self-timer lamp

Shutter release

Hand grip

of setting, such as shutter speed. The other setting, say, the aperture, is made using an alternate control, such as spinning the Main dial while holding down an additional button like the Exposure Compensation button (which resides conveniently under the thumb on the back of the camera).

- **Red-eye reduction/self-timer lamp.** This LED provides a blip of light shortly before a flash exposure to cause the subjects' pupils to close down, reducing the effect of red-eye reflections off their retinas. When using the self-timer, this lamp also flashes to mark the countdown until the photo is taken.

- **Hand grip.** This provides a comfortable handhold, and also contains the XS's battery.

You'll find more controls on the other side of the XS, shown in Figure 2.3.

- **Flash button.** This button releases the built-in flash so it can flip up (see Figure 2.4) and start the charging process. If you decide you do not want to use the flash, you can turn it off by pressing the flash head back down.

- **Lens Release button.** Press and hold this button to unlock the lens so you can rotate the lens to remove it from the camera.

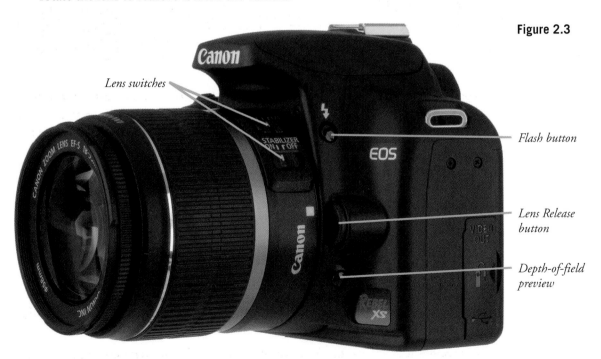

Figure 2.3

Lens switches

Flash button

Lens Release button

Depth-of-field preview

Figure 2.4
Pressing the Flash button (which has an arrow/lightning bolt symbol) pops up the built-in flash unit and starts the charging process.

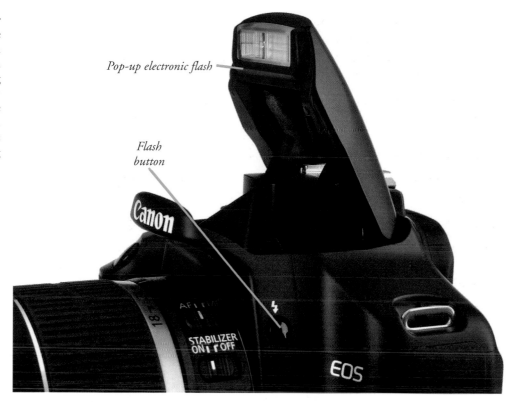

Pop-up electronic flash

Flash button

- **Depth-of-Field Preview button.** This button, adjacent to the lens mount, stops down the lens to the aperture that will be used to take the picture, so you can see in the viewfinder how much of the image is in focus. The view grows dimmer as the aperture is reduced.

- **Lens switches.** Canon autofocus lenses have a switch to allow changing between automatic focus and manual focus, and, in the case of IS lenses, another switch to turn image stabilization on and off.

The main feature on this side of the Rebel XS is a rubber cover (see Figure 2.5) that protects the three connector ports underneath from dust and moisture, plus one of two neck strap mounts (the other is on the other side of the camera). The three connectors, shown in Figure 2.6, are as follows:

- **Video out port.** You can link this connector with a television to view your photos on a large screen.

- **Remote control terminal.** You can plug various Canon remote release switches, timers, and wireless controllers into this connector.

- **USB port.** Plug in the USB cable furnished with your Rebel XS and connect the other end to a USB port in your computer to transfer photos or to operate the camera when linked to the computer.

Figure 2.5

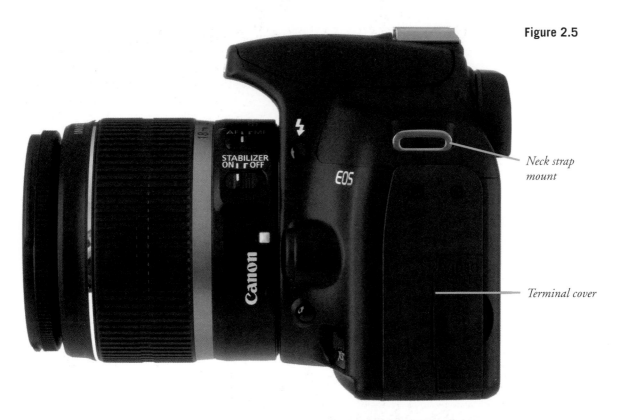

Neck strap mount

Terminal cover

Figure 2.6

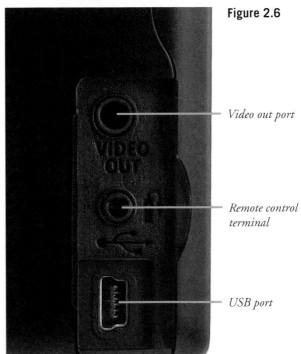

Video out port

Remote control terminal

USB port

The Canon EOS Rebel XS's Business End

The back panel of the Rebel XS (see Figure 2.7) bristles with more than a dozen different controls, buttons, and knobs. That might seem like a lot of controls to learn, but you'll find, as I noted earlier, that it's a lot easier to press a dedicated button and spin a dial than to jump to a menu every time you want to change a setting.

You can see the controls clustered on the left side of the XS in Figure 2.7. The key buttons and components and their functions are as follows:

■ **Viewfinder eyepiece.** You can frame your composition by peering into the viewfinder. It's surrounded by a soft rubber frame that seals out extraneous light when pressing your eye tightly up to the viewfinder, and it also protects your eyeglass lenses (if worn) from scratching. It can be removed and replaced by the cap attached to your neck strap when you use the camera on a tripod, to ensure that light coming from the back of the camera doesn't venture inside and possibly affect the exposure reading.

Figure 2.7

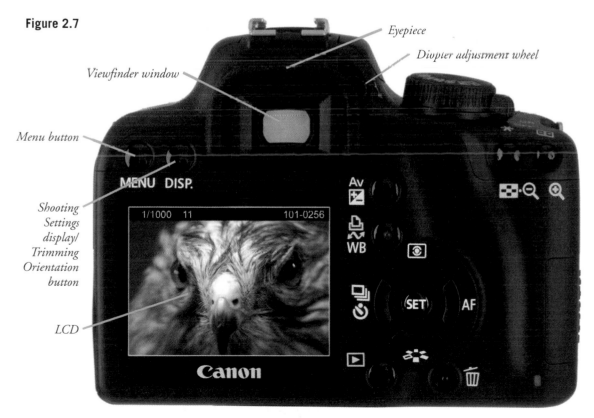

Eyepiece

Diopter adjustment wheel

Viewfinder window

Menu button

Shooting Settings display/ Trimming Orientation button

LCD

- **Menu button.** Summons/exits the menu displayed on the rear LCD of the XS. When you're working with submenus, this button also serves to exit a submenu and return to the main menu.

- **DISP button.** When pressed repeatedly, changes the amount of picture information displayed. In Playback mode, pressing the DISP button cycles among basic displays of the image; a detailed display with a thumbnail of the image, shooting parameters, and a brightness histogram; and a display with less detail but with separate histograms for brightness, red, green, and blue channels. (I'll show you what these look like later in the chapter.) When setting Picture Styles, the DISP button is used to select a highlighted Picture Style for modification. In Live View mode, the DISP button adjusts the amount of information overlaid on the live image that appears on the LCD screen. When trimming an image, the DISP button selects the orientation. If you press the DISP button after you press the Menu button, you are shown a media Freespace, My Menu settings, and date and time display. All these options are explained in Chapter 3.

- **LCD.** This is the 2.5-inch display that shows your Live View preview, image review after the picture is taken, Shooting Setting display before the photo is snapped, and all the menus used by the Rebel XS.

The most-used controls reside on the right side of the Rebel XS. (See Figure 2.8.) There are 11 buttons in all, many of which do double-duty to perform several functions. I've divided them into two groups; here's the first:

- **Cross keys.** This array of four-directional keys provides left/right/up/down movement to navigate menus, and is used to cycle among various options (usually with the left/right buttons) and to choose amounts (with the up/down buttons). The four cross keys also have secondary functions to adjust metering mode, Autofocus mode, Picture Styles, and drive mode (I'll describe these separately).

- **Set button.** Used to confirm a selection or activate a feature.

- **Aperture value (AV)/Exposure compensation button.** When using Manual exposure mode, hold down this button and rotate the Main dial to specify a lens aperture; rotate the Main dial alone to choose the shutter speed. In other Creative Zone exposure modes—Aperture Priority (Av), Shutter Priority (Tv), or Program (P)—hold down this button and rotate the Main dial to the right to add Exposure Compensation (EV) to an image (making it brighter), or rotate to the left to subtract EV and make the image darker.

- **White Balance/Print/Share button.** Press this button when using one of the Creative Zone modes (A-DEP, M, Av, Tv, or P) to produce the White Balance screen. Use the left/right cross keys to select a white balance, and press Set to confirm.

Figure 2.8

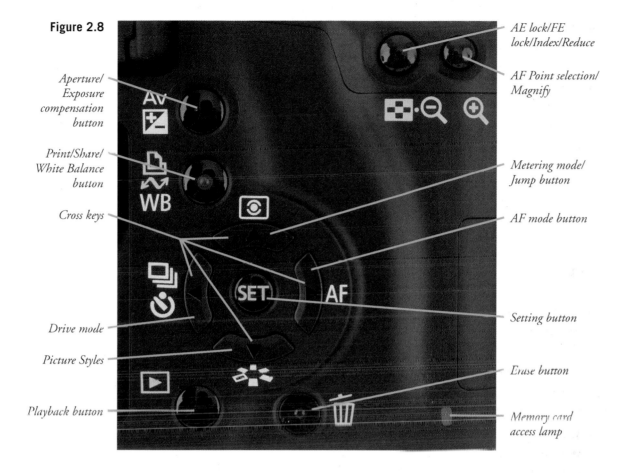

*Aperture/
Exposure
compensation
button*

*Print/Share/
White Balance
button*

Cross keys

Drive mode

Picture Styles

Playback button

*AE lock/FE
lock/Index/Reduce*

*AF Point selection/
Magnify*

*Metering mode/
Jump button*

AF mode button

Setting button

Erase button

*Memory card
access lamp*

(I'll explain more about white balance in Chapter 3.) The button can also be used when the XS is connected to a printer or personal computer to initiate transfer, as described in Chapter 8.

- **Playback button.** Displays the last picture taken. Thereafter, you can move back and forth among the available images by pressing the left/right cross keys to advance or reverse one image at a time, or the Main dial, to jump forward or back using the jump method you've selected. (See the sidebar, below.) To quit playback, press this button again. The XS also exits Playback mode automatically when you press the shutter button (so you'll never be prevented from taking a picture on the spur of the moment because you happened to be viewing an image).

- **Erase button.** Press to erase the image shown on the LCD. A menu will pop up displaying Cancel and Erase choices. Use the left/right cross buttons to select one of these actions, then press the Set button to activate your choice.

JUMPING AROUND

Once you've selected a Jump method, you can leap forward among the images on your memory card using the increment/method you choose just by rotating the Main dial.

- To select a Jump method, when viewing a single full-screen image during playback, press the up cross key. An overlay appears that allows you to choose the method (see Figure 2.9).

- Select from 1 image, 10 images, 100 images, or Jump by Date. Press Set to confirm your choice.

- Rotate the Main dial to jump using the increment you selected. To view the next/previous picture after a jump, just use the left/right cross keys.

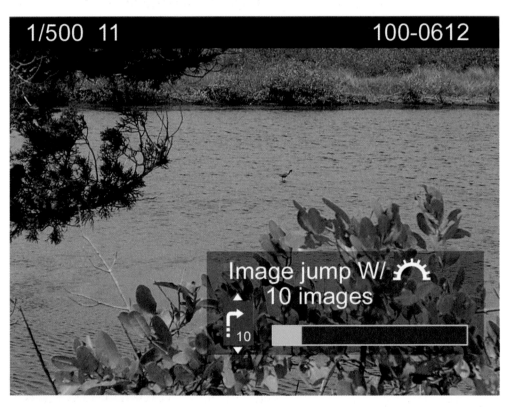

Figure 2.9
Choose a Jump method by pressing the up cross key while viewing an image.

The next group of buttons allow you to change settings:

■ **AE/FE (Auto exposure/Flash exposure) lock/Thumbnail Index/Zoom Out button.** This button, which has a * label above it, has several functions, which differ depending on the AF point and metering mode. You can find more about these variations in Chapter 4.

In Shooting mode, it locks the exposure or flash exposure that the camera sets when you partially depress the shutter button. In Evaluative exposure mode, exposure is locked at the AF point that achieved focus. In Partial or Center-Weighted modes, exposure is locked at the AF center point. The exposure lock indication (*) appears in the viewfinder and on the Shooting Settings display. If you want to recalculate exposure with the shutter button still partially depressed, press the * button again. The exposure will be unlocked when you release the shutter button or take the picture. To retain the exposure lock for subsequent photos, keep the * button pressed while shooting.

When using flash, pressing the * button fires an extra preflash that allows the unit to calculate and lock exposure prior to taking the picture. The characters FEL will appear momentarily in the viewfinder, and the exposure lock indication and a flash indicator appear. (See the description of the viewfinder display later in this chapter.)

In Playback mode, press this button to switch from single-image display to nine-image thumbnail index. (See Figure 2.10.) Move highlighting among the thumbnails with the cross keys or Main dial. To view a highlighted image, press the Zoom In button.

In Playback mode, when an image is zoomed in, press the * button to zoom out.

■ **AF Point Selection/Zoom In button.** In Shooting mode, this button activates autofocus point selection. (See Chapter 4 for information on setting autofocus/exposure point selection.) In Playback mode, if you're viewing a single image, this button zooms in on the image that's displayed. If thumbnail indexes are shown, pressing this button switches from nine thumbnails to four thumbnails, or from four thumbnails to a full screen view of a highlighted image.

■ **Metering mode/Jump.** In Shooting mode, the up cross key produces a screen that allows choosing from Evaluative, Partial, or Center-Weighted Averaging metering modes. (See Figure 1.11 in the previous chapter.) Keep pressing the Metering Mode button until the choice you want is highlighted. Press Set to confirm. In Playback mode, it allows you to choose a Jump mode.

■ **AF mode.** Press the right cross key to produce a screen that allows choosing Autofocus mode from among One Shot, AI Focus, and AI Servo. Press repeatedly until the focus mode you want is selected. Then press Set to confirm your focus mode. (See Figure 1.12 in the previous chapter.)

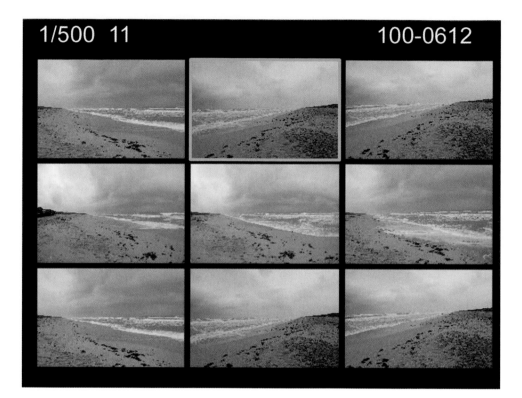

Figure 2.10
The Thumbnail Index/
Zoom Out
button changes
the playback
display from
single image to
four or nine
thumbnails.

- **Drive mode.** Press the left cross key to produce a screen that allows choosing a drive mode. Then press the right cross key to select the 10-second self-timer (which also can be used with the optional IR remote controls), 2-second self-timer, or Self-timer: Continuous, which allows you to specify a number of shots to be taken (from 2 to 10) with the up/down keys. Press Set to confirm your choice. (See Figure 1.15 in the previous chapter.) Then, subsequent photos will be taken using the drive mode you have selected whenever the shutter release is pressed.

- **Picture Styles Selection button.** Press the down cross key to pop up the Picture Styles menu on the LCD, so you can select a given style, or gain access to user-defined styles. To modify a Picture Style, you'll need to use Shooting Menu 2, as described in Chapter 3.

- **Set button.** Selects a highlighted setting or menu option.

- **Access lamp.** When lit or blinking, this lamp indicates that the memory card is being accessed.

Going Topside

The top surface of the Canon EOS Rebel XS has a few frequently accessed controls of its own. The key controls, shown in Figure 2.11, are as follows:

- **Mode dial.** Rotate this dial to switch among Basic Zone and Creative Zone modes. You'll find these modes and options described in more detail in Chapter 4.

- **Sensor focal plane.** Precision macro and scientific photography sometimes requires knowing exactly where the focal plane of the sensor is. The symbol on the side of the pentaprism marks that plane.

Figure 2.11

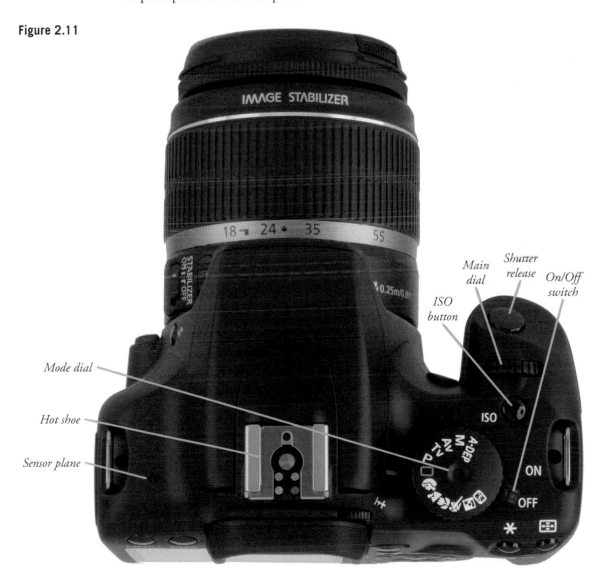

- **Flash hot shoe.** Slide an electronic flash into this mount when you need a more powerful speedlight. A dedicated flash unit, like those from Canon, can use the multiple contact points shown to communicate exposure, zoom setting, white balance information, and other data between the flash and the camera. There's more on using electronic flash in Chapter 7.

- **ISO.** Press this button (just aft of the Main dial) and use the cross keys or Main dial to navigate until the setting you want appears on the LCD. Press the Set button to confirm your choice. You'll find more about ISO options in Chapter 3, and flash EV settings in Chapter 7.

- **Main dial.** This dial is used to make many shooting settings. When settings come in pairs (such as shutter speed/aperture in Manual shooting mode), the Main dial is used for one (for example, shutter speed), while pressing the Av button while rotating the Main dial is used to adjust the other (aperture).

- **Shutter release button.** Partially depress this button to lock in exposure and focus. Press all the way to take the picture. Tapping the shutter release when the camera has turned off the auto exposure and autofocus mechanisms reactivates both. When a review image is displayed on the back-panel color LCD, tapping this button removes the image from the display and reactivates the autoexposure and autofocus mechanisms.

- **On/Off switch.** Flip forward to turn the Rebel XS on, and back to turn it off again.

Underneath Your Rebel XS

There's not a lot going on with the bottom panel of your Rebel XS. You'll find a tripod socket, which secures the camera to a tripod, and is also used to lock on the optional BG-E5 battery grip, which provides more juice to run your camera to take more exposures with a single charge. It also adds a vertically oriented shutter release, Main dial, AE lock/FE lock, and AF point selection controls for easier vertical shooting. To mount the grip, slide the battery door latch to open the door, then push gently towards the outside edge of the camera to free the hinge pins from their sockets. That will let you remove the battery door. Then slide the grip into the battery cavity, aligning the pin on the grip with the small hole on the other side of the tripod socket. Tighten the grip's tripod socket screw to lock the grip onto the bottom of your XS. Figure 2.12 shows the underside view of the camera.

Figure 2.12

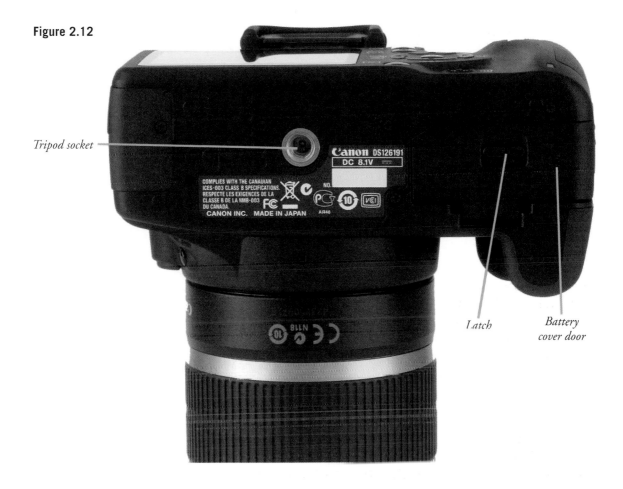

Lens Components

The typical lens, like the ones shown in Figures 2.13 and 2.14, has seven or eight common features. Not every component appears on every lens. The 18-55mm lens on the left, for example, lacks the distance scale and distance indicator that the 17-85mm lens on the right has. Lenses that lack image stabilization will not have a stabilization switch.

- **Filter thread.** Lenses have a thread on the front for attaching filters and other add-ons. Some also use this thread for attaching a lens hood (you screw on the filter first, and then attach the hood to the screw thread on the front of the filter).

- **Lens hood bayonet.** This is used to mount the lens hood for lenses that don't use screw mount hoods (the majority).

- **Zoom ring.** Turn this ring to change the zoom setting.

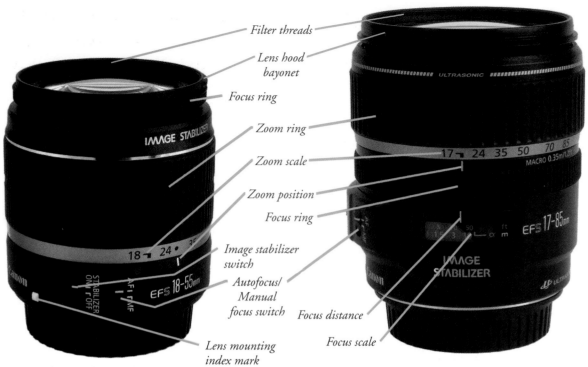

Filter threads

Lens hood
bayonet

Focus ring

Zoom ring

Zoom scale

Zoom position

Focus ring

Image stabilizer
switch

Autofocus/
Manual
focus switch

Focus distance

Focus scale

Lens mounting
index mark

Figure 2.13

Figure 2.14

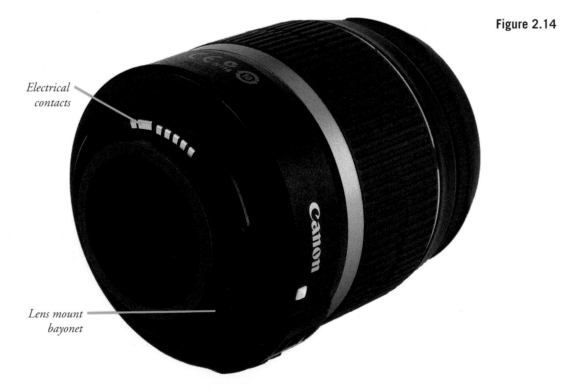

Electrical
contacts

Lens mount
bayonet

- **Zoom scale.** These markings on the lens show the current focal length selected.

- **Focus ring.** This is the ring you turn when you manually focus the lens.

- **Distance scale.** This is a readout that rotates in unison with the lens's focus mechanism to show the distance at which the lens has been focused. It's a useful indicator for double-checking autofocus, roughly evaluating depth-of-field, and for setting manual focus guesstimates.

- **Autofocus/Manual switch.** Allows you to change from automatic focus to manual focus.

- **Image stabilization switch.** Lenses with IS include a separate switch for adjusting the stabilization feature.

- **Electrical contacts.** On the back of the lens (see Figure 2.14) are electrical contacts that the camera uses to communicate focus, aperture setting, and other information.

- **Lens bayonet.** This mount is used to attach the lens to a matching bayonet on the camera body.

LCD Panel Readouts

The Rebel XS does not have a monochrome status LCD, like the one found on the top panel of the EOS 50D, and underneath the back-panel color LCD as the original Digital Rebel and Rebel XT did. Lacking this auxiliary information display, the XS uses the 2.5-inch color LCD to show you everything you need to see, from images to a collection of informational data displays. Here's an overview of these displays, and how to access them:

- **Image playback displays.** When the XS shows you a picture for review, you can select from among four different information overlays. To switch among them, press the DISP button while the image is on the screen. The LCD will cycle among the Single image display (Figure 2.15); Single image display with recording quality (Figure 2.16); Histogram display, which shows basic shooting information as well as a brightness histogram at bottom right, with individual histograms for the red, green, and blue channels above (Figure 2.17); and a complete Shooting information display (Figure 2.18), which includes most of the relevant shooting settings, plus a brightness histogram. I'll explain how to work with histograms in Chapter 4.

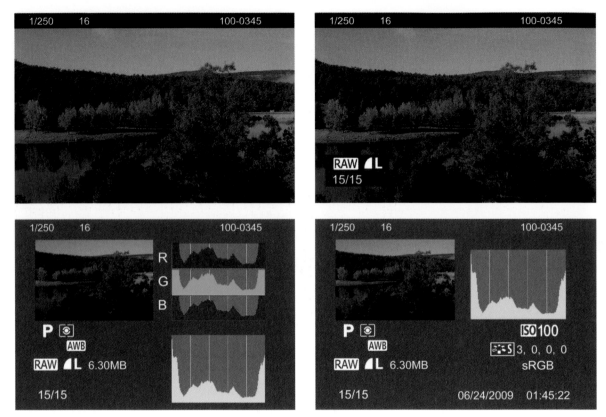

Figures 2.15, 2.16, 2.17, 2.18 Image playback displays include Single image, Single image with recording quality, Histogram, and Shooting information.

- **Shooting Settings display.** While you are taking pictures, this screen will be shown, with information like that in Figure 2.19. Not all of the data pictured will be seen at one time; only the settings that are appropriate for the current shooting mode will be displayed. I'll explain how to make and use each of these settings later in this book. You can turn this display off by pressing the DISP button, and restore it again by pressing the DISP button a second time. When the Shooting Settings display is active, you can return to it when there is a menu screen or image review on the LCD by tapping the shutter release button. The display turns off when you press the shutter release halfway.

- **Camera function settings.** When any menu is displayed, you can switch to the Camera Functions settings screen by pressing the DISP button. A screen like the one shown in Figure 2.20 will appear, with key camera function settings arrayed.

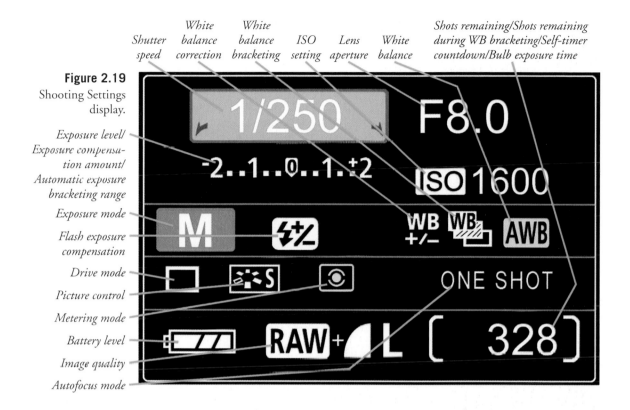

Figure 2.19
Shooting Settings
display.

Shutter
speed

*White
balance
correction*

*White
balance
bracketing*

*ISO
setting*

*Lens
aperture*

*White
balance*

*Shots remaining/Shots remaining
during WB bracketing/Self-timer
countdown/Bulb exposure time*

*Exposure level/
Exposure compensa-
tion amount/
Automatic exposure
bracketing range*

Exposure mode

*Flash exposure
compensation*

Drive mode

Picture control

Metering mode

Battery level

Image quality

Autofocus mode

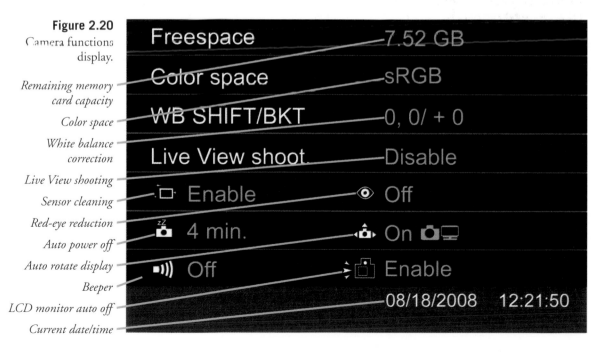

Figure 2.20
Camera functions
display.

*Remaining memory
card capacity*

Color space

*White balance
correction*

Live View shooting

Sensor cleaning

Red-eye reduction

Auto power off

Auto rotate display

Beeper

LCD monitor auto off

Current date/time

Looking Inside the Viewfinder

Much of the important shooting status information is shown inside the viewfinder of the Rebel XS. As with the displays shown on the color LCD, not all of this information will be shown at any one time. Figure 2.21 shows what you can expect to see. I'll explain all of these readouts later in this book, with those pertaining to exposure in Chapter 4, and those relating to flash in Chapter 7. These readouts include:

- **Autofocus zones.** Shows the seven areas used by the XS to focus. The camera can select the appropriate focus zone for you, or you can manually select one or all of the zones, as described in Chapters 1 and 4.

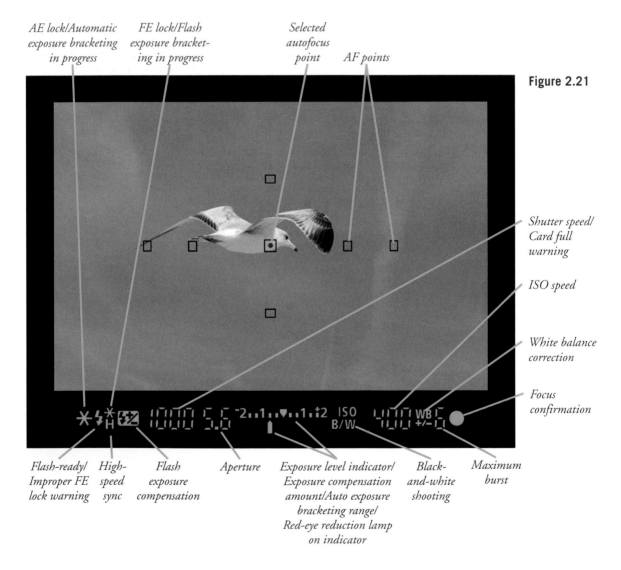

Figure 2.21

AE lock/Automatic exposure bracketing in progress

FE lock/Flash exposure bracketing in progress

Selected autofocus point

AF points

Shutter speed/ Card full warning

ISO speed

White balance correction

Focus confirmation

Flash-ready/ Improper FE lock warning

High-speed sync

Flash exposure compensation

Aperture

Exposure level indicator/ Exposure compensation amount/Auto exposure bracketing range/ Red-eye reduction lamp on indicator

Black-and-white shooting

Maximum burst

■ **Auto exposure lock.** Shows that exposure has been locked. This icon also appears when an automatic exposure bracketing sequence is in progress.

■ **Flash ready indicator.** This icon appears when the flash is fully charged. It also shows when the flash exposure lock has been applied for an inappropriate exposure value.

■ **Flash status indicator.** Appears along with the flash-ready indicator: The H is shown when high speed (focal plane) flash sync is being used. The * appears when flash exposure lock or a flash exposure bracketing sequence is underway.

■ **Flash exposure compensation.** Appears when flash EV changes have been made.

■ **Shutter speed/aperture readouts.** Most of the time, these readouts show the current shutter speed and aperture. This pair can also warn you of memory card conditions (full, error, or missing), ISO speed, flash exposure lock, and a buSY indicator when the camera is busy doing other things (including flash recycling).

■ **Exposure level indicator.** This scale shows the current exposure level, with the bottom indicator centered when the exposure is correct as metered. The indicator may also move to the left or right to indicate under- or overexposure (respectively). The scale is also used to show the amount of EV and flash EV adjustments, the number of stops covered by the current automatic exposure bracketing range, and is used as a red-eye reduction lamp indicator.

■ **ISO Sensitivity.** This useful indicator shows the current ISO setting value. Those who have accidentally taken dozens of shots under bright sunlight at ISO 1600 because they forgot to change the setting back after some indoor shooting will treasure this addition.

■ **B/W indicator.** Illuminates when the Monochrome Picture Style is being used. There's no way to restore color when you're shooting JPEGs without RAW, so this indicator is another valuable warning.

■ **White balance correction.** Shows that white balance has been tweaked.

■ **Maximum burst available.** Changes to a number to indicate the number of frames that can be taken in Continuous mode using the current settings.

■ **Focus confirmation.** This green dot appears when the subject covered by the active autofocus zone is in sharp focus.

3

Setting Up Your Canon EOS Rebel XS

For an entry-level camera, the Rebel XS has a remarkable number of options and settings you can use to customize the way your camera operates. Not only can you change shooting settings used at the time the picture is taken, but you can adjust the way your camera behaves. Indeed, if your XS doesn't operate in exactly the way you'd like, chances are you can make a small change in the pair of Shooting menus, the Playback menu, or three (count 'em) Setup menus to tailor the camera to your needs. If you don't like the organization of the menus themselves, you can collect your favorite functions into one group called My Menu.

This chapter will help you sort out the settings for all the XS's menus. These include the aforementioned Shooting and Playback menus, which determine how the XS uses many of its shooting features to take a photo and how it displays images on review. Later in the chapter, I'll show you how to use the Setup menu to adjust power-saving timers, specify Live View options, control your built-in flash, and work with the Rebel XS's 12 useful Custom Functions.

As I've mentioned before, this book isn't intended to replace the manual you received with your XS, nor have I any interest in rehashing its contents. You'll still find the original manual useful as a standby reference that lists every possible option in exhaustive (if mind-numbing) detail—without really telling you how to use those options to take better pictures. There is, however, some unavoidable duplication between the Canon manual and this chapter, because I'm going to explain all the key menu choices and the options you may have in using them. You should find, though, that I will give you the information you need in a much more helpful format, with plenty of detail on why you should make some settings that are particularly difficult to understand.

I'm not going to waste a lot of space on some of the more obvious menu choices in these chapters. For example, you can probably figure out, even without my help, that the Beep option deals with the solid-state beeper in your camera that sounds off during various activities (such as the self-timer countdown). You can certainly decipher the import of the two options available for the Beep entry (On and Off). In this chapter, I'll devote no more than a sentence or two to the blatantly obvious settings and concentrate on the more confusing aspects of XS setup, such as autofocus. I'll start with an overview of using the XS's menus themselves.

Anatomy of the Rebel XS's Menus

The XS has one of the best-designed menu systems of any digital SLR in its price class, with a remarkable amount of consistency (finally!) with other cameras in the Canon product line. In fact, it's virtually identical to the menu found in the Rebel XSi, and if you used any other newer Canon dSLR before you purchased your Rebel XS, you're probably already familiar with the basic menu lineup. The camera has a series of seven separate tabbed menus when using one of the Creative Zone exposure modes (and four when using one of the Basic Zone modes), each with a single screen of entries, arranged in rows (so you won't need to scroll within a menu to see all the entries). The new menus are much cleaner, too.

With the revamped system, just press the Menu button, located in the upper-left corner of the back of the camera, and use either the left/right cross keys or spin the Main dial to highlight the menu tab you want to access. Then, scroll up and down within a menu with the up/down cross keys. What could be easier?

Pressing the Menu button brings up a typical menu like the one shown in Figure 3.1. (If the camera goes to "sleep" while you're reviewing a menu, you may need to wake it up again by tapping the shutter release button.) There are seven menu tabs: Shooting 1, Shooting 2, Playback, Set-Up 1, Set-Up 2, Set-Up 3, and My Menu. (When using Basic exposure modes, Set-Up 3 and My Menu tabs do not appear.) The tabs are color-coded: red for Shooting menus, blue for the Playback menu, yellow for Set-up menus, and green for the My Menu tab. The currently selected menu's icon is white within a white border, on a background corresponding to its color code. All the inactive menus are grayed out and the icon and their borders are color-coded. The top line of the menu screen also has a DISP indicator to remind you that you can press the DISP button at any time to switch to a screen that shows many of the current settings. (Review Figure 2.20 in the previous chapter; I'm not going to repeat that figure here.)

Figure 3.1
The Rebel XS's menus are arranged in a series of seven tabs.

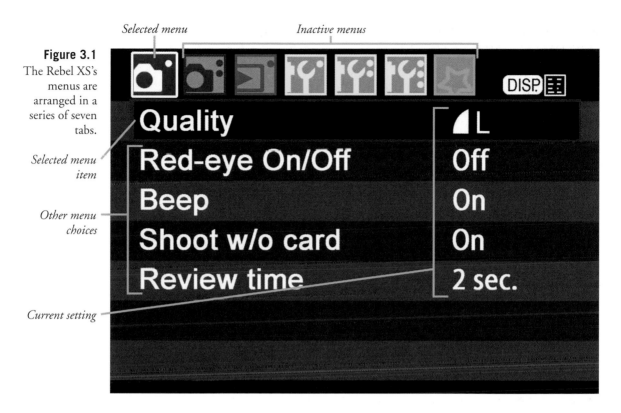

Selected menu

Inactive menus

Selected menu item

Other menu choices

Current setting

Quality	◢ L
Red-eye On/Off	Off
Beep	On
Shoot w/o card	On
Review time	2 sec.

Here are the things to watch for as you navigate the menus:

■ **Menu tabs.** In the top row of the menu screen, the menu that is currently active will be highlighted as described earlier. One, two, or three dots in the tab lets you know if you are in, say Set-Up 1, Set-Up 2, or Set-Up 3. Just remember that the two red camera icons stand for shooting options; the blue right-pointing triangle represents playback options; the three yellow wrench/hammer icons stand for set-up options; and the green star stands for personalized menus defined for the star of the show—you.

■ **Selected menu item.** The currently selected menu item will have a black background and will be surrounded by a box the same hue as its color code.

■ **Other menu choices.** The other menu items visible on the screen will have a medium or dark gray background (alternating).

■ **Current setting.** The current settings for visible menu items are shown in the right-hand column, until one menu item is selected (by pressing the Set key). At that point, all the settings vanish from the screen except for those dealing with the active menu choice.

When you've moved the menu highlighting with the up/down cross keys to the menu item you want to work with, press the Set button to select it. A submenu with a list of options for the selected menu item will appear. Within the submenu options, you can scroll up or down with the up/down cross keys to choose a setting, and then press Set to confirm the choice you've made. Press the Menu button again to exit.

Shooting Menu 1 & 2 Options

The various direct setting buttons on the top and back panels of the camera, for Autofocus mode, white balance, Drive mode, ISO sensitivity, metering mode, and flash, along with exposure compensation (EV) adjustments are likely to be the most common settings changes you make, with changes during a particular session fairly common. You'll find that the Shooting menu options are those that you access second-most frequently when you're using your Rebel XS. You might make such adjustments as you begin a shooting session, or when you move from one type of subject to another. Canon makes accessing these changes very easy.

This section explains the options of the two Shooting menus and how to use them. The options you'll find in these red-coded menus include:

- Quality
- Red-Eye On/Off
- Beep
- Shoot w/o card
- Review time
- AEB (Automatic Exposure Bracketing)

- Flash exp comp
- Custom WB
- WB Shift/BKT
- Color Space
- Picture Style
- Dust Delete Data

Quality Settings

You can choose the image quality settings used by the XS to store its files. You have three choices to make:

- **Resolution.** The number of pixels captured determines the absolute resolution of the photos you shoot with your Rebel XS. Your choices range from 10.2 megapixels (Large or L), measuring 3,888 × 2,592 pixels; 5.2 megapixels (Medium or M), measuring 2,816 × 1,880; to 2.5 megapixels (Small or S), 1,936 × 1,288 pixels.

- **JPEG compression.** To reduce the size of your image files and allow more photos to be stored on a given memory card, the XS uses JPEG compression to squeeze the images down to a smaller size. This compacting reduces the image quality a little, so you're offered your choice of Fine compression or Normal compression. The symbols help you remember that Fine compression (represented by a quarter-circle) provides the smoothest results, while Normal compression (signified by a stair-step icon) provides "jaggier" images.

- **JPEG, RAW, or both.** You can elect to store only JPEG versions of the images you shoot (about 3.8MB per photo), or you can save your photos as uncompressed, loss-free RAW files, which consume more than 2.5 times as much space on your memory card (9.8MB). Or, you can store both at once as you shoot. Many photographers elect to save *both* JPEG and a RAW file, so they'll have a JPEG version that might be usable as-is, as well as the original "digital negative" RAW file in case they want to do some processing of the image later. You'll end up with two different versions of the same file: one with a .jpg extension, and one with the .cr2 extension that signifies a Canon RAW.

To choose the combination you want, access the menus, scroll to Quality, and press the Set button. A screen similar to the one shown in Figure 3.2 will appear. Use the cross keys to cycle among the eight choices. In practice, you'll probably use only the Large (Fine), RAW+L (Large Fine), or RAW selections. Note that you can select different quality settings for Basic Zone and Creative Zone modes, which is why the Mode dial with the appropriate zone highlighted appears as a reminder at the left side of the screen. However, when setting quality for a Basic Zone mode, RAW and RAW+L are not available; you can select only Large, Medium, and Small resolutions and Fine or Normal compression. If you have previously set RAW or RAW+L when using a Creative Zone mode, and then switch to a Basic Zone mode, the setting will be automatically changed to Large JPEG Fine format.

Figure 3.2
Choose your resolution, JPEG compression, and file format from this screen.

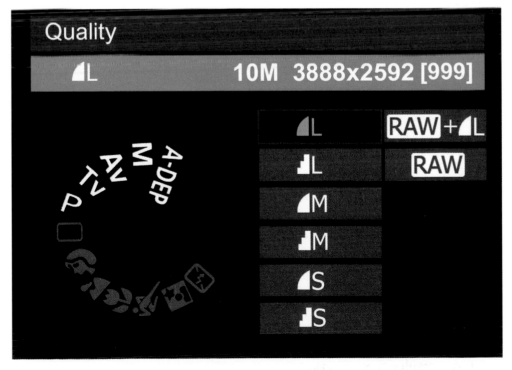

There are some limited advantages to using the Medium and Small resolution settings, and Normal JPEG compression settings. They all allow stretching the capacity of your memory card so you can shoehorn quite a few more pictures onto a single memory card. That can come in useful when on vacation and you're running out of storage, or when you're shooting non-critical work that doesn't require full resolution (such as photos taken for real estate listings, web page display, photo ID cards, or similar applications).

For most work, using lower resolution and extra compression is false economy. You never know when you might actually need that extra bit of picture detail. Your best bet is to have enough memory cards to handle all the shooting you want to do until you have the chance to transfer your photos to your computer or a personal storage device.

However, reduced image quality can sometimes be beneficial if you're shooting sequences of photos rapidly, as the XS is able to hold more of them in its internal memory buffer before transferring to the memory card. Using the RAW+L or RAW settings, the largest burst you can expect will be four to five shots. Eschew RAW and go for JPEG Fine at maximum resolution, and, according to Canon's tests, you might get more than 500 photos in a single burst, and even more using JPEG Standard. (I've never checked this out, because I don't have the patience or inclination to fire off more than 500 pictures at one time.) For most sports and other applications, you'd probably rather have better, sharper pictures than longer periods of continuous shooting, so the JPEG Fine setting will work best.

JPEG vs. RAW

You'll sometimes be told that RAW files are the "unprocessed" image information your camera produces, before it's been modified. That's nonsense. RAW files are no more unprocessed than your camera film is after it's been through the chemicals to produce a negative or transparency. A lot can happen in the developer that can affect the quality of a film image—positively and negatively—and, similarly, your digital image undergoes a significant amount of processing before it is saved as a RAW file. Canon even applies a name (Digic III) to the digital image processing (DIP) chip used to perform this magic in the Rebel XS.

A RAW file is more similar to a film camera's processed negative. It contains all the information, captured in 14-bit channels per color (and stored in a 16-bit space), with no compression, no sharpening, no application of any special filters or other settings you might have specified when you took the picture. Those settings are *stored* with the RAW file so they can be applied when the image is converted to a form compatible with your favorite image editor. However, using RAW conversion software such as Adobe Camera Raw or Canon's Digital Photo Professional, you can override those settings and apply settings of your own. You can select essentially the same changes there that you might have specified in your camera's picture-taking options.

RAW exists because sometimes we want to have access to all the information captured by the camera, before the camera's internal logic has processed it and converted the image to a standard file format. RAW doesn't save as much space as JPEG. What it does do is preserve all the information captured by your camera after it's been converted from analog to digital form.

So, why don't we always use RAW? Although some photographers do save only in RAW format, it's more common to use either RAW plus the JPEG option or just shoot JPEG and eschew RAW altogether. While RAW is overwhelmingly helpful when an image needs to be fine-tuned, in other situations working with a RAW file can slow you down significantly. RAW images take longer to store on the memory card, and require more post-processing effort, whether you elect to go with the default settings in force when the picture was taken, or make minor adjustments.

As a result, those who depend on speedy access to images or who shoot large numbers of photos at once may prefer JPEG over RAW. Wedding photographers, for example, might expose several thousand photos during a bridal affair and offer hundreds to clients as electronic proofs for inclusion in an album. Wedding shooters take the time to make sure that their in-camera settings are correct, minimizing the need to post-process photos after the event. Given that their JPEGs are so good, there is little need to get bogged down shooting RAW. Sports photographers also eschew RAW files for similar reasons.

JPEG was invented as a more compact file format that can store most of the information in a digital image, but in a much smaller size. JPEG predates most digital SLRs and was initially used to squeeze down files for transmission over slow dialup connections. Even if you were using an early dSLR with 1.3 megapixel files for news photography, you didn't want to send them back to the office over a modem at 1,200 bps.

But, as I noted, JPEG provides smaller files by compressing the information in a way that loses some image data. JPEG remains a viable alternative because it offers several different quality levels. At the highest quality Fine level, you might not be able to tell the difference between the original RAW file and the JPEG version, even though the RAW file occupies, by Canon's estimate, 9.8MB on your memory card, while the Fine JPEG takes up only 3.8MB of space. You've squeezed the image by two-thirds without losing much visual information at all. If you don't mind losing some quality, you can use more aggressive Standard compression with JPEG to cut the size almost in half again, to 2MB.

In my case, I shoot virtually everything at RAW+L. Most of the time, I'm not concerned about filling up my memory cards, as I usually have a minimum of three 8GB memory cards with me. If I know I may fill up all those cards, I have a tiny battery-operated personal storage device that can copy an 8GB card in about 15 minutes. As I mentioned earlier, when shooting sports I'll shift to JPEG FINE (with no RAW file) to squeeze a little extra speed out of my XS's Continuous Shooting mode, and to reduce the need to wade through eight-photo bursts taken in RAW format. On my last trip to Europe, I took only RAW photos (rather than shooting both RAW and JPEG) to fit more images onto my 60GB personal storage device, shown in Figure 3.3, as I planned on doing at least some post-processing on many of the images for a travel book I was working on.

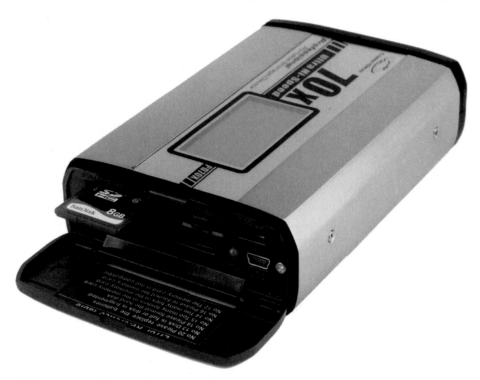

Figure 3.3
If RAW storage space is a concern, consider a portable storage device like this one.

MANAGING LOTS OF FILES

The only long-term drawback to shooting everything in RAW+JPEG is that it's easy to fill up your computer's hard drive if you are a prolific photographer. Here's what I do. My most recent photos are stored on my working hard drive in a numbered folder, say XS-01, with subfolders named after the shooting session, such as 080601Trees, for pictures of trees taken on June 1, 2008. An automatic utility copies new and modified photos to a different hard drive for temporary backup four times daily.

When the top-level folder accumulates about 30GB of images, I back it up to DVDs and then move the folder to a 500GB drive dedicated solely for storage of folders that have already been backed up onto DVD. Then I start a new folder, such as XS-02, on the working hard drive and repeat the process. I always have at least one backup of every image taken, either on another hard drive or on a DVD.

Red-Eye Reduction

Your Rebel XS has a fairly effective Red-Eye Reduction flash mode. Unfortunately, your camera is unable, on its own, to *eliminate* the red-eye effects that occur when an electronic flash (or, rarely, illumination from other sources) bounces off the retinas of the eye and into the camera lens. Animals seem to suffer from yellow or green glowing pupils, instead; the effect is equally undesirable. The effect is worst under low-light conditions (exactly when you might be using a flash) as the pupils expand to allow more light to reach the retinas. The best you can hope for is to *reduce* or minimize the red-eye effect.

The best way to truly eliminate red-eye is to raise the flash up off the camera so its illumination approaches the eye from an angle that won't reflect directly back to the retina and into the lens. The extra height of the built-in flash may not be sufficient, however. That alone is a good reason for using an external flash. If you're working with your XS's built-in flash, your only recourse may be to switch the Red-Eye Reduction feature on with the menu choice shown in Figure 3.4. It causes a lamp on the front of the camera to illuminate with a half-press of the shutter release button, which may cause your subjects' pupils to contract, decreasing the amount of the red-eye effect. (You may have to ask your subject to look at the lamp to gain maximum effect.) Figure 3.5 shows the effects of wider pupils (left) and those that have been contracted using the XS's Red-Eye Reduction feature.

Figure 3.4
Turn on your camera's Red-Eye Reduction feature to help eliminate demon-red pupils.

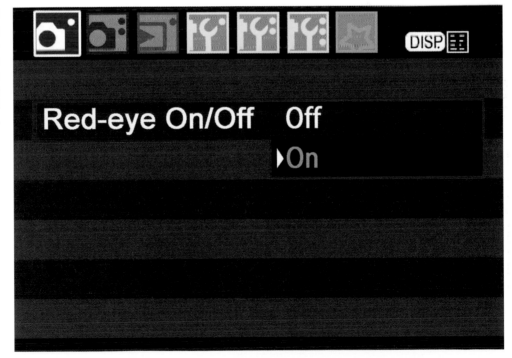

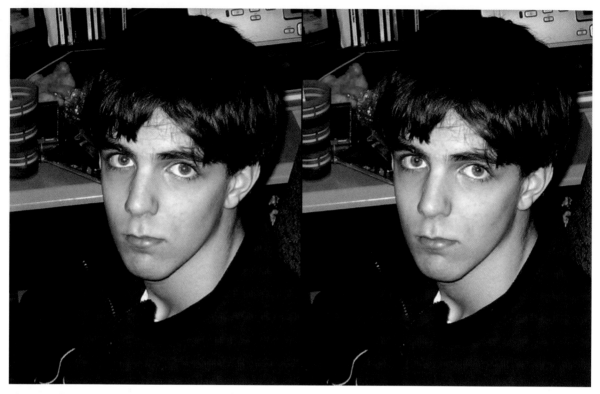

Figure 3.5 Red-eye (left) is tamed (right), thanks to the Rebel XS's Red-Eye reduction lamp.

Beep

The Rebel XS's internal beeper provides a helpful chirp to signify various functions, such as the countdown of your camera's self-timer. You can switch it off if you want to avoid the beep because it's annoying, impolite, or distracting (at a concert or museum), or undesired for any other reason. (I've actually had new dSLR owners ask me how to turn off the "shutter sound" the camera makes; such an option was available in the point-and-shoot camera they'd used previously.) Select Beep from the menu, press Set, and use the cross keys to choose On or Off, as you prefer, as shown in Figure 3.6. Press Set again to activate your choice.

Shoot without a Memory Card Installed

This entry in the Set-Up 1 menu (see Figure 3.7) gives you the ability to snap off "pictures" without a memory card installed—or to lock the camera shutter release if that is the case. It is sometimes called Play mode, because you can experiment with your camera's features or even hand your XS to a friend to let him fool around, without any danger of pictures actually being taken. Back in our film days, we'd sometimes finish a roll, rewind the film back into its cassette surreptitiously, and then hand the camera to a child

Figure 3.6
Silence your
camera's beep
when it
might prove
distracting.

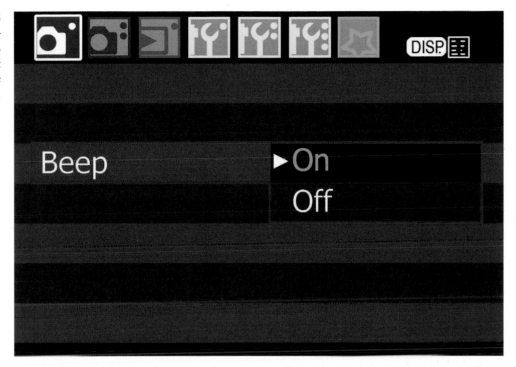

Figure 3.7
You can enable
triggering the
shutter even
when no
memory card
is present.

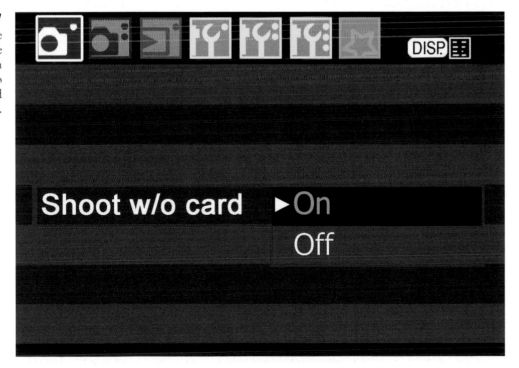

to take a few pictures—without actually wasting any film. It's hard to waste digital film, but Shoot Without Card mode is still appreciated by some, especially camera vendors who want to be able to demo a camera at a store or trade show, but don't want to have to equip each and every demonstrator model with a memory card. To choose this menu item, press Set, select On or Off, and press Set again to enable or disable this capability.

Review Time Out

You can adjust the amount of time an image is displayed for review on the LCD after each shot is taken. You can elect to disable this review entirely (Off), or choose display times of 2, 4, or 8 seconds. You can also select Hold, an indefinite display, which will keep your image on the screen until you use one of the other controls, such as the shutter button or Main dial. Turning the review display off or choosing a brief duration can help preserve battery power. However, the XS will always override the review display when the shutter button is partially or fully depressed, so you'll never miss a shot because a previous image was on the screen. Choose Review Time from the Shooting 1 menu, and select Off, 2 sec., 4 sec., 8 sec., or Hold, as shown in Figure 3.8. If you want to retain an image on the screen for a longer period, but don't want to use Hold as your default, press the Erase button located just southeast of the cross keys. The image will display until you choose Cancel or Erase from the menu that pops up at the bottom of the screen. While those choices remain on the screen, they generally don't obscure much of the picture area.

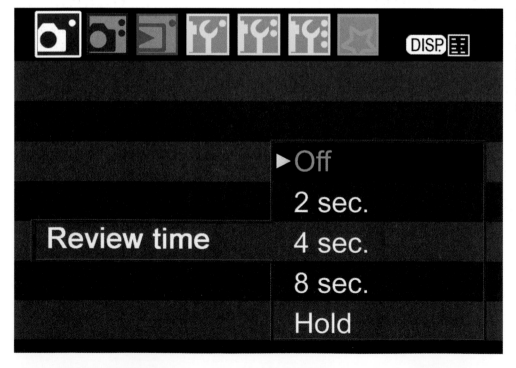

Figure 3.8
Adjust the time an image is displayed on the LCD for review after a picture is taken.

Automatic Exposure Bracketing

The first entry on the Shooting 2 menu is AEB, or Automatic Exposure Bracketing. As you'll learn in Chapter 4, bracketing using the XS's AEB feature is a way to shoot several consecutive exposures using different settings, to improve the odds that one will be exactly right. Select this menu choice, then use the left and right cross keys to spread or contract the three dots beneath the –2/+2 scale until you've defined the range you want the bracket to cover, shown as two-thirds-stop jumps in Figure 3.9.

As you take pictures, the amount of bracketing will be shown as three indicators in the analog exposure display that flash when the shutter release button is pressed halfway. When AEB is activated, the three bracketed shots will be exposed in this sequence: metered exposure, decreased exposure, increased exposure. To cancel bracketing, select this menu option again, and use the left cross key to converge all the bracket indicators once more. You'll find more information about exposure bracketing in Chapter 4.

Figure 3.9
Set the range of the three bracketed exposures.

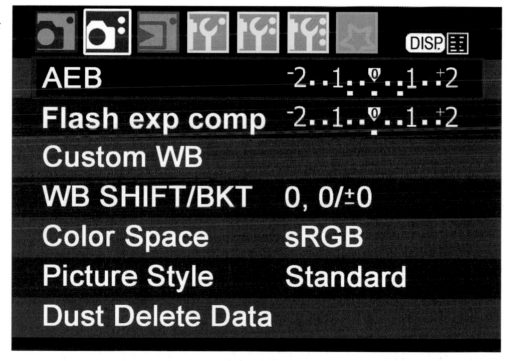

Flash Exposure Compensation

If you'd rather adjust flash exposure using the Shooting 2 menu than with the same function buried several levels deep in the Set-Up 2 menu (under Flash Control), you can do that here. I'll explain how to set this same parameter with the Set-Up 2 menu later in this chapter.

Select this option, then dial in the amount of flash EV compensation you want using the left/right cross keys. Then press Set to confirm your choice; then press the Menu button twice to exit. Once you've activated flash exposure compensation, when you press the shutter release button halfway, the Flash EV icon will flash in the viewfinder and will be displayed on the LCD monitor. To reset or change flash exposure compensation, choose this menu entry again and press the left/right cross keys to restore the pointer to zero, or to another point on the scale.

Tip

If you've activated the Rebel XS's Auto Lighting Optimizer (described later in this chapter), any Flash EV changes you make may not provide the brightening effect you're looking for, as the Auto Lighting Optimizer may cancel out your EV change. Disable Auto Lighting Optimizer (C.Fn.II #5 in the Set-Up 3 menu).

Custom White Balance

If automatic white balance or one of the six preset settings available by pressing the WB button (Auto, Daylight, Shade, Cloudy/Twilight/Sunset, Tungsten, White Fluorescent, or Flash) aren't suitable, you can set a custom white balance using this menu option. The custom setting you establish will then be applied whenever you select Custom using the WB button.

To set the white balance to an appropriate color temperature under the current ambient lighting conditions, follow these steps:

1. Focus manually (with the lens set on MF) on a plain white or gray object, such as a card or wall, making sure the object fills the Spot metering circle in the center of the viewfinder.

2. Take a photo.

3. Press the Menu button and select Custom WB from the Shooting 2 menu.

4. The reference image you just took appears. If you want to use a different picture, use the left/right cross keys to navigate to the photo you'd like to use.

5. Press the Set button to store the white balance of the image as your custom setting.

6. Henceforth, you can access this customized setting by pressing the WB button and choosing the Custom icon. It's the one at the extreme left of the screen that pops up.

A WHITE BALANCE LIBRARY

Shoot a selection of blank-card images under a variety of lighting conditions on a spare memory card. If you want to "recycle" one of the color temperatures you've stored, insert the card and set the Custom white balance to that of one of the images in your white balance library, as described above.

White Balance Shift and Bracketing

White balance shift allows you to dial in a white balance color bias along the Blue/Yellow (Amber) dimensions, and/or Magenta/Green scale. In other words, you can set your color balance so that it is a little bluer or yellower (only), a little more magenta or green (only), or a combination of the two bias dimensions. You can also bracket exposures, taking several consecutive pictures, each with a slightly different color balance biased in the directions you specify.

The process is a little easier to visualize if you look at Figure 3.10. The center intersection of lines BA and GM (remember high school geometry!) is the point of zero bias. Move the point at that intersection using the left/right and up/down cross keys to locate it at any point on the graph using the Blue-Yellow (Amber) and Green-Magenta coordinates. The amount of shift will be displayed in the SHIFT box to the right of the graph.

Figure 3.10
Use the Main dial to specify color balance bracketing using Green/Magenta bias or to specify Blue-Yellow/Amber bias.

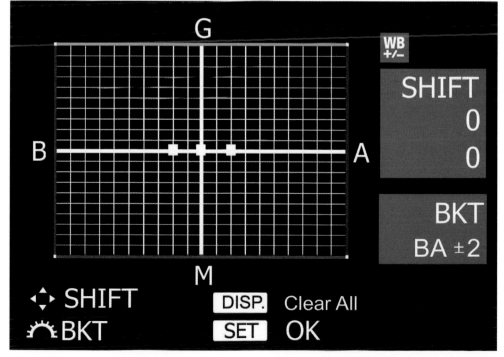

White balance bracketing is like white balance shifting, only the bracketed changes occur along the bias axis you specify. The three squares in Figure 3.10 show that the white balance bracketing will occur in two stop steps along the blue-yellow (amber) axis. The amount of the bracketing is shown in the lower box to the right of the graph.

This form of bracketing is similar to exposure bracketing, but with the added dimension of hue instead of brightness/darkness. Bias bracketing can be performed in any JPEG-only mode. You can't use RAW or RAW+JPEG, because the RAW files already contain the information needed to fine-tune the white balance and white balance bias.

White Balance Bracketing

Follow these steps to bracket white balance.

1. **Activate white balance shift/bracketing.** Select WB SHIFT/BKT from the Shooting 2 menu.

2. **Choose the amount of the WB bracketing.** Rotate the Main dial to select the amount of shift (how much each photo will vary). Spin to the right to separate the three indicator dots by 1 to 3 increments in the horizontal Blue/Amber axis. Spin to the left to separate the three dots in the vertical Green/Magenta direction. The bracket amount (BA) will be shown in the BKT box at the right side of the screen.

3. **Select the WB bias.** Unless you adjust the white balance bias, the bracketing will take place along one axis only; that is, blue-to-amber changes or green-to-magenta changes, either progressing from the center neutral point that's the intersection of axes BA and GM. You can use the left/right and up/down cross keys to add some *bias* to the white balance bracketing (described next).

4. **Confirm your white balance bracketing.** Press DISP to cancel the WB shift/bracketing changes you've made, or press Set to confirm the setting and return to the Shooting 2 menu.

5. **Take your bracket sets.** Subsequent pictures you take will have their white balance bracketed in sets of three, using the parameters you've just entered. The order will be Standard WB (representing the middle dot of the three); More Blue/More Magenta (either the left or top dot, depending on whether you used the Blue/Amber or Magenta/Green axes); More Amber/More Green.

Note

If you use the Rebel XS's continuous shooting feature, you can snap off all three shots in a bracket set quickly and automatically. Note that if High ISO speed noise reduction is set to On in the Custom Functions menu (described later in this chapter), WB bracketing is disabled.

BIASING YOUR WHITE BALANCE

White balance bracketing is confusing enough, until you start adding some bias to the equation. Fortunately, the concept is easy to understand with a little explanation. As I noted above, white balance bracketing usually proceeds along a single axis, either the Blue/Amber (horizontal) or Green/Magenta (vertical axis). If you stick to those directions, the bracketing dot indicators will confine themselves to the thicker center lines that bisect the grid shown in Figure 3.10. You can move the bracket dots along either center line with the left/right (for horizontal movement) or up/down (for vertical movement) cross keys to give your bracketing an unambiguous bias towards the blue, amber, green, or magenta tones.

The potentially confusing part comes into play when you use the up/down keys to adjust the bracket range for Blue/Amber (horizontal) bracketing, or the left/right keys to adjust the bracket range for the Green/Magenta (vertical bracketing). When you do that, the bracket indicators drift into one of the four quadrants of the grid, so you end up with Blue/Amber bracketing that has a bit of a green or magenta bias as well, or a Green/Magenta bracketing with some blue or amber bias, as shown in Figure 3.11. This is the kind of ultra-fine tuning that the Rebel XS makes available to you, and of which you might want to afford yourself as you gain experience. In most cases, it's fairly easy to determine if you want your image to be more green, more magenta, more blue, or more yellow, although judging your current shots on the LCD screen can be tricky unless you view the screen in a darkened location so it will be bright and easy to see. You'll find more about bracketing in Chapter 4.

Figure 3.11
The up/down and left/right cross keys can be used to maneuver the bracketing into any quadrant.

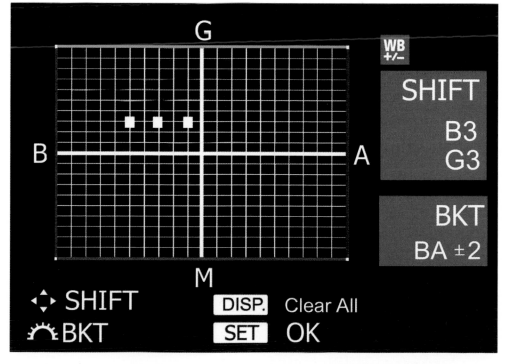

Color Space

You can select one of two color gamuts (the range of colors available to represent an image) using this menu entry, shown previously among the other menu choices in Figure 3.9. Adobe RGB is an expanded color space useful for commercial and professional printing, and it can reproduce a wider range of colors. Canon recommends against using this color space if your images will be displayed primarily on your computer screen or output by your personal printer. The sRGB setting is recommended for images that will be output locally on the user's own printer, as this color space matches that of the typical inkjet printer fairly closely. Strictly speaking, both color spaces can reproduce the exact same absolute number of colors (16.8 million when reduced to a 24-bit file from the original capture), but Adobe RGB spreads those colors over a larger space. Think of a box of crayons (the jumbo 16.8 million crayon variety). Some of the basic crayons from the original sRGB set have been removed and replaced with new hues not contained in the original box. Your "new" box contains colors that can't be reproduced by your computer monitor, but which work just fine with a commercial printing press.

BEST OF BOTH WORLDS

If you plan to use RAW+JPEG for most of your photos, go ahead and set sRGB as your color space. You'll end up with JPEGs suitable for output on your own printer, but you can still extract an Adobe RGB version from the RAW file at any time. It's like shooting two different color spaces at once—sRGB and Adobe RGB—and getting the best of both worlds.

Picture Style

Picture Styles let you choose a combination of sharpness, contrast, color saturation, and color tone settings that you can apply to all the pictures you take using a particular style. The Canon EOS Rebel XS has a "Standard" Picture Style, plus preset styles for Portrait, Landscape, Neutral, and Faithful pictures (which can all be customized with your preferences), plus three user-definable settings you can apply to any sort of shooting situation you want, such as sports, architecture, or baby pictures. There is also a Monochrome Picture Style that allows you to adjust filter effects or add color toning to your black-and-white images.

The Picture Style feature, introduced to the EOS camera line with the Canon EOS 30D, is one of the most important tools for customizing the way your XS renders its photos. Picture Styles are extremely flexible. If you don't like one of the predefined styles, you can adjust it to suit your needs. You can also use those three User Definition files to create styles that are all your own. If you want rich, bright colors to emulate Velvia film or the work of legendary photographer Pete Turner, you can build your own color-soaked style. If you want soft, muted colors and less sharpness to create a romantic look, you can do that, too. Perhaps you'd like a setting with extra contrast for shooting outdoors on hazy or cloudy days.

Once your styles are set up, Picture Styles are easy to access. Press the Picture Styles button (the down cross key) next to the color LCD, and use the up/down cross keys to move through the list of available styles. (See Figure 3.12.) As each style is highlighted, its current settings for Sharpness, Contrast, Saturation, and Color Tone are shown at the left side of the screen. Press Set to activate the style of your choice. You can also select a Picture Style from the Shooting 1 menu entry (although it takes a few seconds longer). You'll primarily use this menu item to define or redefine your Picture Styles. (You can also set up Picture Styles using the XS's Picture Styles Editor, as described in this book's Chapter 8.)

Figure 3.12
Press the Picture Style button (down cross key) to quickly select one of the available styles.

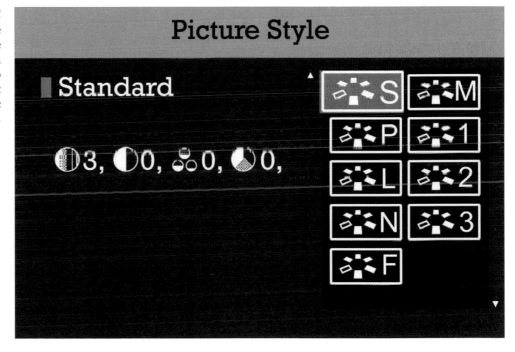

To select a style from this menu, choose Picture Style from Shooting 2 menu and press Set to produce the menu screen shown in Figure 3.13. Use the up/down cross keys to scroll among the nine choices (the ones shown, plus User Def. 1, User Def. 2, and User Def. 3) and press Set to activate your choice. Then press the Menu button to exit the menu system. You can see that switching among Picture Styles is fast and easy enough to allow you to shift gears as often as you like during a shooting session.

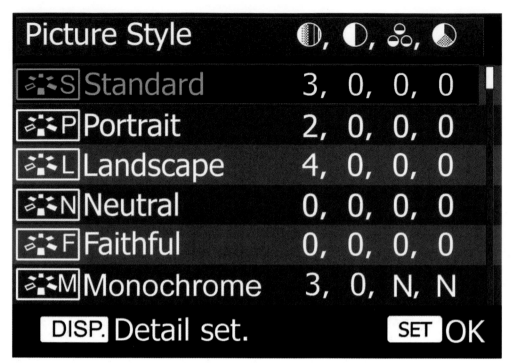

Figure 3.13
Nine different
Picture Styles
are available;
these six plus
three User Def
styles not
shown.

The Rebel XS is smart enough to use Picture Styles on its own. When using one of the Basic Zone modes, the camera selects the Standard Picture Style automatically, except if you select the Portrait or Landscape modes. The Portrait and Landscape Picture Styles will be used (respectively) instead.

Defining Picture Styles

Canon makes interpreting current Picture Style settings and applying changes very easy. The current settings are shown as numeric values on the menu screen shown in Figure 3.13. Some camera vendors use word descriptions, like Sharp, Extra Sharp, or Vivid, More Vivid that are difficult to relate to. The XS's settings, on the other hand, are values on uniform scales, with seven steps (from 1 to 7) for sharpness, and plus/minus four steps clustered around a zero (no change) value for contrast and saturation (so you can change from low contrast/low saturation, –4, to high contrast/high saturation, +4), as well as color tone (–4/reddish to +4/yellowish). The individual icons shown at the top of Figure 3.13 represent (left to right) Sharpness, Contrast, Saturation, and Color Tone. To change one of the existing Picture Styles, or to define your own, just follow these steps:

1. Access the Picture Style menu from the Shooting 2 menu, and press the up/down cross keys to scroll to the style you'd like to adjust.

2. Press the DISP button to choose Detail set. and produce the screen shown in Figure 3.14. The up/down cross keys can scroll among the four parameters, plus Default set. at the bottom of the screen, which restores the values to the preset numbers.

Figure 3.14
Each parameter can be changed separately.

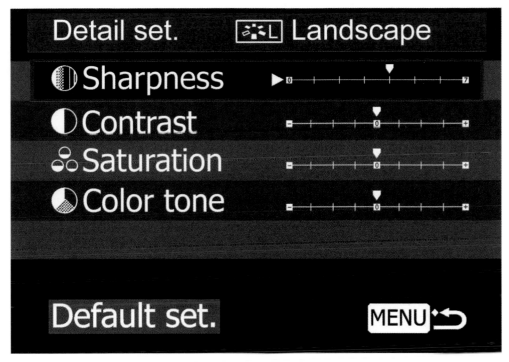

3. Press Set to change the values of one of the four parameters. If you're redefining one of the default presets, the menu screen will look like the figure, which represents the Landscape Picture Style.

4. Use the left/right cross keys to move the triangle to the value you want to use. Note that the previous value remains on the scale, represented by a gray triangle. This makes it easy to return to the original setting if you want.

5. Press the Set button to lock in that value, then press the Menu button to back out of the menu system.

Any Picture Style that has been changed from its defaults will be shown in the Picture Style menu with blue highlighting the altered parameter. You don't have to worry about changing a Picture Style and then forgetting that you've modified it. A quick glance at the Picture Style menu will show you which styles and parameters have been changed.

Making changes in the Monochrome Picture Style is slightly different, as the Saturation and Color Tone parameters are replaced with Filter Effect and Toning Effect options. (Keep in mind that once you've taken a JPEG photo using a Monochrome Picture Style, you can't convert the image back to full color.) You can choose from Yellow, Orange, Red, or Green filters, or None, and specify Sepia, Blue, Purple, or Green toning, or None. You can still set the Sharpness and Contrast parameters that are available with the other Picture Styles. Figure 3.15 shows filter effects being applied to the Monochrome Picture Style.

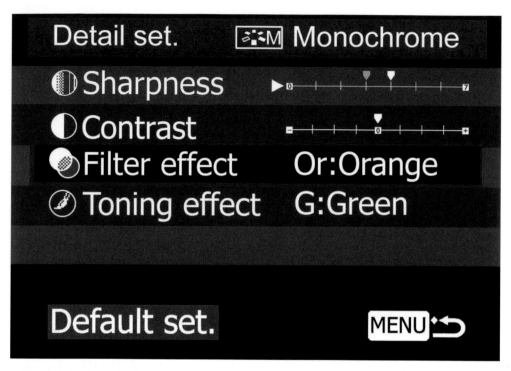

Figure 3.15
Select from among four color filters in the Monochrome Picture Style.

FILTERS VS. TONING

Although some of the color choices overlap, you'll get very different looks when choosing between Filter Effects and Toning Effects. Filter Effects add no color to the monochrome image. Instead, they reproduce the look of black-and-white film that has been shot through a color filter. That is, yellow will make the sky darker and the clouds will stand out more, while orange makes the sky even darker and sunsets more full of detail. The red filter produces the darkest sky of all and darkens green objects, such as leaves. Human skin may appear lighter than normal. The green filter has the opposite effect on leaves, making them appear lighter in tone. Figure 3.16 shows the same scene shot with no filter, then yellow, green, and red filters.

The Sepia, Blue, Purple, and Green toning effects, on the other hand, all add a color cast to your monochrome image. Use these when you want an old-time look or a special effect, without bothering to recolor your shots in an image editor.

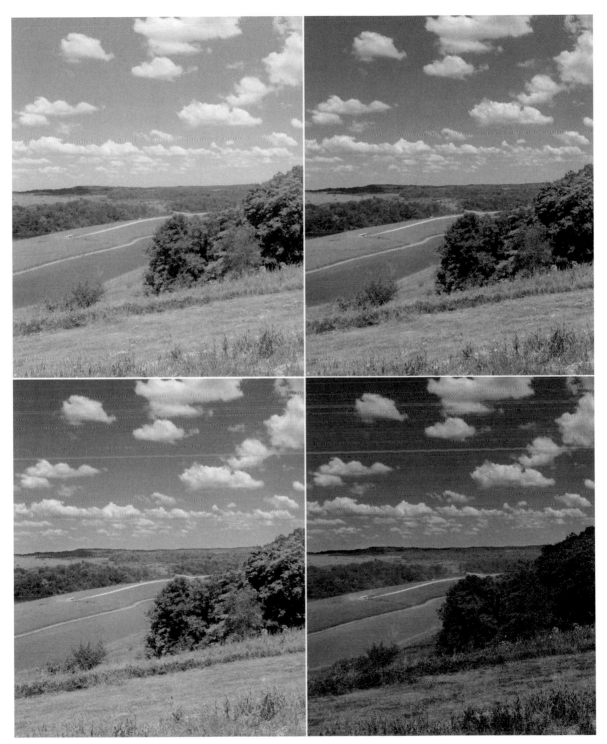

Figure 3.16 No filter (upper left); yellow filter (upper right); green filter (lower left); and red filter (lower right).

Dust Delete Data

This menu choice lets you "take a picture" of any dust or other particles that may be adhering to your sensor. The XS will then append information about the location of this dust to your photos, so that the Digital Photo Professional software can use this reference information to identify dust in your images and remove it automatically. You should capture a Dust Delete Data photo from time to time as your final line of defense against sensor dust.

To use this feature, select Dust Delete Data to produce the screen shown in Figure 3.17. Select OK and press the Set button. The camera will first perform a self-cleaning operation by applying ultrasonic vibration to the low-pass filter that resides on top of the sensor. Then, a screen will appear asking you to press the shutter button. Point the XS at a solid white card with the lens set on Manual focus and rotate the focus ring to infinity. When you press the shutter release, the camera takes a photo of the card using Aperture Priority and f/22 (which provides enough depth-of-field [actually, in this case *depth-of-focus*] to image the dust sharply). The "picture" is not saved to your memory card but, rather, is stored in a special memory area in the camera. Finally, a "Data obtained" screen appears. If the Rebel XS was unable to capture the data, you'll be asked to repeat the process. Make sure the camera is pointed at a plain white surface that's evenly illuminated.

The Delete Dust Data information is retained in the camera until you update it by taking a new "picture." The XS adds the information to each image file automatically.

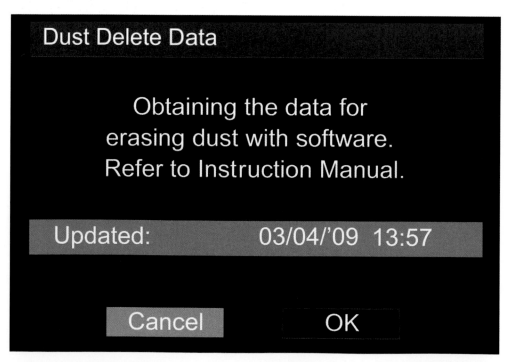

Figure 3.17
Capture updated dust data for your sensor to allow Digital Photo Professional to remove it automatically.

Playback Menu Options

The single blue-coded Playback menu is where you select options related to the display, review, transfer, and printing of the photos you've taken (see Figure 3.18). The choices you'll find include:

- Protect images
- Rotate
- Erase images
- Print order
- Transfer order
- Histogram
- Auto Play

Figure 3.18
The Playback menu includes options for viewing, printing, and transferring images.

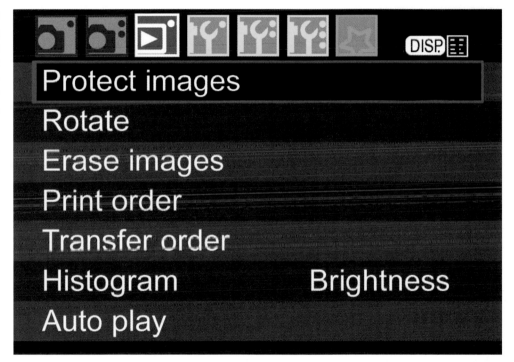

Protect

If you want to keep an image from being accidentally erased (either with the Erase button or by using the Erase images menu), you can mark that image for protection. To protect one or more images, press the Menu button and choose Protect. Then use the left/right cross keys to view the image to be protected. Press the Set button to apply the protection. A key icon will appear at the upper edge of the information display while still in the protection screen, and when reviewing that image later (see Figure 3.19). To remove protection, repeat the process. You can scroll among the other images on your memory card and protect/unprotect them in the same way. Image protection will not save your images from removal when the card is reformatted.

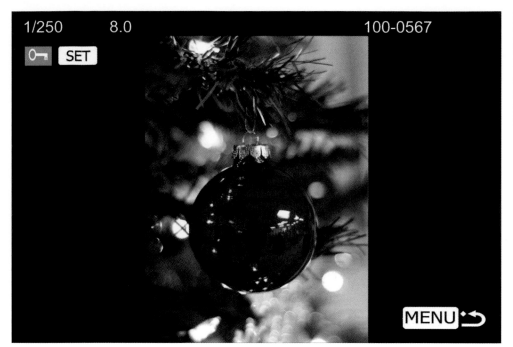

Figure 3.19
Protected images can be locked against accidental erasure (but not preserved from formatting).

Rotate

While you can set the Rebel XS to automatically rotate images taken in a vertical orientation using the Auto Rotate option in the Set-up menu, you can manually rotate an image during playback using this menu selection. Select Rotate from the Playback menu, use the left/right cross keys to page through the available images on your memory card until the one you want to rotate appears, then press Set. The image will appear on the screen rotated 90 degrees. Press Set again, and the image will be rotated 270 degrees.

Erase Images

Choose this menu entry and you'll be given two choices: Select and erase images and All images on card. The former option displays the most recent image. Press the up/down cross keys to mark or unmark an image for deletion (a check mark will appear in a box in the upper-left corner). Then, use the left/right cross keys to view other images and mark/unmark them for deletion. If you try to mark a protected image for deletion, a Protected warning appears on the screen.

When finished marking pictures, press the Trash button, and you'll see a screen that says Erase selected images with two options, Cancel and OK. Choose OK, then press the

Set button to erase the images, or select Cancel and press the Set button to return to the selection screen. Press the Menu button to unmark your selections and return to the menu.

The All images on card choice removes all the pictures on the card, except for those you've marked with the Protect command, and does not reformat the memory card.

Print Order

The Rebel XS supports the DPOF (Digital Print Order Format) that is now almost universally used by digital cameras to specify which images on your memory card should be printed, and the number of prints desired of each image. This information is recorded on the memory card, and can be interpreted by a compatible printer when the camera is linked to the printer using the USB cable, or when the memory card is inserted into a card reader slot on the printer itself. Photo labs are also equipped to read this data and make prints when you supply your memory card to them.

You can read more about assembling print orders in Chapter 8.

Transfer Order

You can specify which images are to be transferred to your personal computer when the Rebel XS is linked to the computer with the USB cable. Individual images are "marked" using a review and selection system similar to the one used to specify print orders. You'll find more about creating a transfer order in Chapter 8.

Histogram

The XS can show either a Brightness histogram or set of three separate Red, Green, and Blue histograms in the full Shooting Information display during picture review. Brightness histograms give you information about the overall tonal values present in the image. The RGB histograms can show more advanced users valuable data about specific channels that might be "clipped" (details are lost in the shadows or highlights). Select Histogram from the Playback menu and choose Brightness or RGB. You can read more about using histograms in Chapter 4.

To view histograms during picture review, you can press the DISP button and use the up/down cross keys to cycle among the Single image, Single image with recording quality, Histogram, and Shooting Information displays as described in Chapter 2. This menu entry changes only the type of histogram displayed in the full Shooting Information screen. You can also view histograms—both brightness and RGB—in the Histogram display, but with a reduced amount of shooting information (see Figure 3.20).

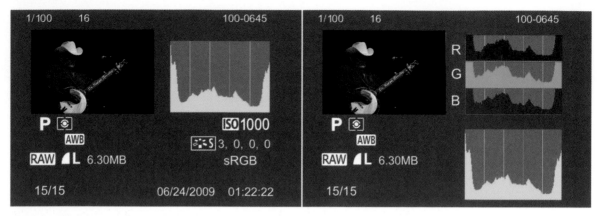

Figure 3.20 You can specify whether brightness or RGB histogram is displayed in the full Shooting Information screen; both types are always visible in the Histogram display.

Auto Play

Auto Play is a convenient way to review images one after another, without the need to manually switch between them. To activate, just choose Auto Play from the Playback menu. During playback, you can press the Set button to pause the "slide show" (in case you want to examine an image more closely), or the DISP button to change the amount of information displayed on the screen with each image. For example, you might want to review a set of images and their histograms to judge the exposure of the group of pictures. When you've finished using Auto Play, press the Menu button to return to the menu display.

Set-Up Menu 1, 2, and 3 Options

There are three yellow-coded Set-up menus where you make adjustments on how your camera *behaves* during your shooting session, as differentiated from the Shooting menu, which adjusts how the pictures are actually taken. Your choices include:

- Auto power off
- File numbering
- Auto rotate
- Format
- LCD auto off
- Screen color
- LCD brightness
- Date/Time
- Language

- Video system
- Sensor cleaning
- Live View function settings
- Flash control
- Camera user setting
- Custom Functions (C.Fn.)
- Clear settings
- Firmware Ver.

Auto Power Off

This setting allows you to determine how long the Rebel XS remains active before shutting itself off. As you can see in Figure 3.21, you can select 30 seconds, 1, 2, 4, 8, or 15 minutes, or Off, which leaves the camera turned on indefinitely—or until 30 minutes have passed. However, even if the camera has shut itself off, if the power switch remains in the On position, you can bring the camera back to life by pressing the shutter button halfway, or the DISP, Playback, or Set buttons.

Figure 3.21
Select an automatic shut-off period to save battery power.

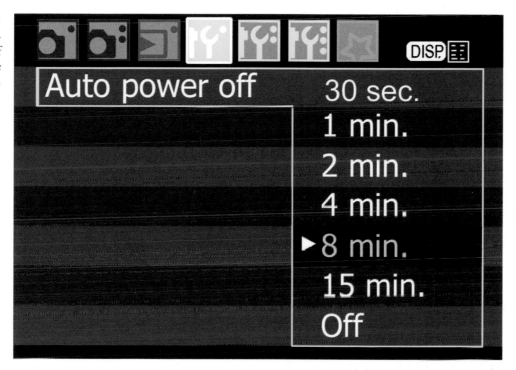

SAVING POWER WITH THE Rebel XS

There are three settings and several techniques you can use to help you stretch the longevity of your XS's battery. The first setting is the Review Time option described earlier under the Shooting 1 menu. That big 2.5-inch LCD uses a lot of juice, so reducing the amount of time it is used can boost the effectiveness of your battery. Auto Power Off turns off most functions based on the delay you specify. The third setting is the LCD Brightness adjustment. If you're willing to shade the LCD with your hand, you can often get away with lower brightness settings outdoors. Use the internal flash as little as possible; no flash at all or fill flash use less power than a full blast. Turn off image stabilization if your lens has that feature and you feel you don't need it. When transferring pictures from your XS, use a card reader instead of the USB cable. Using the cable takes longer and uses a lot more power.

File Numbering

The Rebel XS will automatically apply a file number to each picture you take, using consecutive numbering for all your photos over a long period of time, spanning many different memory cards, starting over from scratch when you insert a new card, or when you manually reset the numbers. Numbers are applied from 0001 to 9999, at which time the camera creates a new folder on the card (100, 101, 102, and so forth), so you can have 0001 to 9999 in folder 100, then numbering will start over in folder 101.

The camera keeps track of the last number used in its internal memory. That can lead to a few quirks you should be aware of. For example, if you insert a memory card that had been used with a different camera, the XS may start numbering with the next number after the highest number used by the previous camera. (I once had a brand new XS start numbering files in the 8,000 range.) I'll explain how this can happen next.

On the surface, the numbering system seems simple enough: In the menu, you can choose Continuous, Automatic Reset, or Manual Reset. Here is how each works:

- **Continuous.** If you're using a blank/reformatted memory card, the XS will apply a number that is one greater than the number stored in the camera's internal memory. If the card is not blank and contains images, then the next number will be one greater than the highest number on the card *or* in internal memory. (In other words, if you want to use continuous file numbering consistently, you must always use a card that is blank or freshly formatted.) Here are some examples.

    - You've taken 4,235 shots with the camera, and you insert a blank/reformatted memory card. The next number assigned will be 4,236, based on the value stored in internal memory.

    - You've taken 4,235 shots with the camera, and you insert a memory card with a picture numbered 2,728. The next picture will be numbered 4,236.

    - You've taken 4,235 shots with the camera, and you insert a memory card with a picture numbered 8,281. The next picture will be numbered 8,282, and that value will be stored in the camera's menu as the "high" shot number (and will be applied when you next insert a blank card).

- **Automatic Reset.** If you're using a blank/reformatted memory card, the next photo taken will be numbered 0001. If you use a card that is not blank, the next number will be one greater than the highest number found on the memory card. Each time you insert a memory card, the next number will either be 0001, or one higher than the highest already on the card.

- **Manual Reset.** The XS creates a new folder numbered one higher than the last folder created, and restarts the file numbers at 0001. Then, the camera uses the numbering scheme that was previously set, either Continuous or Automatic Reset, each time you subsequently insert a blank or non-blank memory card.

Auto Rotate

You can turn this feature On or Off. When activated, the Rebel XS rotates pictures taken in vertical orientation on the LCD screen so you don't have to turn the camera to view them comfortably. However, this orientation also means that the longest dimension of the image is shown using the shortest dimension of the LCD, so the picture is reduced in size. You have three options, shown in Figure 3.22. The image can be autorotated when viewing in the camera *and* on your computer screen using your image editing/viewing software. The image can be marked to autorotate *only* when reviewing your image in your image editor or viewing software. This option allows you to have rotation applied when using your computer, while retaining the ability to maximize the image on your LCD in the camera. The third choice is Off. The image will not be rotated when displayed in the camera or with your computer. Note that if you switch Auto Rotate off, any pictures shot while the feature is disabled will not be automatically rotated when you turn Auto Rotate back on; information embedded in the image file when the photo *is taken* is used to determine whether autorotation is applied.

Figure 3.22
Choose Autorotation both in the camera and on your computer display (top); only on your computer display (middle); or no automatic rotation (bottom).

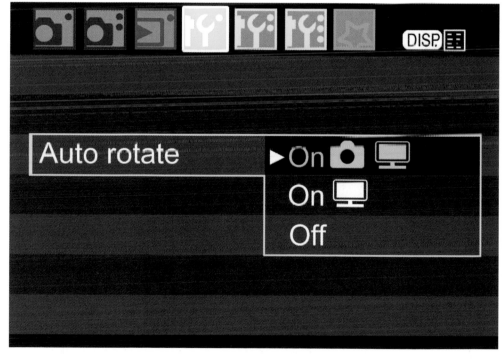

Format

Use this item to erase everything on your memory card and set up a fresh file system ready for use. When you select Format, you'll see a display like Figure 3.23, showing the capacity of the card, how much of that space is currently in use, and two choices at the bottom of the screen: Cancel or OK (proceed with the format). A blue-green bar appears on the screen to show the progress of the formatting step. (The optional low level format invoked with the Trash button is a slower, but more thorough reformatting that can help restore a memory card that has picked up some bad sectors that aren't locked out by the normal format step.)

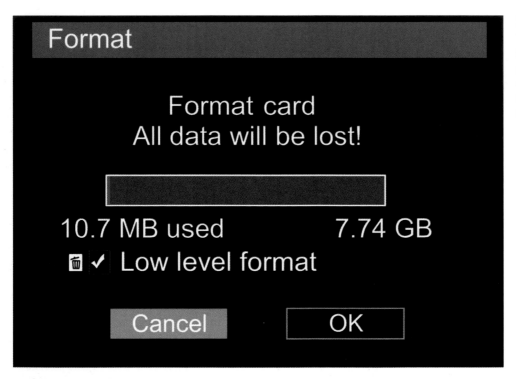

Figure 3.23
You must confirm the format step before the camera will erase a memory card.

LCD Auto Off

The Shooting Settings display on the LCD is turned off when you press the shutter release halfway. If you'd like to modify this behavior, say, to have the LCD display visible at all times (unless you turn it off manually by pressing the DISP button), use this menu option and one of the following options.

- **Shutter btn.** The Shooting Settings display turns off when you press the shutter release halfway down, but reappears as soon as you release the button.

- **Shutter/DISP.** The display switches off when you press the shutter release halfway and remains off if you release the button. To reactivate the display, you need to press the DISP or Set buttons.

- **Remains on.** The Shooting Settings display remains on when you press the shutter release halfway. To turn it off, press the DISP or Set buttons.

Screen Color

If you find the default color scheme for the Shooting Settings display (black text on white) distracting or hard to read, you can change to one of three alternates: white text on black, white text on dark blue, and black text on tan.

LCD Brightness

Choose this menu option, the first on the second Set-up menu tab, and a thumbnail image with a grayscale strip appears on the LCD, as shown in Figure 3.24. Use the left/right cross keys to adjust the brightness to a comfortable viewing level. Brighter settings use more battery power, but can allow you to view an image on the LCD outdoors in bright sunlight. When you have the brightness you want, press the Set button to lock it in and return to the menu.

Figure 3.24
Adjust LCD brightness for easier viewing under varying ambient lighting conditions.

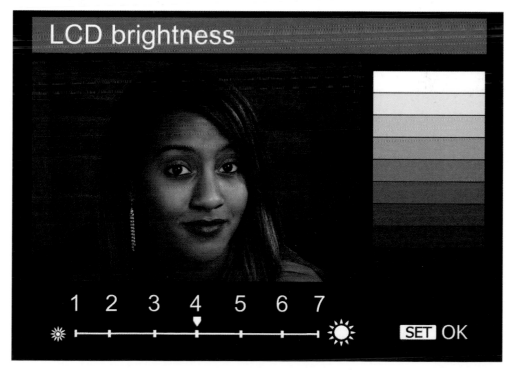

Date/Time

Use this option to set the date and time, which will be embedded in the image file along with exposure information and other data.

Language

Choose from 20 languages for menu display, using the cross keys until the language you want to select is highlighted. Press the Set button to activate. Your choices include English, German, French, Dutch, Danish, Portuguese, Finnish, Italian, Norwegian, Swedish, Spanish, Greek, Russian, Polish, Czech, Magyar, Simplified Chinese, Traditional Chinese, Korean, and Japanese.

If you accidentally set a language you don't read and find yourself with incomprehensible menus, don't panic. Just choose the third option from the top of the Set-Up 2 menu, and select the idioma, sprache, langue, or kieli of your choice.

Video System

This setting controls the output of the XS through the AV cable when you're displaying images on an external monitor. You can select either NTSC, used in the United States, Canada, Mexico, many Central, South American, and Caribbean countries, much of Asia, and other countries; or PAL, which is used in the UK, much of Europe, Africa, India, China, and parts of the Middle East.

Sensor Cleaning

One of the Canon EOS Rebel XS's best features is the automatic sensor cleaning system that reduces or eliminates the need to clean your camera's sensor manually using brushes, swabs, or bulb blowers (you'll find instructions on how to do that in Chapter 9). Canon has applied anti-static coatings to the sensor and other portions of the camera body interior to counter charge build-ups that attract dust. A separate filter over the sensor vibrates ultrasonically each time the XS is powered on or off, shaking loose any dust, which is captured by a sticky strip beneath the sensor.

Use this menu entry to enable or disable automatic sensor cleaning on power up (select Auto Cleaning to choose power-up cleaning) or to activate automatic cleaning during a shooting session (select Clean Now). You can also choose the Clean manually option to flip up the mirror and clean the sensor yourself with a blower, brush, or swab, as described in Chapter 9. If the battery level is too low to safely carry out the cleaning operation, the XS will let you know and refuse to proceed, unless you use the optional AC adapter kit.

Live View Function Settings

Here is where you adjust the Rebel XS's Live View functions, which enable you to work with a real-time LCD display as you preview and compose your image. I'm going to provide detailed instructions for using Live View in Chapter 5, as some functions are controlled here, and some are set in the Custom Functions menus (described later in this chapter). You'll want to review the Live View section of Chapter 5 for detailed information on how to use the three settings you can make from this menu entry.

- **Live View shooting.** Activates Live View. Choose Disable to turn the feature off; select Enable and Live View will be activated when you press the Set button.

- **Grid Display.** Overlays a "rule of thirds" grid on the LCD to help with alignment and composition.

- **Metering Timer.** This option turns off the exposure meter after a specified period of time (4, 16, or 30 seconds, plus 1, 10, and 30 minutes).

Flash Control

This multi-level menu entry includes five settings for controlling the Canon EOS Rebel XS's built-in, pop-up electronic flash unit, as well as accessory flash units you can attach to the camera (see Figure 3.25). I'll provide in-depth coverage of how you can use these options in Chapter 6, but will list the main options here for reference.

Figure 3.25
The Flash Control menu entry has five setting submenus.

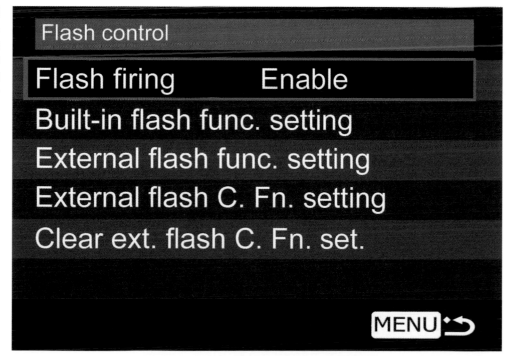

Flash control

| Flash firing | Enable |

Built-in flash func. setting

External flash func. setting

External flash C. Fn. setting

Clear ext. flash C. Fn. set.

MENU ⭮

Flash Firing

Use this option to enable or disable the built-in electronic flash in Custom Zone modes. You might want to totally disable the XS's flash (both built-in and accessory flash) when shooting in sensitive environments, such as concerts, in museums, or during religious ceremonies. When disabled, the flash cannot fire even if you accidentally elevate it, or have an accessory flash attached and turned on when using Custom Zone modes.

Built-in Flash Function Setting

There are three choices for this menu choice (the Flash mode entry is grayed out and cannot be selected):

- **Shutter sync.** You can choose 1st Curtain sync, which fires the flash as soon as the shutter is completely open (this is the default mode). Alternatively, you can select 2nd Curtain sync, which fires a pre-flash used to measure exposure as soon as the shutter release is pressed down all the way, but before the shutter opens, and then triggers a second flash at the end of the exposure, just before the shutter starts to close. This action allows photographing a blurred trail of light of moving objects with sharp flash exposures at the beginning and the end of the exposure. This type of flash exposure is slightly different from what some other cameras produce using 2nd Curtain sync. I'll explain how it works in Chapter 6.

- **Flash exp. comp.** This entry is an alternate method of setting flash exposure compensation. Select this option with the Set button, then dial in the amount of flash EV compensation you want using the left/right cross keys. The EV that was in force prior to your adjustment is shown with a blue indicator. Press Set again to confirm your change, and then press the Menu button to exit.

- **E-TTL II.** You can choose Evaluative (Matrix) or Average metering modes for the electronic flash exposure meter. Evaluative metering looks at selected areas in the scene to calculate exposure, while Average metering calculates flash exposure by reading the entire scene.

External Flash Function Setting

You can access this menu only when you have a compatible electronic flash attached and switched on. The settings available are shown in Figure 3.26. If you press the DISP button while adjusting flash settings, both the changes made to the settings of an attached external flash and to the built-in flash will be cleared.

- **Flash mode.** This entry allows you to set the flash mode for the external flash, from E-TTL II, A-TTL, or TTL. All three provide through-the lens flash metering, but with different degrees of sophistication. E-TTL (Evaluative Through-The-Lens) uses a preflash just prior to taking the picture to allow the camera's metering sensor to read the flash exposure and compare it with ambient light to provide the best exposure. A-TTL (Advanced Through-The-Lens) metering is an earlier system used with some Canon speedlights to read illumination through the lens, but concentrate sensitivity on the active focus point, also using a preflash. The TTL (Through-The-Lens) system is a less sophisticated flash exposure control system used by some flash units. It doesn't use a preflash. You should always choose E-TTL if your flash supports it, or select one of the other systems compatible with the Speedlite you are using. (As I'll explain in Chapter 7, you should be careful when using non-dedicated and non-Canon flash units, because their triggering voltage may be too high for your camera's electronics.)

■ **Shutter sync.** As with the XS's internal flash, you can choose 1st Curtain sync, which fires the flash as soon as the shutter is completely open (this is the default mode). Alternatively, you can select 2nd Curtain sync, which fires the flash as soon as the shutter opens, and then triggers a second flash at the end of the exposure, just before the shutter starts to close.

■ **FEB.** Flash Exposure Bracketing (FEB) operates similarly to ordinary exposure bracketing, providing a series of different exposures to improve your chances of getting the exact right exposure, or to provide alternative renditions for creative purposes.

Figure 3.26
External flash units can be controlled from the Canon EOS Rebel XS using this menu.

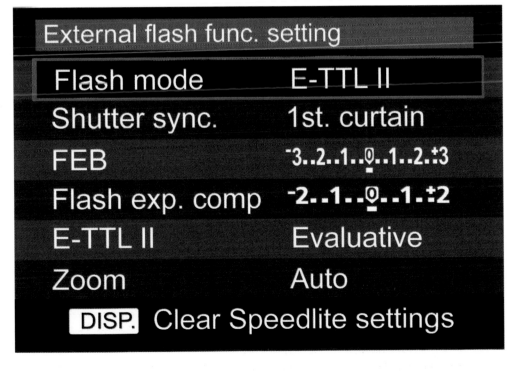

- **Flash exposure compensation.** You can adjust flash exposure using a menu here. Select this option with the Set button, then dial in the amount of flash EV compensation you want using the left cross key to make the next image darker, and the right cross key to make it lighter. The EV that was in place before you started to make your adjustment is shown as a blue indicator, so you can return to that value quickly. Press Set again to confirm your change, then press the Menu button twice to exit.

- **E-TTL II.** You can choose Evaluative (Matrix) or Average metering modes for the electronic flash exposure meter. Evaluative looks at selected areas in the scene to calculate exposure, while Average calculates flash exposure by reading the entire scene.

- **Zoom.** Some flash units can vary their coverage to better match the field of view of your lens at a particular focal length. You can allow the external flash to zoom automatically, based on information provided, or manually, using a zoom button on the flash itself.

External Flash Custom Function Setting

Many external Speedlites from Canon include their own list of Custom Functions, which can be used to specify things like flash metering mode and flash bracketing sequences, as well as more sophisticated features, such as modeling light/flash (if available), use of external power sources (if attached), and functions of any slave unit attached to the external flash. This menu entry allows you to set an external flash unit's Custom Functions from your XS's menu.

Clear External Flash Custom Function Setting

This entry allows you to zero-out any changes you've made to your external flash's Custom Functions, and return them to their factory default settings.

Custom Functions I, II, III, IV

Custom Functions, the first choice in the Set-Up 3 menu, let you customize the behavior of your camera in a variety of different ways, ranging from whether the flash fires automatically to the function carried out when the Set button is pressed. If you don't like the default way the camera carries out a particular task, you just may be able to do something about it. You can find the Custom Functions in their own screen with 12 choices, divided into four groups of settings, as indicated by the title bar at the top of the screen: Exposure (I, C.Fn 01 and 02); Image (II, C.Fn 03-05); Auto focus/Drive (III C.Fn 06-08); and Operation/Others (IV, C.Fn. 09-12). The Roman numeral divisions within a single screen with a single line of choices seem odd until you realize that other Canon EOS models, from the EOS 40D up, separate each of these groups into separate screens (with larger numbers of options).

Note

The Rebel XSi, "sister" camera to the XS, has one additional Custom Function, for Highlight Tone Optimizer, a feature not found in the Rebel XS. I mention this for the benefit of those who have both cameras, to avoid some confusion: the Custom Functions described in this section are numbered one *lower* in the XSi for Fns 5-12 (that is C.Fn. 05 in the XS is C.Fn. 06 in the XSi, and so on). Because both cameras display only the function numbers and don't show the function name until you select that function, it's easy to get confused when you're in a hurry.

Each of the Custom Functions is set in exactly the same way, so I'm not going to bog you down with a bunch of illustrations showing how to make this setting or that. One quick run-through using Figure 3.27 should be enough. Here are the key parts of the Custom Function screen:

■ **Custom Function category.** At the top of the Settings screen is a label that tells you which category that screen represents.

■ **Current Function name.** Use the left/right cross keys to select the function you want to adjust. The name of the function currently selected appears at the top of

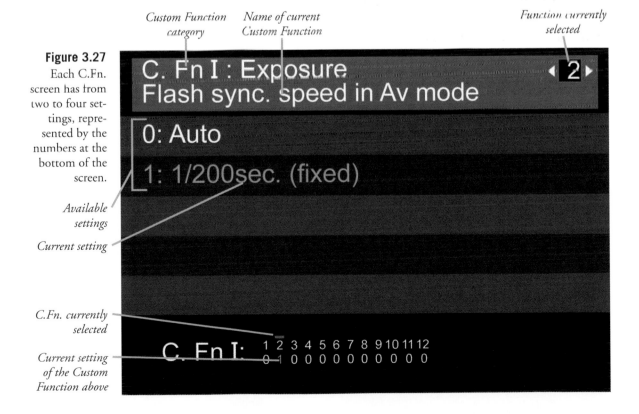

Figure 3.27
Each C.Fn. screen has from two to four settings, represented by the numbers at the bottom of the screen.

the screen, and its number is marked with an over score in the row of numbers at the bottom of the screen. You don't need to memorize the function numbers.

■ **Function currently selected.** The function number appears in two places. In the upper-right corner you'll find a box with the current function clearly designated. In the lower half of the screen are two lines of numbers. The top row has numbers from 1 to 13, representing the Custom Function. The second row shows the number of the current setting. If the setting is other than the default value (a zero), it will be colored blue, so you can quickly see which Custom Functions have been modified. The currently selected function will have an orange line above it.

■ **Available settings.** Within the alternating medium gray/dark gray blocks appear numbered setting options. The current setting is highlighted in blue. You can use the up/down cross keys to scroll to the option you want and then press the Set button to select it; then press the Menu button twice to back out of the Custom Functions menus.

■ **Current setting.** Underneath each Custom Function is a number from 0 to 4 that represents the current setting for that function.

■ **Option selection.** When a function is selected, the currently selected option appears in a highlighted box. As you scroll up and down the option list, the setting in the box changes to indicate an alternate value.

In the listings that follow, I'm going to depart from the sometimes-cryptic labels Canon assigns to each Custom Function in the menu, and instead categorize them by what they actually do. I'm also going to provide you with a great deal more information on each option and what it means to your photography.

C.Fn.I-01: Size of Exposure Adjustments

Exposure level increments. This setting tells the Rebel XS the size of the "jumps" it should use when making exposure adjustments—either one-third or one-half stop. The increment you specify here applies to f/stops, shutter speeds, EV changes, and autoexposure bracketing.

■ **0: 1/3 stop.** Choose this setting when you want the finest increments between shutter speeds and/or f/stops. For example, the XS will use shutter speeds such as 1/60th, 1/80th, 1/100th, and 1/125th second, and f/stops such as f/5.6, f/6.3, f/7.1, and f/8, giving you (and the autoexposure system) maximum control.

■ **1: 1/2 stop.** Use this setting when you want larger and more noticeable changes between increments. The XS will apply shutter speeds such as 1/60th, 1/125th, 1/250th, and 1/500th second, and f/stops including f/5.6, f/6.7, f/8, f/9.5, and f/11. These coarser adjustments are useful when you want more dramatic changes between different exposures.

C.Fn.I-02: Flash Synchronization Speed when Using Aperture Priority

Flash sync. Speed in Av mode. You'll find this setting useful when using flash. When you're set to Aperture Priority mode (Av), you select a fixed f/stop and the Rebel XS chooses an appropriate shutter speed. That works fine when you're shooting by available light. However, when you're using flash, the flash itself provides virtually all of the illumination that makes the main exposure, and the shutter speed determines how much, if any, of the ambient light contributes to a second, non-flash exposure. Indeed, if the camera or subject is moving, you can end up with two distinct exposures in the same frame: the sharply defined flash exposure, and a second, blurry "ghost" picture created by the ambient light.

If you *don't* want that second exposure, you should use the highest shutter speed that will synchronize with your flash (that's 1/200th second with the Rebel XS). If you do want the ambient light to contribute to the exposure (say, to allow the background to register in night shots, or to use the ghost image as a special effect), use a slower shutter speed. For brighter backgrounds, you'll need to put the camera on a tripod or other support to avoid the blurry ghosts.

- **0: Auto.** The XS will vary the shutter speed in Av mode, allowing ambient light to partially illuminate the scene in combination with the flash exposure, as at right in Figure 3.28.

- **1: 1/200th sec. (fixed).** The camera always uses 1/200th second as its shutter speed in Av mode, reducing the effect of ambient light and, probably, rendering the background dark.

C.Fn.II-03: Reducing Noise Effects at Shutter Speeds of One Second or Longer

Long exposure noise reduction. Visual noise is that graininess that shows up as multicolored specks in images, and this setting helps you manage it. In some ways, noise is like the excessive grain found in some high-speed photographic films. However, while photographic grain is sometimes used as a special effect, it's a fad that hasn't caught on in the digital world, and is rarely desirable in a digital photograph.

The visual noise-producing process is something like listening to a CD in your car, and then rolling down all the windows. You're adding sonic noise to the audio signal, and while increasing the CD player's volume may help a bit, you're still contending with an unfavorable signal to noise ratio that probably mutes tones (especially higher treble notes) that you really want to hear.

The same thing happens when the analog signal is amplified: You're increasing the image information in the signal, but boosting the background fuzziness at the same time. Tune in a very faint or distant AM radio station on your car stereo. Then turn up the volume. After a certain point, turning up the volume further no longer helps you hear better.

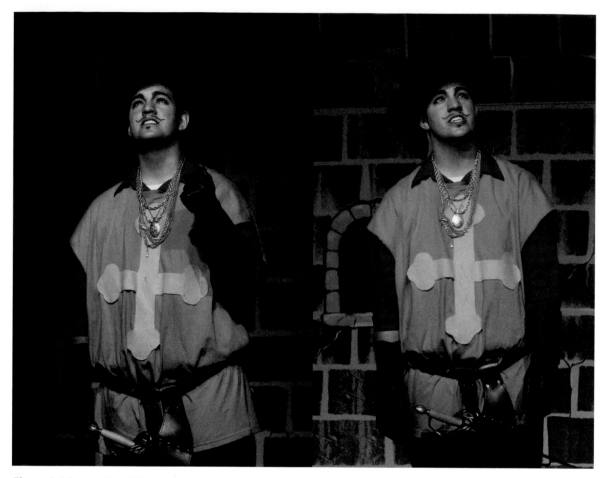

Figure 3.28 At left, a 1/200th second shutter speed eliminated ambient light so only the flash illuminated the scene; at right, a 1/60th second shutter speed let the ambient light supplement the electronic flash.

There's a similar point of diminishing returns for digital sensor ISO increases and signal amplification as well.

These processes create several different kinds of noise. Noise can be produced from high ISO settings. As the captured information is amplified to produce higher ISO sensitivities, some random noise in the signal is amplified along with the photon information. Increasing the ISO setting of your camera raises the threshold of sensitivity so that fewer and fewer photons are needed to register as an exposed pixel. Yet, that also increases the chances of one of those phantom photons being counted among the real-life light particles, too.

Fortunately, the Rebel XS's sensor and its digital processing chip are optimized to produce the low noise levels, so ratings as high as ISO 800 can be used routinely (although there will be some noise, of course), and even ISO 1600 can generate good results.

A second way noise is created is through longer exposures. Extended exposure times allow more photons to reach the sensor, but increase the likelihood that some photosites will react randomly even though not struck by a particle of light. Moreover, as the sensor remains switched on for the longer exposure, it heats, and this heat can be mistakenly recorded as if it were a barrage of photons. This Custom Function can be used to tailor the amount of noise-canceling performed by the digital signal processor.

■ **0: Off.** Disables long exposure noise reduction. Use this setting when you want the maximum amount of detail present in your photograph, even though higher noise levels will result. This setting also eliminates the extra time needed to take a picture caused by the noise reduction process. If you plan to use only lower ISO settings (thereby reducing the noise caused by ISO amplification), the noise levels produced by longer exposures may be acceptable. For example, you might be shooting waves crashing into the shore at ISO 100 with the camera mounted on a tripod, using a neutral density filter and long exposure to cause the pounding water to blur slightly, as shown in Figure 3.29. To maximize detail in the non-moving portions of your photos, you can switch off long exposure noise reduction.

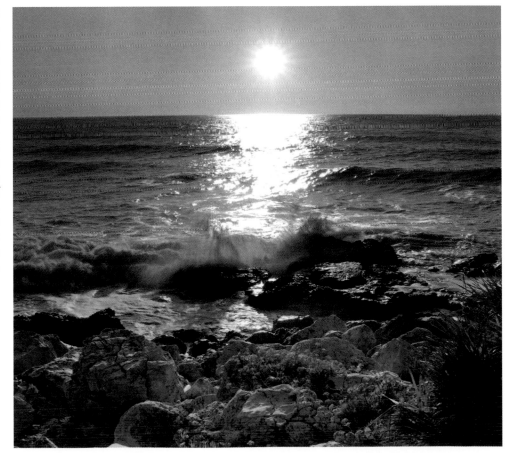

Figure 3.29
When lower ISO settings are used, as in this two-second exposure of waves crashing on the shore (made through a "split" neutral density filter to darken the upper half of the frame), long exposure noise reduction might not be needed.

- **1: Auto.** The Rebel XS examines your photo taken with an exposure of one second or longer, and if long exposure noise is detected, a second, blank exposure is made and compared to the first image. Noise found in the "dark frame" image is subtracted from your original picture, and only the noise-corrected image is saved to your memory card. Because the noise-reduction process effectively doubles the time required to take a picture, this is a good setting to use when you want to avoid this delay when possible, but still have noise reduction applied when appropriate.

- **2: On.** When this setting is activated, the XS applies dark frame subtraction to all exposures longer than one second. You might want to use this option when you're working with high ISO settings (which will already have noise boosted a bit) and want to make sure that any additional noise from long exposures is eliminated, too. Noise reduction will be applied to some exposures that would not have caused it to kick in using the Auto setting.

Note

While the "dark frame" is being exposed, the LCD screen will be blank during Live View mode, and the number of shots you can take in Continuous shooting mode will be reduced. White balance bracketing is disabled during this process.

C.Fn.II-04: Eliminating Noise Caused by Higher ISO Sensitivities

High ISO speed noise reduct'n. This setting applies noise reduction that is especially useful for pictures taken at high ISO sensitivity settings. The default is 0 (Off), but you can specify 1 (On) to apply additional noise reduction at *all* ISO settings. At lower ISO values, noise reduction improves the appearance of shadow areas without affecting highlights; at higher ISO settings, noise reduction is applied to the entire photo. Note that when this function is activated, the maximum number of continuous shots that can be taken will decrease significantly, because of the additional processing time for the images.

Figure 3.30 shows how high ISO noise reduction can improve the look of photographs taken in dim light.

- **0: Off.** No additional noise reduction will be applied.

- **1: On.** Activates ISO noise reduction. At lower ISO values, noise reduction is applied primarily to shadow areas; at higher ISO settings, noise reduction affects the entire image.

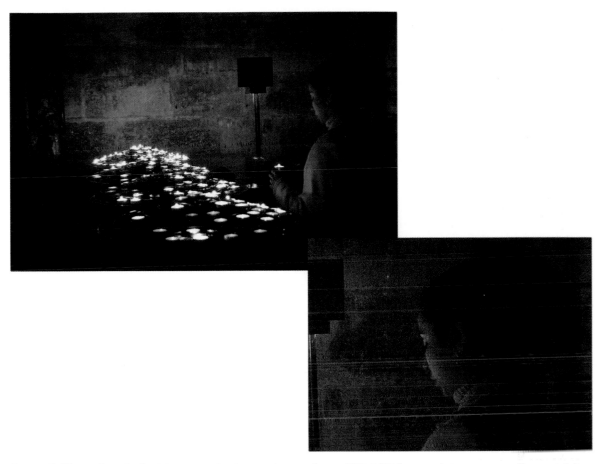

Figure 3.30 Without high ISO noise reduction, an image taken at ISO 1600 has a grainy appearance (lower right), but with noise reduction applied, the texture is more subdued (upper left).

C.Fn.II-O5: Fixing Dark, Low Contrast Images.

Auto lighting optimizer. This setting automatically provides a partial fix for images that are too dark or flat (low in contrast) by boosting the brightness and contrast as required. The feature is used automatically in Basic Zone modes, but can be activated here for Creative Zone modes, Program, Aperture Priority, Shutter Priority, and Manual modes. You might want to use it to provide some extra snap in photos with murky areas and no true white tones, such as foggy scenes. However, this setting can increase the amount of image noise, so you might want to shut it off when you're already using ISO settings above ISO 800.

- **0: Enable.** Adjusts brightness and contrast of dark, flat images.

- **1: Disable.** No adjustments are applied.

C.Fn.III-06: Activation of the Autofocus Assist Lamp

AF-assist beam firing. This setting determines when the electronic flash is activated to emit a pulse of light that helps provide enough contrast for the Rebel XS to focus on a subject.

- **0: Emits.** The AF assist light is emitted by the camera's built-in flash whenever light levels are too low for accurate focusing using the ambient light.

- **1: Does not emit.** The AF assist illumination is disabled. You might want to use this setting when shooting at concerts, weddings, or darkened locations where the light might prove distracting or discourteous.

- **2: Only external flash emits.** The built-in AF assist light is disabled, but if a Canon EX dedicated flash unit is attached to the camera, its AF assist feature will be used when needed. Because the flash unit's AF assist is more powerful, you'll find this option useful when you're using flash and are photographing objects in dim light that are more than a few feet away from the camera (and thus not likely to be illuminated usefully by the Rebel XS's built-in light source). Note that if AF-assist beam firing is disabled within the flash unit's own Custom Functions, this setting will not override that.

C.Fn.III-07: AF During Live View Shooting

AF during Live View shooting. Because the Rebel XS uses a sensor in the viewfinder to autofocus, autofocusing is not possible when you're viewing a Live View image on the LCD screen. (The mirror is flipped up, and no image is available in the viewfinder.) This setting allows interrupting the Live View image long enough to allow autofocusing. Simply press the AF-ON button, and release it to return to Live View. I'll explain more about using Live View and autofocus in Chapter 7.

- **0: Disable.** Live View is continuous, and focus must be achieved manually.

- **1: Quick mode.** Pressing the * button in the upper-right corner of the back of the camera flips the mirror back down so the XS can autofocus. When focus is achieved, the beeper will sound. The mirror flips back up, restoring Live View when you release the * button.

- **2: Live mode.** Pressing the * button activates autofocus using the image on the LCD, which takes longer, but does not interrupt the Live View display.

C.Fn.III-08: Whether It Is Possible to Lock Up the Viewing Mirror Prior to an Exposure

Mirror lockup. The Mirror lockup function determines whether the reflex viewing mirror will be flipped up out of the way in advance of taking a picture, thereby eliminating any residual blurring effects caused by the minuscule amount of camera shake that can be produced if (as is the case normally) the mirror is automatically flipped up an instant before the actual exposure. When shooting telephoto pictures with a very long lens, or close-up photography at extreme magnifications, even this tiny amount of vibration can have an impact.

You'll want to make this adjustment immediately prior to needing the mirror lockup function, because once it's been enabled, the mirror *always* flips up, and picture taking becomes a two-press operation. That is, you press the shutter release once to lock exposure and focus, and to swing the mirror out of the way. Your viewfinder goes blank (of course, the mirror's blocking it). Press the shutter release a second time to actually take the picture. Because the goal of mirror lockup is to produce the sharpest picture possible, and because of the viewfinder blackout, you can see that the camera should be mounted on a tripod prior to taking the picture, and, to avoid accidentally shaking the camera yourself, using an off-camera shutter release mechanism is a good idea.

- **0:Disable.** Mirror lockup is not possible.

- **1: Enable.** Mirror lockup is activated and will be used for every shot until disabled.

Canon lists some important warnings and techniques related to using mirror lockup in the Rebel XS manual, and I want to emphasize them here and add a few of my own, even if it means a bit of duplication. Better safe than sorry!

- **Don't use ML for sensor cleaning.** Though locked up, the mirror will flip down again automatically after 30 seconds, which you don't want to happen while you're poking around the sensor with a brush, swab, or air jet. There's a separate menu item—sensor cleaning—for sensor housekeeping. You can find more about this topic in Chapter 9.

- **Avoid long exposure to extra-bright scenes.** The shutter curtain, normally shielded from incoming light by the mirror, is fully exposed to the light being focused on the focal plane by the lens mounted on the XS. When the mirror is locked up, you certainly don't want to point the camera at the sun, and even beach or snow scenes may be unsafe if the shutter curtain is exposed to their illumination for long periods. (This advice also applies to Live View, of course, because the sensor is similarly exposed while you're previewing the image on the LCD.)

- **ML can't be used in continuous shooting modes.** The Rebel XS will use Single Shot mode for mirror lockup exposures, regardless of the sequence mode you've selected.

- **Use self-timer to eliminate second button press.** If you've activated the self-timer, the mirror will flip up when you press the shutter button down all the way, and then the picture will be taken two seconds later. This technique can help reduce camera shake further if you don't have a remote release available and have to use a finger to press the shutter button. You can also use the Remote Controller RC-1 or RC5. Set the RC-1 to a two-second delay. With the RC-5, press the transmit button to lock up the mirror; the shot will be taken automatically two seconds later.

C.Fn.IV-09: What Happens When You Partially Depress the Shutter Release/Press the AE Lock Button

Shutter button/AE Lock button (*). This setting controls the behavior of the shutter release and the AE Lock button (*) when you are using Creative Zone exposure modes. With Basic Zone modes, the Rebel XS always behaves as if it has been set to Option 0, described below. Options 1, 2, and 3 are designed to work with AI Servo mode, which locks focus as it is activated, but refocuses if the subject begins to move. The options allow you to control exactly when focus and exposure are locked when using AI Servo mode.

In the option list, the first action in the pair represents what happens when you press the shutter release; the second action says what happens when the AE Lock button is pressed.

- **0: AF/AE lock.** With this option, pressing the shutter release halfway locks in focus; pressing the * button locks exposure. Use this when you want to control each of these actions separately.

- **1: AE lock/AF.** Pressing the shutter release halfway locks exposure; pressing the * button locks autofocus. This setting swaps the action of the two buttons compared to the default 0 option.

- **2: AF/AF lock, no AE lock.** Pressing the AE lock button interrupts the autofocus and locks focus in AI Servo mode. Exposure is not locked at all until the actual moment of exposure when you press the shutter release all the way. This mode is handy when moving objects may pass in front of the camera (say, a tight end crosses your field of view as you focus on the quarterback) and you want to be able to avoid change of focus. Note that you can't lock in exposure using this option.

- **3: AE/AF, no AE lock.** Pressing the shutter release halfway locks in autofocus, except in AI Servo mode, in which you can use the * button to start or stop autofocus. Exposure is always determined at the moment the picture is taken, and cannot be locked.

C.Fn.IV-10: Using the Set Button as a Function Key

SET button when shooting. You already know that the Set button is used to select a choice or option when navigating the menus. However, when you're taking photos, it has no function at all. You can easily remedy that with this setting. This setting allows you to assign one of four different actions to the Set key. Because the button is within easy reach of your right thumb, that makes it quite convenient for accessing a frequently used function. When this Custom Function is set to 0, the Set button has no additional function during shooting mode (except to activate Live View when it is turned on), and options 1 through 4 assign an action to the button during shooting.

> **CAUTION**
>
> One thing to keep in mind when redefining the behavior of controls (including other controls that can be modified within the Custom Functions menus) is that any non-standard customization you do will definitely be confusing to others who use your camera, and may even confuse you if you've forgotten that you've changed a control from its default function.

- **0: Default (no function).** This is the default during shooting. Nothing happens when you press the Set button while in shooting mode.

- **1: Change quality.** Pressing the Set button produces the Shooting 1 Menu's Quality menu screen on the color LCD. You can cycle among the various quality options with the up/down and left/right cross keys. Press Set again to lock in your choice.

- **2: Flash exposure comp.** The Set button summons the Flash Exposure Compensation screen. Use the left/right cross keys to adjust flash exposure plus or minus two stops. If you're using an external flash unit, its internal flash exposure compensation settings override those set from the camera. Press Set to confirm your choice.

- **3: LCD monitor On/Off.** Assigns to the Set button the same functions as the DISP button. Because the Set button can be accessed with the thumb, you may find it easier to use when turning the LCD monitor on or off.

- **4: Menu display.** Pressing Set produces the XS's Menu screen on the LCD, with the last menu entry you used highlighted. Press Set again to work with that menu normally, or press the Menu button to cancel and back out of the menus. This setting duplicates the Menu button's function, but some find it easier to locate the Set button with their thumb.

C.Fn.IV-11: LCD Display When Power On

LCD display when power on. Controls the behavior of the LCD when the Rebel XS is switched on. There are two options:

- **0: Display.** When the XS is powered on, the Shooting Settings screen will be shown. You can turn this screen on and off by pressing the DISP button. Use this option if you always want the settings screen to be displayed when the camera is turned on.

- **1: Retain power OFF status.** When the Rebel XS is turned on, the LCD monitor will display the Shooting Settings screen if it was turned on when the camera was last powered down. If the screen had been turned off (by pressing the DISP button), it will not be displayed when the XS is next powered up. Use this option if you frequently turn off the settings screen, and want the camera to "remember" whether the screen was on display when the XS was last powered down.

C.Fn.IV-12: Activating Data Verification Feature

Add original decision data. The Rebel XS has a special feature that allows determining whether a specific image has been modified using a special Canon Original Data Security Kit OSK-E3. Data Verification Kit DVK-E2, a nifty $650 add-on, consists of a data security card and dedicated USB card reader-writer and verification software that must be used with a computer to verify an image. The Add original decision data function determines whether the information needed to verify an image is included in the image file. Data verification is especially useful for law enforcement, legal, and scientific purposes, but not required for everyday shooting (which is why the feature is turned off by default).

- **0: Off.** Data verification information is not added to the image file.

- **1: On.** Data verification information is included in the image file.

Clear All Camera Settings

This menu choice resets all the settings to their default values. You can choose Clear all camera settings or Clear all Custom Func. (C.Fn.). When you choose Clear all camera settings, regardless of how you've set up your Rebel XS, it will be adjusted for One-Shot AF mode, automatic AF point selection, Evaluative metering, JPEG Fine Large image quality, automatic ISO, sRGB color mode, automatic white balance, and Standard Picture Style. Any changes you've made to exposure compensation, flash exposure compensation, and white balance will be canceled, and any bracketing for exposure or white balance nullified. Custom white balances and Dust Delete Data will be erased.

The Clear all Custom Func. (C.Fn) choice can be used to clear all camera Custom Functions. Press the Set button, then rotate the left/right cross keys to either Cancel or OK. Press the Set button to confirm. All Custom Functions will be reset to their default 0 values.

Firmware Version

You can see the current firmware release in use in the menu listing. If you want to update to a new firmware version, insert a memory card containing the binary file, and press the Set button to begin the process. You can read more about firmware updates in Chapter 9.

My Menu

The Canon EOS Rebel XS has a great new feature that allows you to define your own menu, with just the items listed that you want. Remember that the XS always returns to the last menu and menu entry accessed when you press the Menu button, so you can set up My Menu to include just the items you want, and jump to those items instantly by pressing the Menu button. To create your own My Menu, you have to *register* the menu items you want to include. Registered items will be grayed out and unavailable elsewhere, making My Menu a good place to park "dangerous" menu entries, such as Format. Just follow these steps:

1. Press the Menu button and use the left/right cross keys to select the My Menu tab. When you first begin, the personalized menu will be empty except for the My Menu Settings entry. Press the Set button to select it. You'll then see a screen like the one shown in Figure 3.31.

2. Use the up/down cross keys to select Register, then press the Set button.

3. Use the up/down cross keys to scroll down through the continuous list of all menu entries that can be registered to find one you would like to add. Press Set.

4. Confirm your choice by selecting OK in the next screen and pressing Set again.

5. Continue to select up to six menu entries for My Menu.

6. When you're finished, press the Menu button twice to return to the My Menu screen to see your customized menu, which might look like Figure 3.32.

In addition to registering menu items, you can perform other functions at the My Menu Settings screen:

- **Changing the Order.** Choose Sort to reorder the items in My Menu. Select the menu item to be moved and press the Set button. Press the up/down cross keys to move the item up and down within the menu list. When you've placed it where you'd like it, press the Menu button to lock in your selection and return to the previous screen.

- **Delete/Delete All Items.** Use these to remove an individual menu item or all menu items you've registered in My Menu.

- **Display from My Menu.** As I mentioned earlier, the XS (almost) always shows the last menu item accessed. That's convenient if you used My Menu last, but if you happen to use another menu, then pressing the Menu button will return to that item instead. If you enable the Display from My Menu option, pressing the Menu button will *always* display My Menu first. You are free to switch to another menu tab if you like, but the next time you press the Menu button, My Menu will come up again. Use this option if you work with My Menu a great deal and make settings with other menu items less frequently.

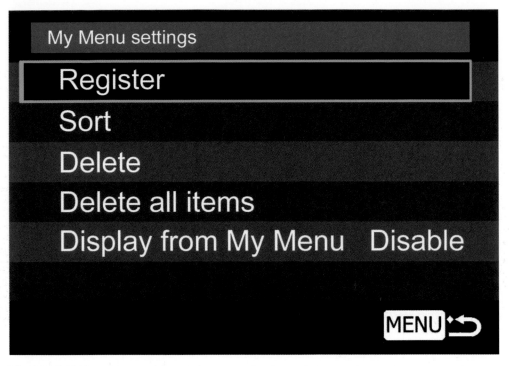

Figure 3.31
In the My Menu Settings screen, you can add menu items, delete them, and specify whether My Menu always pops up when the Menu button is pressed.

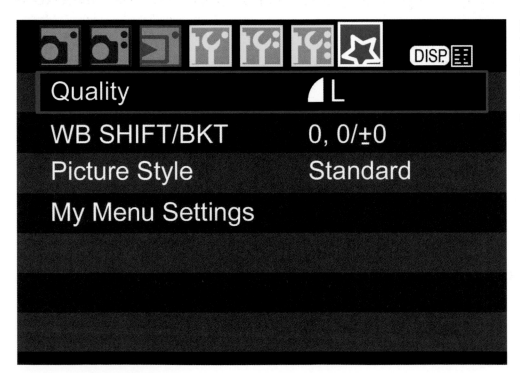

Figure 3.32
You can add one to six menu entries to My Menu. Three entries are shown.

4

Getting the Right Exposure

The Canon EOS Rebel XS offers the best of two worlds when it comes to capturing exactly the right exposure—a picture with the optimum balance of tones and colors that are neither too light nor too dark to reveal all the detail in the original subject. You can select one of the Basic Zone modes suitable for your subject matter—portrait, landscape, close-up, sports, or nighttime subjects, and the camera will do an excellent job of calculating the right settings to give you an outstanding picture with little input on your part beyond the initial Mode dial selection. If you can't decide which Basic Zone mode is best, you can select the green Auto icon instead, and the XS will still do a fine job.

On the other hand, it's likely that you purchased a sophisticated digital SLR like the Rebel XS because you wanted to apply a little creativity to your images, perhaps making a particular picture a little brighter to produce a high-key look, or to use backlighting to create a silhouette. If that sort of picture is your goal, the XS offers the aptly named Creative Zone modes, which give you complete control over many of the basic functions of the camera that you'll need to produce your visual masterpieces.

These parameters include exposure, sensitivity (ISO settings), color balance, focus, and image attributes like sharpness and contrast. While you can choose to let the camera set any or all of these for you automatically, you can also opt to fine-tune how the XS applies its automatic settings. And if you want absolute creative control over any of these functions, you can set them manually, too. That's why the XS is such a versatile tool for creating images.

You'll find in this chapter complete explanations of the shooting basics of exposure. When you finish, you'll understand everything you need to know to take photographs in a broad range of situations.

Understanding Exposure

Exposure determines the look, feel, and tone of an image, in more ways than one. Incorrect exposure can impair even the best-composed image by cloaking important tones in darkness, or by washing them out so they become featureless to the eye. On the other hand, correct exposure brings out the detail in the areas you want to picture, and provides the range of tones and colors you need to create the desired image. However, getting the perfect exposure can be tricky, because digital sensors can't capture all the tones we are able to see. If the range of tones in an image is extensive, embracing both inky black shadows and bright highlights, the sensor may not be able to capture them all. Sometimes, we must settle for an exposure that renders most of those tones—but not all—in a way that best suits the photo we want to produce. You'll often need to make choices about which details are important, and which are not, so that you can grab the tones that truly matter in your image. That's part of the creativity you bring to bear in realizing your photographic vision.

For example, look at the two typical tourist snapshots presented side by side in Figure 4.1. For the image on the left, the camera calculated exposure based—mostly—on the buildings in the background that are visible between the columns. The columns' shadows that wrap around the columns themselves are underexposed. Stepping back and pointing the camera upward produced the image at right. The ornate ceiling now receives the right amount of exposure, but the buildings in the background are badly overexposed. The camera's sensor simply can't capture detail in both dark areas and bright areas in a single shot.

The solution, such as it is, can be seen in Figure 4.2. The photo was reframed as a horizontal image, with no attempt to capture the detail in the ceiling. But by exposing for the intermediate areas of the column, it was possible to capture some detail in the bright highlights of the buildings in the background. The structures aren't perfectly exposed, but they aren't completely washed out, either. In some situations, this may be the best you can do without resorting to manipulation in an image-editing program like Photoshop or Photoshop Elements.

To understand exposure, you need to understand the six aspects of light that combine to produce an image. Start with a light source—the sun, an interior lamp, or the glow from a campfire—and trace its path to your camera, through the lens, and finally to the sensor that captures the illumination.

Figure 4.1
At left, the image is exposed for the background highlights, losing shadow detail. At right, the exposure captures detail in the shadows, but the background highlights are washed out.

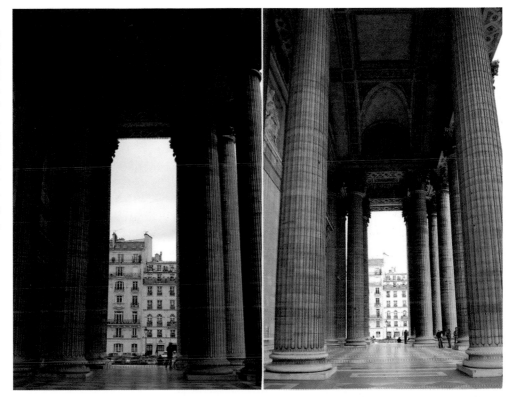

Figure 4.2
Reframing the shot and exposing for the middle shadows produces the best compromise exposure.

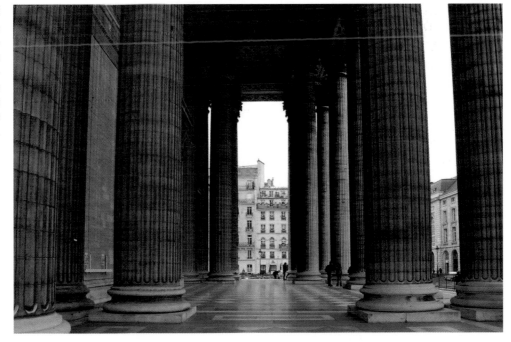

Here's a brief review of the things within our control that affect exposure.

- **Light at its source.** Our eyes and our cameras—film or digital—are most sensitive to that portion of the electromagnetic spectrum we call *visible light.* That light has several important aspects that are relevant to photography, such as color, and harshness (which is determined primarily by the apparent size of the light source as it illuminates a subject). But, in terms of exposure, the important attribute of a light source is its *intensity.* We may have direct control over intensity, which might be the case with an interior light that can be brightened or dimmed. Or, we might have only indirect control over intensity, as with sunlight, which can be made to appear dimmer by introducing translucent light-absorbing or reflective materials in its path.

- **Light's duration.** We tend to think of most light sources as continuous. But, as you'll learn in Chapter 7, the duration of light can change quickly enough to modify the exposure, as when the main illumination in a photograph comes from an intermittent source, such as an electronic flash.

- **Light reflected, transmitted, or emitted.** Once light is produced by its source, either continuously or in a brief burst, we are able to see and photograph objects by the light that is reflected from our subjects towards the camera lens; transmitted (say, from translucent objects that are lit from behind); or emitted (by a candle or television screen). When more or less light reaches the lens from the subject, we need to adjust the exposure. This part of the equation is under our control to the extent we can increase the amount of light falling on or passing through the subject (by adding extra light sources or using reflectors), or by pumping up the light that's emitted (by increasing the brightness of the glowing object).

- **Light passed by the lens.** Not all the illumination that reaches the front of the lens makes it all the way through. Filters can remove some of the light before it enters the lens. Inside the lens barrel is a variable-sized aperture called a *diaphragm* that dilates and contracts to control the amount of light that enters the lens. You, or the XS's autoexposure system, can control exposure by varying the size of the aperture. The relative size of the aperture is called the *f/stop.*

- **Light passing through the shutter.** Once light passes through the lens, the amount of time the sensor receives it is determined by the XS's shutter, which can remain open for as long as 30 seconds (or even longer if you use the Bulb setting) or as briefly as 1/4,000th second.

- **Light captured by the sensor.** Not all the light falling onto the sensor is captured. If the number of photons reaching a particular photosite doesn't pass a set threshold, no information is recorded. Similarly, if too much light illuminates a pixel in the sensor, then the excess isn't recorded or, worse, spills over to contaminate adjacent pixels. We can modify the minimum and maximum number of pixels that contribute to image detail by adjusting the ISO setting. At higher ISOs, the incoming light is amplified to boost the effective sensitivity of the sensor.

These factors—the quantity of light produced by the light source, the amount reflected or transmitted towards the camera, the light passed by the lens, the amount of time the shutter is open, and the sensitivity of the sensor—all work proportionately and reciprocally to produce an exposure. That is, if you double the amount of light that's available, increase the aperture by one stop, make the shutter speed twice as long, or boost the ISO setting 2X, you'll get twice as much exposure. Similarly, you can increase any of these factors while decreasing one of the others by a similar amount to keep the same exposure.

F/STOPS AND SHUTTER SPEEDS

If you're *really* new to more advanced cameras, you might need to know that the lens aperture, or f/stop, is a ratio, much like a fraction, which is why f/2 is larger than f/4, just as 1/2 is larger than 1/4. However, f/2 is actually *four times* as large as f/4. (If you remember your high school geometry, you'll know that to double the area of a circle, you multiply its diameter by the square root of two: 1.4.)

Lenses are usually marked with intermediate f/stops that represent a size that's twice as much/half as much as the previous aperture. So, a lens might be marked:

f/2, f/2.8, f/4, f/5.6, f/8, f/11, f/16, or f/22,

with each larger number representing an aperture that admits half as much light as the one before, as shown in Figure 4.3.

Shutter speeds are actual fractions (of a second), but the numerator is omitted, so that 60, 125, 250, 500, 1,000, and so forth represent 1/60th, 1/125th, 1/250th, 1/500th, and 1/1,000th second. To avoid confusion, Canon uses quotation marks to signify longer exposures: 2", 2"5, 4", and so forth represent 2.0, 2.5, and 4.0 second exposures, respectively.

Figure 4.3
Top row (left to right): f/2, f/2.8, f/4; bottom row, f/5.6, f/8, f11.

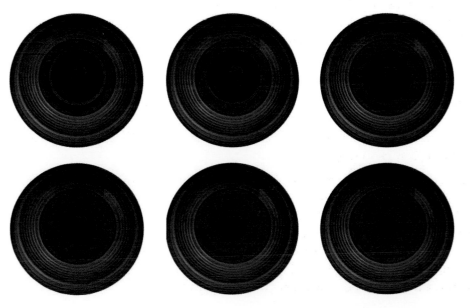

Most commonly, exposure settings are made using the aperture and shutter speed, followed by adjusting the ISO sensitivity if it's not possible to get the preferred exposure (that is, the one that uses the "best" f/stop or shutter speed for the depth-of-field or action-stopping we want). Table 4.1 shows equivalent exposure settings using various shutter speeds and f/stops.

Table 4.1 Equivalent Exposures

Shutter speed	f/stop	Shutter speed	f/stop
1/30th second	f/22	1/500th second	f/5.6
1/60th second	f/16	1/1,000th second	f/4
1/125th second	f/11	1/2,000th second	f/2.8
1/250th second	f/8	1/4,000th second	f/2

When the XS is set for P mode, the metering system selects the correct exposure for you automatically, but you can change quickly to an equivalent exposure by holding down the shutter release button halfway ("locking" the current exposure), and then spinning the Main dial until the desired equivalent exposure combination is displayed. This program shift mode does not work when you're using flash.

In Aperture Priority (Av) and Shutter Priority (Tv) modes, you can change to an equivalent exposure, but only by adjusting either the aperture (the camera chooses the shutter speed) or shutter speed (the camera selects the aperture). I'll cover all these exposure modes later in the chapter.

How the Rebel XS Calculates Exposure

Your XS calculates exposure by measuring the light that passes through the lens using a metering pattern you can select (more on that later) and based on the assumption that each area being measured reflects about the same amount of light as a neutral gray card with 18-percent reflectance. That assumption is necessary, because different subjects reflect different amounts of light.

In a photo containing a white cat and a dark gray cat, the white cat might reflect five times as much light as the gray cat. An exposure based on the white cat will cause the gray cat to appear to be black, while an exposure based only on the gray cat will make the white cat washed out. Light-measuring devices handle this by assuming that the areas measured average a standard value of 18-percent gray, a figure that's been used as a rough standard (not all vendors calibrate their metering for exactly 18-percent gray) for many years. Black, white, and gray cats have been a standard metaphor for many years, as well, so I'm going to explain this concept using a different, and more cooperative, life form: peppers.

Figure 4.4 shows three peppers. The yellow pepper at upper right represents a white cat, or any object that is very light but which contains detail that we want to see in the light areas. The red pepper in the lower center is a stand-in for a gray cat, because it has most of its details in the middle tones. The green pepper serves as our black cat, because it is a dark object with detail in its shadows.

The colors confuse the issue, so I'm going to convert our color peppers to black-and-white. For the version shown in Figure 4.5, the exposure was optimized for the white (yellow) pepper, changing its tonal value to a medium, 18-percent gray. The dark (green) and medium-toned (red) peppers are now *too* dark. For Figure 4.6, the exposure was

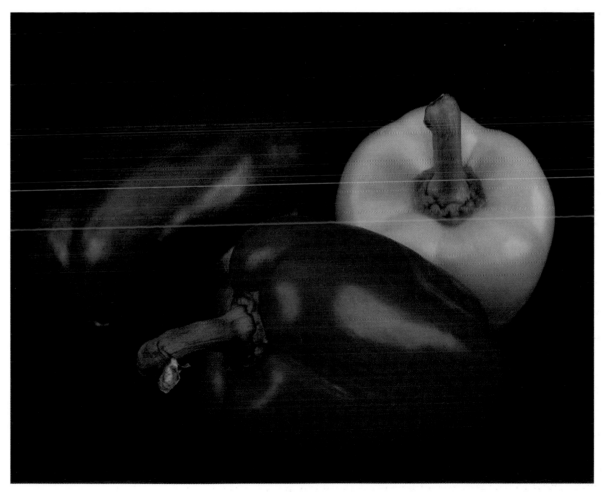

Figure 4.4 The yellow pepper, red pepper, and green pepper represent light, middle, and dark tones.

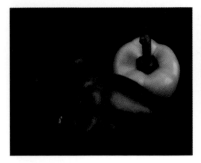

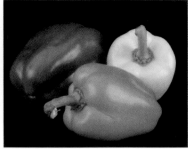

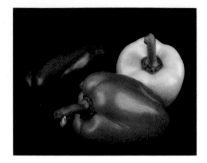

Figure 4.5 Exposing for the light-colored pepper in upper right renders the other two excessively dark.

Figure 4.6 Exposing for the dark pepper (upper left) causes the two vegetables in the right half of the picture to become too light.

Figure 4.7 Exposing for the middle-toned red pepper produces an image in which the tones of all three subjects appear accurately.

optimized for the dark (green) pepper, making most of its surface, now, fall into the middle-tone, 18-percent gray range. The yellow (light) and midtone (red) peppers are now too light.

The solution, of course, is to measure exposure from the object with the middle tones that most closely correspond to the 18-percent gray "standard." Do that, and you wind up with a picture that more closely resembles the original tonality of the red, yellow, and green peppers, and which looks, in black-and-white, like Figure 4.7.

In the real world, you could calculate exposure the hard way, and arrive at accurate settings by pointing your XS at an evenly lit object, such as an actual gray card or the palm of your hand (the backside of the hand is too variable). You'll need to increase the exposure by one stop in the latter case, because the human palm—of any ethnic group—reflects about twice as much light as a gray card. As you'll see, however, it's more practical to use your XS's system to meter the actual scene.

F/STOPS VERSUS STOPS

In photography parlance, *f/stop* always means the aperture or lens opening. However, for lack of a current commonly used word for one exposure increment, the term *stop* is often used. (In the past, EV served this purpose, but Exposure Value and its abbreviation has been inextricably intertwined with its use in describing Exposure Compensation.) In this book, when I say "stop" by itself (no *f/*), I mean one whole unit of exposure, and am not necessarily referring to an actual f/stop or lens aperture. So, adjusting the exposure by "one stop" can mean both changing to the next shutter speed increment (say, from 1/125th second to 1/250th second) or the next aperture (such as f/4 to f/5.6). Similarly, 1/3 stop or 1/2 stop increments can mean either shutter speed or aperture changes, depending on the context. Be forewarned.

In most cases, your camera's light meter will do a good job of calculating the right exposure, especially if you use the exposure tips in the next section. But if you want to double-check, or feel that exposure is especially critical, take the light reading off an object of known reflectance. Photographers sometimes carry around an 18-percent gray card (available from any camera store) and, for critical exposures, actually use that card, placed in the subject area, to measure exposure (or to set a custom white balance if needed).

To meter properly in the Creative Zone, you'll want to choose both the *metering method* (how light is evaluated) and *exposure method* (how the appropriate shutter speeds and apertures are chosen). I'll describe both in the following sections.

Choosing a Metering Method

The XS has three different schemes for evaluating the light received by its exposure sensors. You can choose among them by pressing the Metering Mode button (up cross key) and rotating the Main dial until the mode you want is selected.

■ **Evaluative.** The XS slices up the frame into 35 different zones, shown in Figure 4.8 (the LCD icon is shown in the upper-left corner). The camera evaluates the measurements, paying special attention to the metering zones that indicate sharp focus,

Figure 4.8
Evaluative metering uses 35 zones, linked to the autofocus points shown as red brackets.

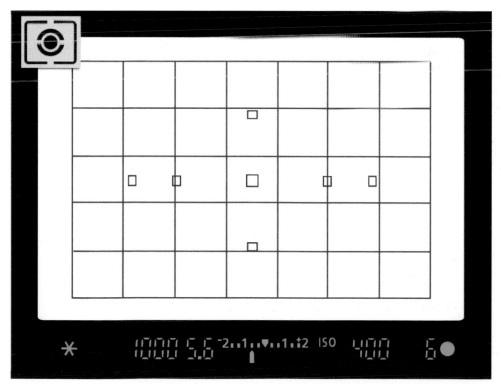

to make an educated guess about what kind of picture you're taking, based on examination of thousands of different real-world photos. For example, if the top sections of a picture are much lighter than the bottom portions, the algorithm can assume that the scene is a landscape photo with lots of sky. This mode is the best all-purpose metering method for most pictures.

- **Partial.** This is a *faux* Spot mode (Spot is available in the Rebel XSi, if you're keeping score), using roughly nine percent of the image area to calculate exposure, which, as you can see in Figure 4.9, is a rather large spot. The status LCD icon is shown in the upper-left corner. Use this mode if the background is much brighter or darker than the subject.

- **Center-Weighted.** In this mode, the exposure meter emphasizes a zone in the center of the frame to calculate exposure, as shown in Figure 4.10, on the theory that, for most pictures, the main subject will be located in the center. Center-weighting works best for portraits, architectural photos, and other pictures in which the most important subject is located in the middle of the frame. As the name suggests, the light reading is *weighted* towards the central portion, but information is also used from the rest of the frame. If your main subject is surrounded by very bright or very dark areas, the exposure might not be exactly right. However, this scheme works well in many situations if you don't want to use one of the other modes.

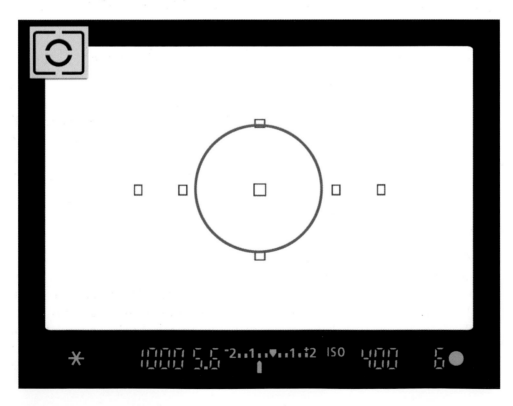

Figure 4.9
Partial metering uses a center spot that's roughly nine percent of the frame area.

Figure 4.10
Center-Weighted metering calculates exposure based on the full frame, but emphasizes the center area.

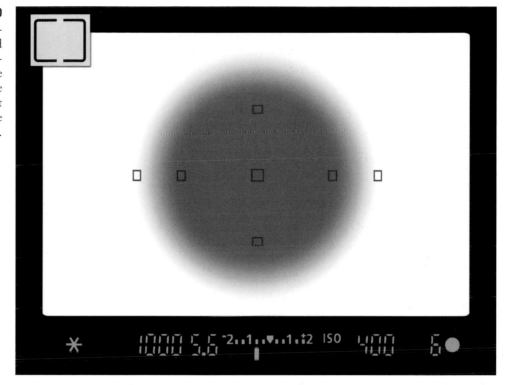

Choosing a Creative Zone Exposure Method

You'll find five methods for choosing the appropriate shutter speed and aperture within the Creative Zone settings. Just spin the Mode dial to choose the method you want to use. (See Figure 4.11.) Your choice of which is best for a given shooting situation will depend on things like your need for lots of (or less) depth-of-field, a desire to freeze action or allow motion blur, or how much noise you find acceptable in an image. Each of the Rebel XS's exposure methods emphasizes one aspect of image capture or another. This section introduces you to all five.

A-DEP

The Automatic Depth-of-Field exposure mode is a handy method to use when you want to maximize the range of sharpness in your image. The camera actually selects an f/stop that will allow as much of the subject matter you've framed as possible to be in sharp focus, and then applies the shutter speed necessary to provide a good exposure at that aperture. The disadvantage of this mode is that you relinquish control over shutter speed, f/stop, and focus distance (which makes A-DEP a bit more like a Basic Zone scene mode than a true Creative Zone mode). You might end up with the required depth-of-field, but a blurry photo because the XS has selected a shutter speed that's too slow for hand-holding!

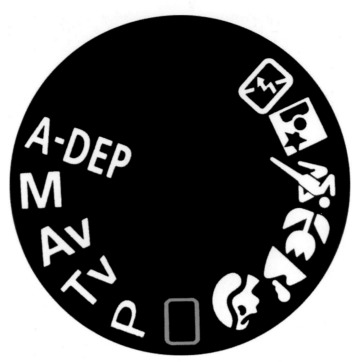

Figure 4.11
Choose Creative Zone modes by spinning the Mode dial to one of the settings shown at left.

A-DEP performs its magic by examining the nine autofocus points in the viewfinder to discover the nearest and farthest objects in the frame. Then, it chooses an aperture and focus point that supplies the required DOF (if possible) and sets the appropriate shutter speed. The focus zones that can be rendered in sharp focus will flash red; other zones that can't be included in the focus range remain black, as shown in Figure 4.12. Press the DOF button on the front of the camera to check the range of focus, if you want. This mode won't work under all conditions, for example, with flash or if you're using manual focus. The viewfinder provides you with status information:

- **Flashing red AF points.** Shows the subjects covered by the DOF range set.

- **Blinking aperture indicator in viewfinder.** The desired DOF range cannot be set because the subjects are separated too widely for sufficient depth-of-field at the smallest available aperture.

- **Blinking 30 shutter speed in viewfinder.** Illumination is too dim to provide requested DOF at the current ISO setting.

- **Blinking 4000 shutter speed in viewfinder.** Illumination is too bright to provide requested DOF at the current ISO setting.

Because of the limitations of A-DEP mode, I don't favor it. However, it's fun to play with and may come in handy in certain situations, especially when you're shooting quickly and don't have time to manipulate depth-of-field manually.

Figure 4.12
A-DEP mode can provide automatic depth-of-field for many types of subjects.

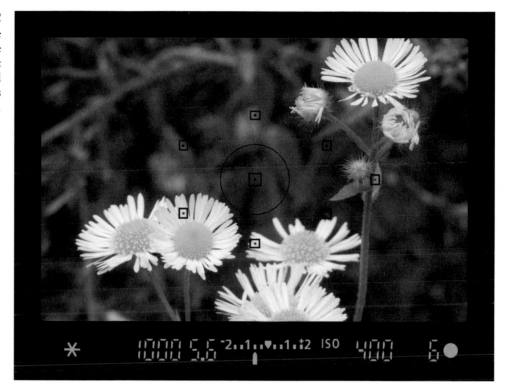

Aperture Priority

In Av mode, you specify the lens opening used, and the XS selects the shutter speed. Aperture Priority is especially good when you want to use a particular lens opening to achieve a desired effect. Perhaps you'd like to use the smallest f/stop possible to maximize depth-of-field in a close-up picture. Or, you might want to use a large f/stop to throw everything except your main subject out of focus, as in Figure 4.13, where the emphasis is on the musician's bass guitar, while his face, in the background, is allowed to blur. Maybe you'd just like to "lock in" a particular f/stop because it's the sharpest available aperture with that lens. Or, you might prefer to use, say, f/2.8 on a lens with a maximum aperture of f/1.4, because you want the best compromise between speed and sharpness.

Aperture Priority can even be used to specify a *range* of shutter speeds you want to use under varying lighting conditions, which seems almost contradictory. But think about it. You're shooting a soccer game outdoors with a telephoto lens and want a relatively high shutter speed, but you don't care if the speed changes a little should the sun duck behind a cloud. Set your XS to Av, and adjust the aperture until a shutter speed of, say, 1/1,000th second is selected at your current ISO setting. (In bright sunlight at ISO 400, that aperture is likely to be around f/11.) Then, go ahead and shoot, knowing that your XS will maintain that f/11 aperture (for sufficient DOF as the soccer players move about

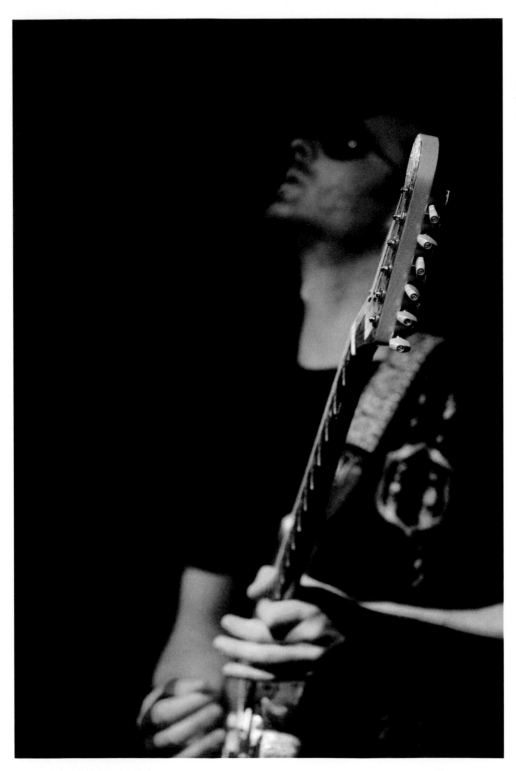

Figure 4.13
Use Aperture Priority to "lock in" a large f/stop when you want to blur the background.

the field), but will drop down to 1/750th or 1/500th second if necessary should the lighting change a little.

A blinking 30 or 4000 shutter speed in the viewfinder indicates that the XS is unable to select an appropriate shutter speed at the selected aperture and that over- and under-exposure will occur at the current ISO setting. That's the major pitfall of using Av: you might select an f/stop that is too small or too large to allow an optimal exposure with the available shutter speeds. For example, if you choose f/2.8 as your aperture and the illumination is quite bright (say, at the beach or in snow), even your camera's fastest shutter speed might not be able to cut down the amount of light reaching the sensor to provide the right exposure. Or, if you select f/8 in a dimly lit room, you might find yourself shooting with a very slow shutter speed that can cause blurring from subject movement or camera shake. Aperture Priority is best used by those with a bit of experience in choosing settings. Many seasoned photographers leave their XS set on Av all the time.

Shutter Priority

Shutter Priority (Tv) is the inverse of Aperture Priority: you choose the shutter speed you'd like to use, and the camera's metering system selects the appropriate f/stop. Perhaps you're shooting action photos and you want to use the absolute fastest shutter speed available with your camera; in other cases you might want to use a slow shutter speed to add some blur to a sports photo that would be mundane if the action were completely frozen. (See Figure 4.14.) Shutter Priority mode gives you some control over how much action-freezing capability your digital camera brings to bear in a particular situation.

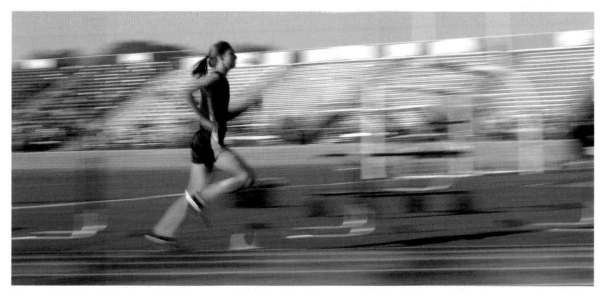

Figure 4.14 Lock the shutter at a slow speed to introduce blur into an action shot, as with this panned image of a track runner.

MAKING EV CHANGES

Sometimes you'll want more or less exposure than indicated by the Rebel XS's metering system. Perhaps you want to underexpose to create a silhouette effect, or overexpose to produce a high key look. It's easy to use the XS's Exposure Compensation system to override the exposure recommendations. It's available in any Creative Zone mode except M (Manual).

Hold down the AV button (located on the back next to the upper-left corner of the LCD) and rotate the Main dial to the right to make the image brighter (add exposure), and to the left to make the image darker (subtract exposure). The exposure scale in the viewfinder and on the LCD indicates the EV change you've made. The EV change you've made remains for the exposures that follow, until you manually zero out the EV setting with the AV button + Main dial. EV changes are ignored when using M or any of the Basic Zone modes.

You'll also encounter the same problem as with Aperture Priority when you select a shutter speed that's too long or too short for correct exposure under some conditions. I've shot outdoor soccer games on sunny Fall evenings and used Shutter Priority mode to lock in a 1/1,000th second shutter speed, only to find my XS refused to shoot when the sun dipped behind some trees and there was no longer enough light to shoot at that speed, even with the lens wide open.

Like Av mode, it's possible to choose an inappropriate shutter speed. If that's the case, the maximum aperture of your lens (to indicate underexposure) or the minimum aperture (to indicate overexposure) will blink.

Program Mode

Program mode (P) uses the XS's built-in smarts to select the correct f/stop and shutter speed using a database of picture information that tells it which combination of shutter speed and aperture will work best for a particular photo. If the correct exposure cannot be achieved at the current ISO setting, the shutter speed indicator in the viewfinder will blink 30 or 4000, indicating under- or overexposure (respectively). You can then boost or reduce the ISO to increase or decrease sensitivity.

The XS's recommended exposure can be overridden if you want. Use the EV setting feature (described later, because it also applies to Tv and Av modes) to add or subtract exposure from the metered value. And, as I mentioned earlier in this chapter, you can change from the recommended setting to an equivalent setting (as shown in Table 4.1) that produces the same exposure, but using a different combination of f/stop and shutter speed.

To accomplish this:

1. Press the shutter release halfway to lock in the current base exposure, or press the AE-Lock button (*) on the back of the camera (in which case the * indicator will illuminate in the viewfinder to show that the exposure has been locked).

2. Spin the Main dial to change the shutter speed (the XS will adjust the f/stop to match).

Your adjustment remains in force for a single exposure; if you want to change from the recommended settings for the next exposure, you'll need to repeat those steps.

Manual Exposure

Part of being an experienced photographer comes from knowing when to rely on your Rebel XS's automation (including P mode and Basic Zone settings), when to go semi-automatic (with Tv or Av), and when to set exposure manually (using M). Some photographers actually prefer to set their exposure manually, as the XS will be happy to indicate when its metering system judges your manual settings provide the proper exposure, using the analog exposure scale at the bottom of the viewfinder and on the status LCD.

Manual exposure can come in handy in some situations. You might be taking a silhouette photo and find that none of the exposure modes or EV correction features give you exactly the effect you want. For example, when I shot the ballet dancer in Figure 4.15 in front of a backlit scrim, there was no way any of my Rebel XS's exposure modes would be able to interpret the scene the way I wanted to shoot it. So, I took a couple test exposures, and set the exposure manually to the exact shutter speed and f/stop I needed. You might be working in a studio environment using multiple flash units. The additional flash are triggered by slave devices (gadgets that set off the flash when they sense the light from another flash, or, perhaps from a radio or infrared remote control). Your camera's exposure meter doesn't compensate for the extra illumination, and can't interpret the flash exposure at all, so you need to set the aperture manually.

Because, depending on your proclivities, you might not need to set exposure manually very often, you should still make sure you understand how it works. Fortunately, the Rebel XS makes setting exposure manually very easy. Just set the Mode dial to M, turn the Main dial to set the shutter speed, and hold down the Av button while rotating the Main dial to adjust the aperture. Press the shutter release halfway or press the AE-Lock button, and the exposure scale in the viewfinder shows you how far your chosen setting diverges from the metered exposure. (Canon helpfully provides the same feedback if you want to *focus* manually, too. Flip the lens barrel switch from AF to MF, turn the focus ring, and watch the focus confirmation light, which will signal when the image is sharp.)

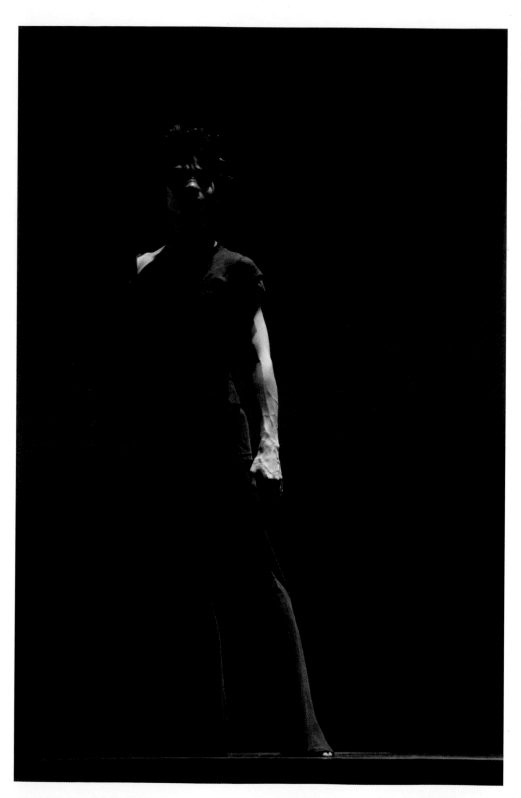

Figure 4.15
Manual mode allowed setting the exact exposure for this partial silhouette shot.

Adjusting Exposure with ISO Settings

Another way of adjusting exposures is by changing the ISO sensitivity setting. Sometimes photographers forget about this option, because the common practice is to set the ISO once for a particular shooting session (say, at ISO 100 or 200 for bright sunlight outdoors, or ISO 800 when shooting indoors) and then forget about ISO. The reason for that is that ISOs higher than ISO 100 or 200 are seen as "bad" or "necessary evils." However, changing the ISO is a valid way of adjusting exposure settings, particularly with the Canon EOS Rebel XS, which produces good results at ISO settings that create grainy, unusable pictures with some other camera models.

Indeed, I find myself using ISO adjustment as a convenient alternate way of adding or subtracting EV when shooting in Manual mode, and as a quick way of choosing equivalent exposures when in Automatic or Semiautomatic modes. For example, I've selected a manual exposure with both f/stop and shutter speed suitable for my image using, say, ISO 200. I can change the exposure in full stop increments by pressing the ISO button on top of the camera, and spinning the Main dial one click at a time. The difference in image quality/noise at the base setting of ISO 200 is negligible if I dial in ISO 100 to reduce exposure a little, or change to ISO 400 to increase exposure. I keep my preferred f/stop and shutter speed, but still adjust the exposure.

Or, perhaps, I am using Tv mode and the metered exposure at ISO 200 is 1/500th second at f/11. If I decide on the spur of the moment I'd rather use 1/500th second at f/8, I can press the ISO button and spin the Main dial to switch to ISO 100. Of course, it's a good idea to monitor your ISO changes, so you don't end up at ISO 1,600 accidentally. ISO settings can, of course, also be used to boost or reduce sensitivity in particular shooting situations. The Rebel XS can use ISO settings from ISO 100 up to 1,600.

The camera can adjust the ISO automatically as appropriate for various lighting conditions. In Basic Zone modes, ISO is normally set between ISO 100-800. When you choose the Auto ISO setting, the XS adjusts the sensitivity dynamically to suit the subject matter. In Basic Zone Auto, Landscape, Close-Up, Night Portrait, and Flash Off modes, the XS adjusts ISO between ISO 100-800 as required. In Sports mode, ISO is set between ISO 400-800. In Portrait mode, ISO is fixed at ISO 100, because the XS attempts to use larger f/stops to blur the background, and the lower ISO setting lends itself to those larger stops.

When Auto ISO is chosen when using Creative Zone modes, sensitivity will be generally set to ISO 100-800 in Program, Av, and A-DEP modes, except when ISO 400 would produce overexposure, and a lower speed (down to ISO 100) will be used instead. In Tv mode, Auto ISO normally produces an ISO 400 setting, but for very bright or dark subjects the XS will change the ISO in the range ISO 100-800. In Manual exposure mode, Auto ISO is fixed at ISO 400. Don't look for any of these specifications in

the Canon manual; I had to figure then   m-
era did in various situations.

When using flash, Auto ISO produce
overexposure would occur (as when s
case a lower setting (down to ISO
ranges aren't suitable for you, indi
Creative Zone modes.

Bracketing

Bracketing is a method for sh   et-
tings, as a way of improving   and
electronic film cameras took over   ures,
shooting, say, a series of three photos at 1/12   from
f/8 to f/11 to f/16. In practice, smaller than whole-stop inc   greater
precision. Plus, it was just as common to keep the same aperture and   shutter
speed, although in the days before electronic shutters, film cameras often had only whole
increment shutter speeds available.

Today, cameras like the XS can bracket exposures much more precisely, and bracket
white balance as well. While WB bracketing is sometimes used when getting color
absolutely correct in the camera is important, Auto Exposure bracketing (AEB) is used
much more often. When this feature is activated, the XS takes three consecutive photos: one at the metered "correct" exposure, one with less exposure, and one with more
exposure, using an increment of your choice up to plus 2/minus 2 stops. (Choose
between increments by setting Custom Function I-01 to 0:1/3 stop or 1:1/2 stop.) In
Av mode, the shutter speed will change, while in Tv mode, the aperture will change.

Using AEB is trickier than it needs to be, but you can follow these steps:

1. Press the Menu button and use the Main dial to select the Shooting 2 tab, and then
   use the up/down cross keys to navigate to the AEB position and press the Set button. A dot is centered on the plus/minus scale.

2. Press the left/right cross keys to spread out or contract the three dots to include the
   desired range you want to cover. For example, with the dots clustered tightly
   together, the three bracketed exposures will be spread out over a single stop.
   Separating the cluster produces a wider range and larger exposure change between
   the three shots in the bracket set, as shown in Figure 4.16.

Figure 4.16
Use the
left/right cross
keys to set the
increment
between brack-
eted shots.

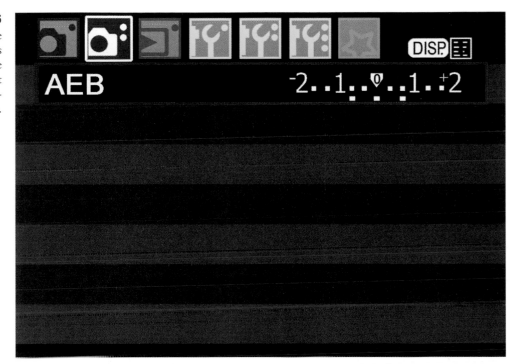

Figure 4.16 Use the left/right cross keys to set the increment between bracketed shots.

3. Press the Set button to enter the settings and then the Menu button to exit the menu system.

4. Press the shutter release button halfway to view the AEB amount in the LCD display.

5. Take your three photos. You can use Single shooting mode to take the trio of pictures yourself, use the self-timer (which will expose all three pictures after the delay), or switch to Continuous shooting mode to take the three pictures in a burst.

6. As the shots are taken, three indicators will appear on the exposure scale in the viewfinder, with one of them flashing for each bracketed photo, showing when the base exposure, underexposure, and overexposure are taken (in that order). The base exposure will be set by the metered exposure *or* the exposure dictated by any exposure compensation you might have dialed in.

7. Bracketing remains in effect when the set is taken so you can continue shooting bracketed exposures until you turn the XS off, use the electronic flash, or return to the menu to cancel bracketing.

Dealing with Noise

Image noise is that random grainy effect that some like to use as a visual effect, but which, most of the time, is objectionable because it robs your image of detail even as it adds that "interesting" texture. Noise is caused by two different phenomena: high ISO settings and long exposures.

High ISO noise commonly appears when you raise your camera's sensitivity setting above ISO 400. With Canon cameras, which are renown for their good ISO noise characteristics, noise may become visible at ISO 800, and is usually fairly noticeable at ISO 1600. This kind of noise appears as a result of the amplification needed to increase the sensitivity of the sensor. While higher ISOs do pull details out of dark areas, they also amplify non-signal information randomly, creating noise.

A similar noisy phenomenon occurs during long time exposures, which allow more photons to reach the sensor, increasing your ability to capture a picture under low-light conditions. However, the longer exposures also increase the likelihood that some pixels will register random phantom photons, often because the longer an imager is "hot" the warmer it gets, and that heat can be mistaken for photons. There's also a special kind of noise that CMOS sensors like the one used in the XS are potentially susceptible to. With a CCD, the entire signal is conveyed off the chip and funneled through a single amplifier and analog-to-digital conversion circuit. Any noise introduced there is, at least, consistent. CMOS imagers, on the other hand, contain millions of individual amplifiers and A/D converters, all working in unison. Because all these circuits don't necessarily process in precisely the same way all the time, they can introduce something called fixed-pattern noise into the image data.

Fortunately, Canon's electronics geniuses have done an exceptional job minimizing noise from all causes in the XS. Even so, you might still want to apply the optional long exposure noise reduction that can be activated using Custom Function II: 03. This type of noise reduction involves the XS taking a second, blank exposure, and comparing the random pixels in that image with the photograph you just took. Pixels that coincide in the two represent noise and can safely be suppressed. This noise reduction system, called *dark frame subtraction,* effectively doubles the amount of time required to take a picture, and is used only for exposures longer than one second. Noise reduction can reduce the amount of detail in your picture, as some image information may be removed along with the noise. So, you might want to use this feature with moderation.

To activate your XS's noise reduction features, go to the Custom Function menu, choose C.Fn.II: Image, and select either C.Fn.II-03 (Long exposure noise reduction) or C.Fn.II-04 (High ISO noise reduction), as explained in Chapter 3.

You can also apply noise reduction to a lesser extent using Photoshop, and when converting RAW files to some other format, using your favorite RAW converter, or an industrial-strength product like Noise Ninja (www.picturecode.com) to wipe out noise after you've already taken the picture.

Fixing Exposures with Histograms

While you can often recover poorly exposed photos in your image editor, your best bet is to arrive at the correct exposure in the camera, minimizing the tweaks that you have to make in post-processing. However, you can't always judge exposure just by viewing the image on your XS's LCD after the shot is made. Nor can you get a 100 percent accurately exposed picture by using the XS's Live View feature. Ambient light may make the LCD difficult to see, and the brightness level you've set can affect the appearance of the playback image.

Instead, you can use a histogram, which is a chart displayed on the Rebel XS's LCD that shows the number of tones being captured at each brightness level. You can use the information to provide correction for the next shot you take. The XS offers two histogram variations that can be shown while viewing images: one that shows overall brightness levels for an image and an alternate version that separates the red, green, and blue channels of your image into separate histograms.

Both types are charts that include a representation of up to 256 vertical lines on a horizontal axis that show the number of pixels in the image at each brightness level, from 0 (black) on the left side to 255 (white) on the right. (The 2.5-inch LCD doesn't have enough pixels to show each and every one of the 256 lines, but, instead provides a representation of the shape of the curve formed.) The more pixels at a given level, the taller the bar at that position. If no bar appears at a particular position on the scale from left to right, there are no pixels at that particular brightness level.

A typical histogram produces a mountain-like shape, with most of the pixels bunched in the middle tones, with fewer pixels at the dark and light ends of the scale. Ideally, though, there will be at least some pixels at either extreme, so that your image has both a true black and a true white representing some details. Learn to spot histograms that represent over- and underexposure, and add or subtract exposure using an EV modification to compensate.

DISPLAYING HISTOGRAMS

To view histograms on your screen, press the DISP button while an image is shown on the LCD. Keep pressing the button until the histogram(s) are shown. The display will cycle between several levels of information, including flashing highlights and two histograms. One histogram shows overall brightness levels (Figure 4.17), while the second type of histogram screen shows both brightness levels and levels for each of the red, green, and blue channels (Figure 4.18). During histogram display, you'll also see a thumbnail at the left side of the screen with your image displayed. Overexposed areas will blink, which is your prompt to use negative exposure compensation if you want to salvage those areas. (See Making EV Changes, above.) To change your default histogram type from Brightness to RGB, use the Histogram setting in the Playback 2 menu.

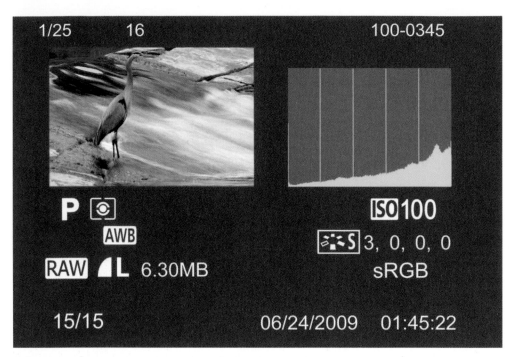

Figure 4.17
A brightness histogram shows the relationship of tones in an image.

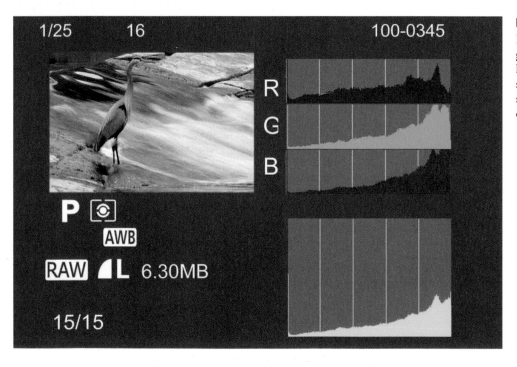

Figure 4.18
Individual red, green, and blue histograms show the exposure for each color channel.

For example, Figure 4.19 shows the histogram for an image that is badly underexposed. You can guess from the shape of the histogram that many of the dark tones to the left of the graph have been clipped off. There's plenty of room on the right side for additional pixels to reside without having them become overexposed. The curve on the right edge of this histogram represents the brightest areas in the clouds.

Figure 4.19
This histogram shows an underexposed image.

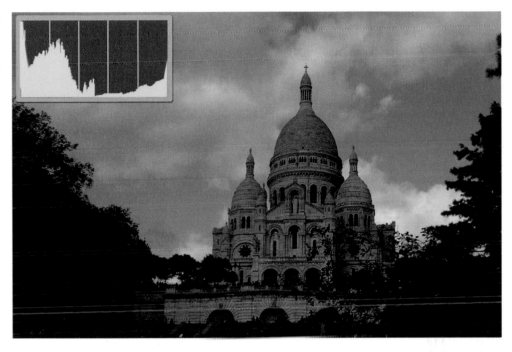

Or, a histogram might look like Figure 4.20, which is overexposed. In either case, you can increase or decrease the exposure (either by changing the f/stop or shutter speed in Manual mode or by adding or subtracting an EV value in Autoexposure mode) to produce the corrected histogram shown in Figure 4.21, in which the tones "hug" the right side of the histogram to produce as many highlight details as possible. See "Making EV Changes," above for information on dialing in exposure compensation.

The histogram can also be used to aid in fixing the contrast of an image, although gauging incorrect contrast is more difficult. For example, if the histogram shows all the tones bunched up in one place in the image, the photo will be low in contrast. If the tones are spread out more or less evenly, the image is probably high in contrast. In either case, your best bet may be to switch to RAW (if you're not already using that format) so you can adjust contrast in post processing. However, you can also change to a user-defined Picture Style (User Def. 1, User Def. 2, or User Def. 3 in the Picture Style menu) with contrast set lower (−1 to −4) or higher (+1 to +4) as required.

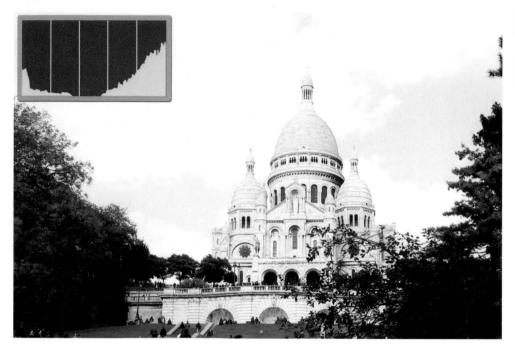

Figure 4.20
This histogram reveals that the image is overexposed.

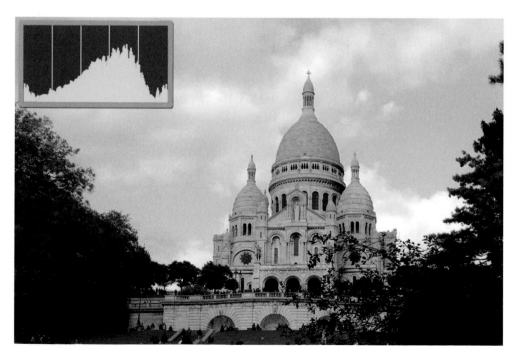

Figure 4.21
A histogram for a properly exposed image should look like this.

Basic Zone Modes

The final tools in your exposure repertoire are the seven Basic Zone shooting modes, which can automatically make all the basic settings needed for certain types of shooting situations, such as portraits, landscapes, close-ups, sports, night portraits, and "no-flash zone" pictures. These "autopilot" modes are especially useful when you suddenly encounter a picture-taking opportunity and don't have time to decide exactly which Creative Zone mode you want to use. Instead, you can spin the Mode dial to the appropriate Basic Zone mode and fire away, knowing that, at least, you have a fighting chance of getting a good or usable photo.

Basic Zone modes are also helpful when you're just learning to use your XS. Once you've learned how to operate your camera, you'll probably prefer one of the Creative Zone modes that provide more control over shooting options. The Basic Zone scene modes may give you few options or none at all. The AF mode, drive mode, and metering mode are all set for you. Here are the modes available:

- **Full Auto.** This is the mode to use when you hand your camera to a total stranger and ask him or her to take your picture posing in front of the Eiffel Tower. All the photographer has to do is press the shutter release button. Every other decision is made by the camera's electronics.

- **Portrait.** This mode tends to use wider f/stops and faster shutter speeds, providing blurred backgrounds and images with no camera shake. If you hold the shutter release down, the XS will take a continuous sequence of photos, which can be useful in capturing fleeting expressions in portrait situations.

- **Landscape.** The XS tries to use smaller f/stops for more depth-of-field, and boosts saturation slightly for richer colors.

- **Close-up.** This mode is similar to the Portrait setting, with wider f/stops to isolate your close-up subjects, and high shutter speeds to eliminate the camera shake that's accentuated at close focusing distances. However, if you have your camera mounted on a tripod or are using an image-stabilized (IS) lens, you might want to use the Creative Zone Aperture Priority (Av) mode instead, so you can specify a smaller f/stop with additional depth-of-field.

- **Sports.** In this mode, the XS tries to use high shutter speeds to freeze action, switches to high-speed continuous drive to allow taking a quick sequence of pictures with one press of the shutter release, and uses AI Servo AF to continually refocus as your subject moves around in the frame. You can find more information on autofocus options in Chapter 5.

- **Night Portrait.** Combines flash with ambient light to produce an image that is mainly illuminated by the flash, but the background is exposed by the available light. This mode uses longer exposures, so a tripod, monopod, or IS lens is a must.

- **Flash Off.** Absolutely prevents the flash from flipping up and firing, which you might want in some situations, such as religious ceremonies, museums, classical music concerts, and your double-naught spy activities. This mode is identical to Full Auto, but with the flash disabled.

5

Advanced Techniques for Your Canon EOS Rebel XS

The typical new user of a sophisticated camera like the Canon EOS Rebel XS passes through three stages on the road to proficiency. When the camera first came out of the box, you probably spent a lot of time learning its basic features, and setting it up to take decent pictures automatically, with little input from you. It probably felt great to gain the confidence to snap off picture after picture, knowing that a large percentage of them were going to be well-exposed, in sharp focus, and rich with color.

After you were comfortable with your camera, you began looking for ways to add your own creativity to your shots. You explored ways of tweaking the exposure, using selective focus, and, perhaps, experimenting with the different looks that various lens zoom settings (*focal lengths*) could offer.

The final, and most rewarding, stage comes when you begin exploring advanced techniques that enable you to get stunning shots that will have your family, friends, and colleagues asking you, "How did you *do* that?" These more advanced techniques deserve an entire book of their own (and I have one for you called *Digital SLR Pro Secrets*, also from Course Technology PTR). But there is plenty of room in this chapter to introduce you to some clever things you can do with your Rebel XS.

Beyond Good Exposure

In Chapter 4, you learned techniques for getting the *right* exposure, but I haven't explained all your exposure options just yet. You'll want to know about the *kind* of exposure settings that are available to you with the Canon EOS Rebel XS. There are options that let you control when the exposure is made, or even how to make an exposure that's out of the ordinary in terms of length (time or bulb exposures). These capabilities all let you take pictures that are surprising and effective.

Short Exposures

Fast shutter speeds stop action because they capture only a tiny slice of time. Electronic flash also freezes motion by virtue of its extremely short duration—as brief as 1/50,000th second or less. The Rebel XS's 1/4,000 second shutter speed and its built-in flash unit both can give you these ultra-quick glimpses of moving subjects. An external flash, such as one of the Canon Speedlites, offers even more versatility. You can read more about using electronic flash to stop action in Chapter 7.

In this chapter, I'm going to emphasize the use of short exposures to capture a moment in time. The XS is fully capable of immobilizing all but the fastest movement using only its shutter speeds, which range all the way up to 1/4,000th second. While some cameras, such as stablemate EOS 40D, have speeds up to 1/8,000 second, those ultra-fast shutters are generally overkill when it comes to stopping action, and are rarely needed for achieving the exposure you desire.

For example, if you wanted to use an aperture of f/1.8 at ISO 100 outdoors in bright sunlight, for some reason, a shutter speed of 1/4,000th second would more than do the job. You'd need a faster shutter speed only if you moved the ISO setting to a higher sensitivity, and you probably wouldn't do that if your goal was to use the widest f/stop possible. Under *less* than full sunlight, 1/4,000th second is more than fast enough for any conditions you're likely to encounter.

When it comes to stopping action, most sports can be frozen at 1/2,000th second or slower, and for many sports a slower shutter speed is actually preferable—for example, to allow the wheels of a racing automobile or motorcycle, or the propeller on a classic aircraft to blur realistically. Figure 5.1 is one example. The 1/500 second shutter speed more or less stopped the soccer players in mid-stride, but there is still enough blur in their legs and the ball to provide a feeling of motion. If the ball were perfectly sharp, it might look on first glance as if it were suspended in mid-air. The blur tells us that this shot wasn't faked.

But if you want to do some exotic action-freezing photography without resorting to electronic flash, the XS's top shutter speed is at your disposal. Here are some things to think about when exploring this type of high-speed photography:

- **You'll need a lot of light.** High shutter speeds cut very fine slices of time and sharply reduce the amount of illumination that reaches your sensor. To use 1/4,000th second at an aperture of f/6.3, you'd need an ISO setting of 1,600—even in full daylight. To use an f/stop smaller than f/6.3 or an ISO setting lower than 1,600, you'd need *more* light than full daylight provides. (That's why electronic flash units work so well for high-speed photography when used as the sole illumination; they provide both the effect of a brief shutter speed and the high levels of illumination needed.)

■ **Forget about reciprocity failure.** If you're an old-time film shooter, you might recall that very brief shutter speeds (as well as very high light levels and very *long* exposures) produced an effect called *reciprocity failure,* in which given exposures ended up providing less than the calculated value because of the way film responded to very short, very intense, or very long exposures of light. Solid-state sensors don't suffer from this defect, so you don't need to make an adjustment when using high shutter speeds (or brief flash bursts).

■ **No elongation effect.** This is another old bugaboo that has largely been solved through modern technology, but I wanted to bring it to your attention anyway. In olden times, cameras used shutters that traveled horizontally. To achieve faster shutter speeds, focal plane shutters (located just in front of the plane of the sensor) open only a smaller-than-frame-sized slit so that, even though the shutter is already

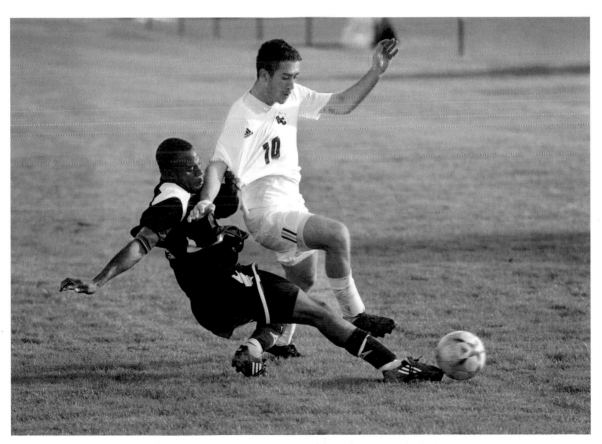

Figure 5.1 A little blur can be a good thing, as the soccer ball adds excitement to this action shot.

traveling at its highest rate of speed, the film/sensor is exposed for a briefer period of time as the slit moves across the surface. At very short shutter speeds, and with subjects moving horizontally at very fast velocities, it was possible for the subject to partially "keep up" with the shutter if it were traveling in the same direction as the slit, producing an elongated effect. Conversely, subjects moving in the opposite direction of shutter motion could be compressed. Today, shutters like those in the XS move vertically and at a higher maximum rate of speed. So, unless you're photographing a rocket blasting into space, and holding the camera horizontally to boot (or shooting a racing car in vertical orientation), it's almost impossible to produce unwanted elongation/compression.

- **Don't combine high shutter speeds with electronic flash.** You might be tempted to use an electronic flash with a high shutter speed. Perhaps you want to stop some action in daylight with a brief shutter speed and use electronic flash only as supplemental illumination to fill in the shadows. Unfortunately, under most conditions, you can't use flash in subdued illumination with your XS at any shutter speed faster than 1/200th second. That's the fastest speed at which the camera's focal plane shutter is fully open: at shorter speeds, the "slit" described above comes into play, so that the flash will expose only the small portion of the sensor exposed by the slit during its duration. This top speed is called the maximum *sync speed.*

Working with Short Exposures

You can have a lot of fun exploring the kinds of pictures you can take using very brief exposure times, whether you decide to take advantage of the action-stopping capabilities of your built-in or external electronic flash or work with the Canon EOS Rebel XS's faster shutter speeds. Here are a few ideas to get you started:

- **Take revealing images.** Fast shutter speeds can help you reveal the real subject behind the façade, by freezing constant motion to capture an enlightening moment in time. Legendary fashion/portrait photographer Philippe Halsman used leaping photos of famous people, such as the Duke and Duchess of Windsor, Richard Nixon, and Salvador Dali to illuminate their real selves. Halsman said, "*When you ask a person to jump, his attention is mostly directed toward the act of jumping and the mask falls so that the real person appears.*" Try some high-speed portraits of people you know in motion to see how they appear when concentrating on something other than the portrait.

- **Create unreal images.** High-speed photography can also produce photographs that show your subjects in ways that are quite unreal. A helicopter in mid-air with its rotors frozen or a motocross cyclist leaping over a ramp, but with all motion stopped so that the rider and machine look as if they were frozen in mid-air, make for an unusual picture. (See Figure 5.2.) When we're accustomed to seeing subjects in motion, seeing them stopped in time can verge on the surreal.

Figure 5.2
Freezing a leaping motocross rider in mid-air makes for an image that verges on the surreal.

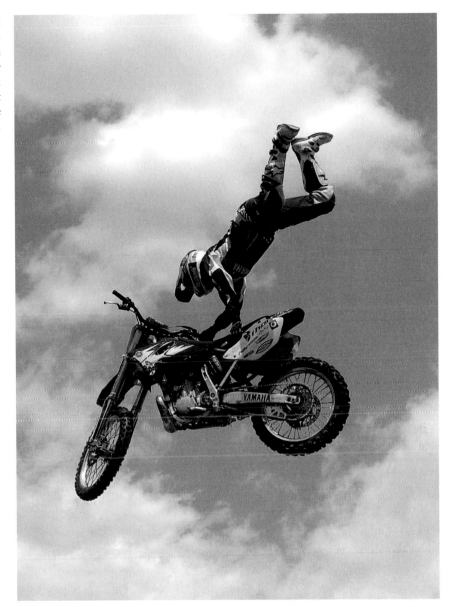

■ **Capture unseen perspectives.** Some things are *never* seen in real life, except when viewed in a stop-action photograph. "Stroboscope" inventor Dr. Harold Edgerton's well-known photographs of balloons burst by bullets at MIT in the 1930s were only a starting point. Freeze a hummingbird in flight for a view of wings that never seem to stop. Or, capture the splashes as liquid falls into a bowl, as shown in Figure 5.3. No electronic flash was required for this image (and wouldn't have illuminated the water in the bowl as evenly). Instead, a clutch of high-intensity lamps and an ISO setting of 1,600 allowed the camera to capture this image at 1/2,000th second.

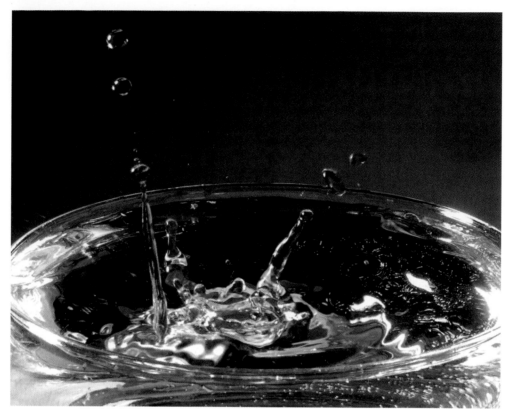

Figure 5.3

A large amount of artificial illumination and an ISO 1,600 sensitivity setting allowed capturing this shot at 1/2,000th second without use of an electronic flash.

- **Vanquish camera shake and gain new angles.** Here's an idea that's so obvious it isn't always explored to its fullest extent. A high enough shutter speed can free you from the tyranny of a tripod, making it easier to capture new angles, or to shoot quickly while moving around, especially with longer lenses. I tend to use a monopod or tripod for almost everything when I'm not using an image-stabilized lens, and I end up missing some shots because of a reluctance to adjust my camera support to get a higher, lower, or different angle. If you have enough light and can use an f/stop wide enough to permit a high shutter speed, you'll find a new freedom to choose your shots. I have a favored 170mm-500mm lens that I use for sports and wildlife photography, almost invariably with a tripod, as I don't find the "reciprocal of the focal length" rule particularly helpful in most cases. (I would *not* handhold this hefty lens at its 500mm setting with a 1/500th second shutter speed under most circumstances.) However, at 1/2,000th second or faster, it's entirely possible for a steady hand to use this lens without a tripod or monopod's extra support, and I've found that my whole approach to shooting animals and other elusive subjects changes in high-speed mode. Selective focus allows dramatically isolating my prey wide open at f/6.3, too.

Long Exposures

Longer exposures are a doorway into another world, showing us how even familiar scenes can look much different when photographed over periods measured in seconds. At night, long exposures produce streaks of light from moving, illuminated subjects like automobiles or amusement park rides. Extra-long exposures of seemingly pitch-dark subjects can reveal interesting views using light levels barely bright enough to see by. At any time of day, including daytime (in which case you'll often need the help of neutral density filters to make the long exposure practical), long exposures can cause moving objects to vanish entirely, because they don't remain stationary long enough to register in a photograph.

Three Ways to Take Long Exposures

There are actually three common types of lengthy exposures: *timed exposures*, *bulb exposures*, and *time exposures*. The Rebel XS offers only the first two, but once you understand all three, you'll see why Canon made the choices it did. Because of the length of the exposure, all of the following techniques should be used with a tripod to hold the camera steady.

- **Timed exposures.** These are long exposures from 1 second to 30 seconds, measured by the camera itself. To take a picture in this range, simply use Manual or Tv modes and use the Main dial to set the shutter speed to the length of time you want, choosing from preset speeds of 1.0, 1.5, 2.0, 3.0, 4.0, 6.0, 8.0, 10.0, 15.0, 20.0, or 30.0 seconds (if you've specified 1/2 stop increments for exposure adjustments), or 1.0, 1.3, 1.6, 2.0, 2.5, 3.2, 4.0, 5.0, 6.0, 8.0, 10.0, 13.0, 15.0, 20.0, 25.0, and 30.0 seconds (if you're using 1/3 stop increments). The advantage of timed exposures is that the camera does all the calculating for you. There's no need for a stop-watch. If you review your image on the LCD and decide to try again with the exposure doubled or halved, you can dial in the correct exposure with precision. The disadvantage of timed exposures is that you can't take a photo for longer than 30 seconds.

- **Bulb exposures.** This type of exposure is so-called because in the olden days the photographer squeezed and held an air bulb attached to a tube that provided the force necessary to keep the shutter open. Traditionally, a bulb exposure is one that lasts as long as the shutter release button is pressed; when you release the button, the exposure ends. To make a bulb exposure with the XS, set the camera on Manual mode and use the Main dial to select the shutter speed immediately after 30 seconds. BULB will be displayed on the LCD and buLb in the viewfinder. Then, press the shutter to start the exposure, and press it again to close the shutter. If you'd like to simulate a time exposure (described below), you can use the Canon RS-80N3 or TC-80N3 remote releases that attach to the remote terminal on the left side of the camera under the rubber cover. Both have a shutter release lock that can be used to keep the shutter open, and the TC-80N3 includes a timer that can expose a picture for any length from 1 second to 99 hours, 59 minutes, and 59 seconds. Or, if you have a lot of money to spend and can find one, you can use the LC-4 infrared wireless transmitter and receiver.

■ **Time exposures.** This is a setting found on some cameras to produce longer exposures. With cameras that implement this option, the shutter opens when you press the shutter release button, and remains open until you press the button again. Usually, you'll be able to close the shutter using a mechanical cable release or, more commonly, an electronic release cable. The advantage of this approach is that you can take an exposure of virtually any duration without the need for special equipment (the tethered release is optional). You can press the shutter release button, go off for a few minutes, and come back to close the shutter (assuming your camera is still there). The disadvantages of this mode are exposures must be timed manually, and with shorter exposures it's possible for the vibration of manually opening and closing the shutter to register in the photo. For longer exposures, the period of vibration is relatively brief and not usually a problem—and there is always the release cable option to eliminate photographer-caused camera shake entirely. While the XS does not have a built-in time exposure capability, you can simulate it with the bulb exposure technique, described previously.

Working with Long Exposures

Because the Rebel XS produces such good images at longer exposures, and there are so many creative things you can do with long-exposure techniques, you'll want to do some experimenting. Get yourself a tripod or another firm support and take some test shots with long exposure noise reduction both enabled and disabled (to see whether you prefer low noise or high detail) and get started. Here are some things to try:

■ **Make people invisible.** One very cool thing about long exposures is that objects that move rapidly enough won't register at all in a photograph, while the subjects that remain stationary are portrayed in the normal way. That makes it easy to produce people-free landscape photos and architectural photos at night or, even, in full daylight if you use a neutral density filter (or two, or three) to allow an exposure of at least a few seconds. At ISO 100, f/22, and a pair of 8X (three-stop) neutral-density filters you can use exposures of nearly two seconds; overcast days and/or even more neutral density filtration would work even better if daylight people-vanishing is your goal. They'll have to be walking *very* briskly and across the field of view (rather than directly toward the camera) for this to work. At night, it's much easier to achieve this effect with the 20- to 30-second exposures that are possible, as you can see in Figure 5.4.

Figure 5.4
This alleyway is thronged with people, but you can't see them in this two-second exposure using only the available illumination.

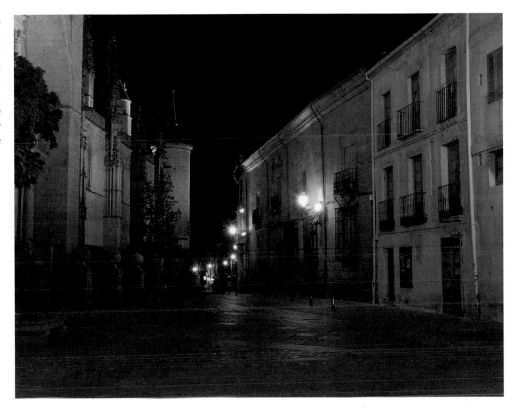

■ **Create streaks.** If you aren't shooting for total invisibility, long exposures with the camera on a tripod can produce some interesting streaky effects. Even a single 8X ND filter will let you shoot at f/22 and 1/6th second in daylight. Indoors, you can achieve interesting streaks with slow shutter speeds, as shown in Figure 5.5. For this shot, the camera lens was mounted on a monopod using the lens's tripod collar, and I loosened the collar and rotated the camera during a one-second exposure.

Tip

Neutral density filters are gray (non-colored) filters that reduce the amount of light passing through the lens, without adding any color of their own.

■ **Produce light trails.** At night, car headlights and taillights and other moving sources of illumination can generate interesting light trails. Your camera doesn't even need to be mounted on a tripod; handholding the XS for longer exposures adds movement and patterns to your trails. If you're shooting fireworks, a longer exposure may allow you to combine several bursts into one picture, as shown in Figure 5.6.

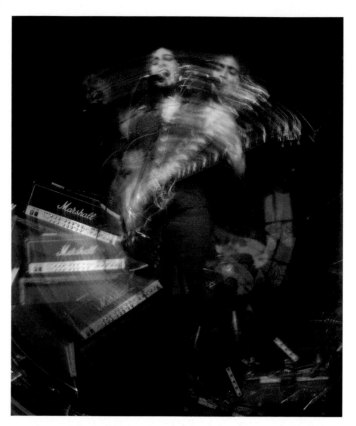

Figure 5.5
A long exposure, and rotating the camera produced this concert shot.

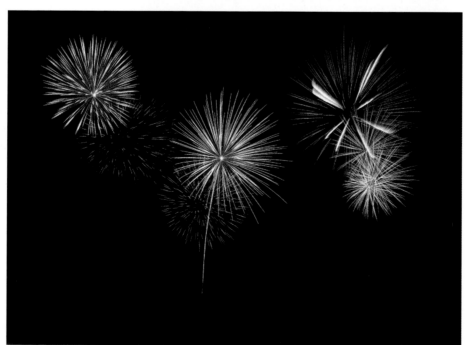

Figure 5.6
I caught the fireworks after a baseball game from a half-mile away, using a four-second exposure to capture several bursts in one shot.

■ **Blur waterfalls, etc.** You'll find that waterfalls and other sources of moving liquid produce a special type of long-exposure blur, because the water merges into a fantasy-like veil that looks different at different exposure times, and with different waterfalls. Cascades with turbulent flow produce a rougher look at a given longer exposure than falls that flow smoothly. Although blurred waterfalls have become almost a cliché, there are still plenty of variations for a creative photographer to explore, as you can see in Figure 5.7.

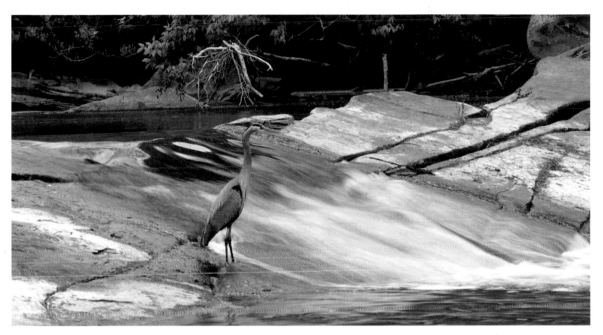

Figure 5.7 Long exposures can transform a waterfall into a display of flowing silk.

■ **Show total darkness in new ways.** Even on the darkest, moonless nights, there is enough starlight or glow from distant illumination sources to see by, and, if you use a long exposure, there is enough light to take a picture, too. I was visiting a riverside park hours after sunset, but found that a 30-second exposure with the lens almost wide open revealed the scene shown in Figure 5.8, even though in real life, there was barely enough light to make out the closest tree. Although the photo appears as if it were taken at twilight or sunset, in fact the shot was made at 11 p.m.

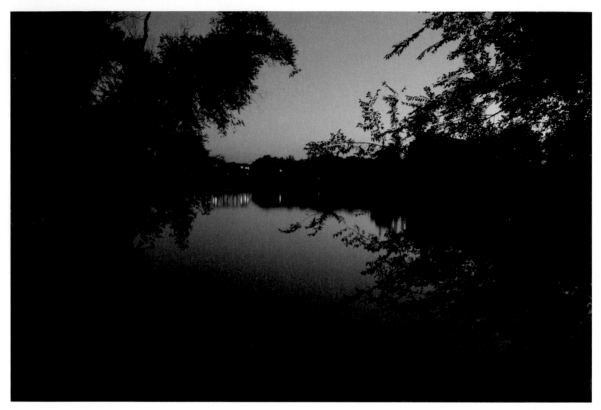

Figure 5.8 A 30-second exposure transformed this night scene into a picture apparently taken at dusk.

Delayed Exposures

Sometimes it's desirable to have a delay of some sort before a picture is actually taken. Perhaps you'd like to get in the picture yourself, and would appreciate it if the camera waited 10 seconds after you press the shutter release to actually take the picture. Maybe you want to give a tripod-mounted camera time to settle down and damp any residual vibration after the release is pressed to improve sharpness for an exposure with a relatively slow shutter speed. It's possible you want to explore the world of time-lapse photography. The next sections present your delayed exposure options.

Self-Timer

The Rebel XS has a built-in self-timer with 10-second and 2-second delays. Your camera also has a self-timer/multiple setting that allows taking 2 to 10 shots after the delay. All these options were described in Chapter 2.

Activate the timer by pressing the Drive button (left cross key) and pressing the left/right cross keys to choose one of the three self-timer icons. Press the Set button to confirm your choice. Then, press the shutter release button halfway to lock in focus on your subjects (if you're taking a self-portrait, focus on an object at a similar distance and use focus lock). When you're ready to take the photo, continue pressing the shutter release the rest of the way. The lamp on the front of the camera will blink slowly for eight seconds (when using the 10-second timer) and the beeper will chirp (if you haven't disabled it in the Shooting 1 menu, as described in Chapter 3). During the final two seconds, the beeper sounds more rapidly and the lamp remains on until the picture is taken. The LCD displays a countdown in the lower-right corner of the screen while all this is going on.

Another way to use the self-timer is with the mirror lockup feature (C.Fn.III-08). This is something you might want to do if you're shooting close-ups, landscapes, or other types of pictures using the self-timer only to trip the shutter in the most vibration-free way possible. Forget to bring along your tripod, but still want to take a close-up picture with a precise focus setting? Set your digital camera to the self-timer function, then put the camera on any reasonably steady support, such as a fence post or a rock. When you're ready to take the picture, press the shutter release. The camera might totter back and forth for a second or two, but it will settle back to its original position before the self-timer activates the shutter. The self-timer remains active until you turn it off—even if you power down the XS.

Remote Control

As outlined in the "Bulb Exposure" description earlier, your Canon EOS Rebel XS can be triggered using a plug-in remote control with an electronic or infrared connection. For example, the Remote Switch RS-80N3 allows triggering a camera attached to the end of its cable.

Time-Lapse/Interval Photography

Who hasn't marveled at a time-lapse photograph of a flower opening, a series of shots of the moon marching across the sky, or one of those extreme time-lapse picture sets showing something that takes a very, very long time, such as a building under construction.

You probably won't be shooting such construction shots, unless you have a spare XS you don't need for a few months (or are willing to go through the rigmarole of figuring out how to set up your camera in precisely the same position using the same lens settings to shoot a series of pictures at intervals). However, other kinds of time-lapse photography are entirely within reach.

Although the Rebel XS can't take time-lapse/interval photographs all by itself, if you're willing to tether the camera to a computer (a laptop will do) using the USB cable, you can take time-lapse photos using the Digital Photo Professional software furnished with your camera. There's more information on using this software in Chapter 8.

If you want freedom to shoot anywhere, Opteka (www.opteka.com) offers a reasonably affordable add-on (around $100) with much more than the self-timer and remote control features mentioned previously. In fact, it has several different modes with an interesting array of delay/interval combinations for time-lapse photography and interval shooting. For example, you can set a delay period that must elapse before the XS begins an exposure. Or, you can choose to shoot a set number of pictures at intervals from 1 second to 99 hours, 59 minutes, and 59 seconds. Canon offers a similar controller for other cameras in its line (the TC-80N3), so until an equivalent model becomes available for the XS, the Opteka device is your best option.

Here are some tips for effective time-lapse photography:

- **Use AC power.** If you're shooting a long sequence, consider connecting your camera to an AC adapter, as leaving the XS on for long periods of time will rapidly deplete the battery. Use the Canon AC Adapter kit ACK-E5, which consists of the Compact Power Adapter CA-PS700 and the DC Coupler DR-E5.

- **Make sure you have enough storage space.** Unless your memory card has enough capacity to hold all the images you'll be taking, you might want to change to a higher compression rate or reduced resolution to maximize the image count.

- **Make a movie.** While time-lapse stills are interesting, you can increase your fun factor by compiling all your shots into a motion picture using your favorite desktop movie-making software.

- **Protect your camera.** If your camera will be set up for an extended period of time (longer than an hour or two), make sure it's protected from weather, earthquakes, animals, young children, innocent bystanders, and theft.

- **Vary intervals.** Experiment with different time intervals. You don't want to take pictures too often or less often than necessary to capture the changes you hope to image.

Getting into Focus

Learning to use the Canon EOS Rebel XS's autofocus system is easy, but you do need to fully understand how the system works to get the most benefit from it. Once you're comfortable with autofocus, you'll know when it's appropriate to use the manual focus option, too. The important thing to remember is that focus isn't absolute. For example, some things that look in sharp focus at a given viewing size and distance might not be in focus at a larger size and/or closer distance. In addition, the goal of optimum focus isn't always to make things look sharp. Not all of an image will be or should be sharp. Controlling exactly what is sharp and what is not is part of your creative palette. Use of depth-of-field characteristics to throw part of an image out of focus while other parts are sharply focused is one of the most valuable tools available to a photographer. But selective focus works only when the desired areas of an image are in focus properly. For the digital SLR photographer, correct focus can be one of the trickiest parts of the technical and creative process.

To make your job easier, the Rebel XS has a precision seven-point autofocus system that uses a separate sensor in the viewing system to measure the contrast of the image. When the contrast is highest at the active autofocus point(s), that part of the image is in sharp focus. The active focus points are represented by the seven sets of brackets visible in the viewfinder (see Figure 5.9), and can be selected automatically by the camera, or manually by you, the photographer. The center autofocus point is of the advanced "cross" type (that is, it measures in both horizontal and vertical directions) that works with all Canon lenses having a maximum aperture of f/5.6 or larger, but has enhanced sensitivity when used with a lens having a maximum aperture of f/2.8 or larger.

Your camera's autofocus sensors require a minimum amount of light to operate, which is why autofocus capabilities are possible only with lenses having an f/5.6 or larger maximum aperture. If necessary, the AF assist burst built into the XS's built-in flash and Canon's dedicated flash units provide additional light that helps assure enough illumination for autofocus.

Figure 5.9
Any of the seven autofocus points can be selected by the photographer manually or by the camera automatically.

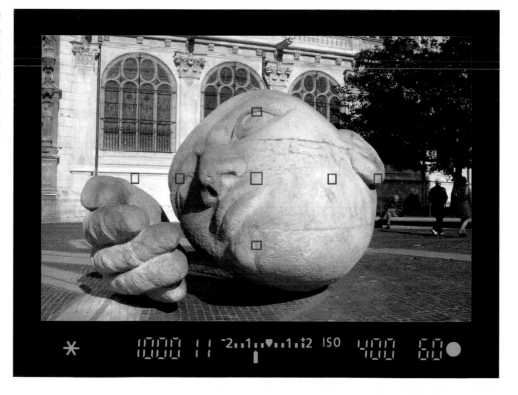

Improved Cross-Type Focus Point

One improvement that new Canon EOS Rebel XS owners sometimes overlook is the upgrade to a cross-type focus point at the center position. Why is this important? It helps to review exactly how the XS determines focus.

The camera looks for contrast between adjacent pixels to determine relative sharpness—specifically, the transitions between those groups of pixels that determine the edges in a subject. At left in the extreme enlargement shown in Figure 5.10, the transitions between pixels are soft and blurred. When the image is brought into focus (right), the transitions are sharp and clear. Although this example is a bit exaggerated so you can see the results on the printed page, it's easy to understand that when the Rebel XS detects maximum contrast in a subject being evaluated by the focus sensor, it is deemed to be in sharp focus.

Of course, the process isn't quite that simple. When focusing using the focus screen, the XS uses a process called *phase detection*; in Live View mode, when focusing using the back-panel color LCD, the method used is called *contrast detection*. I'll explain the

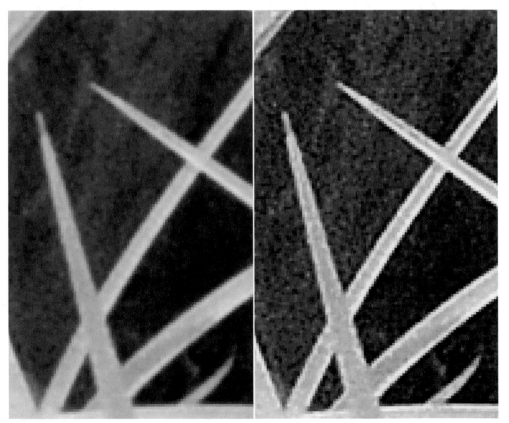

Figure 5.10

Focus sensors detect the increase in contrast in the edges of subjects, starting with a blurry image (left) and producing a sharp, contrasty image (right).

difference between the two methods later in this chapter in the section that deals with Live View.

But when you're not using Live View, the phase detection process (which, as you'll learn, is based on "lining up" the top and bottom halves of edges, like a rangefinder device) benefits from the center cross-type sensor. The cross sensor is able to interpret, or line up, edges in both horizontal and vertical directions, as you can visualize by looking at Figure 5.11. The two upper photos show a horizontal-type sensor evaluating a subject, which happens to be a piece of aged wood siding heavily creased with horizontal lines. At upper left, the sensor sees blurry lines, which become sharper when the wood is brought into focus. This type of subject is of average difficulty for a horizontal sensor: easier to interpret than an image with no pattern at all, and harder to focus than, say, vertical lines, which would stand out more clearly. You can see that a horizontal focus sensor does a good job but has some weaknesses. (A vertical-only focus sensor would have the same reduced performance with vertical lines and better focusing with horizontal lines.)

At the bottom of the figure you'll see the same subject being evaluated by a cross-type sensor. The horizontal lines are still more difficult to interpret with the horizontal arm of the cross, but they stand out in sharp contrast (even in the blurry version at lower left) and allow the camera to snap the image into focus easily, as you can see at lower

Figure 5.11
Horizontal (and vertical) focus sensors can "line up" edges in only one direction (top), while cross-type sensors can evaluate edges in both horizontal and vertical directions.

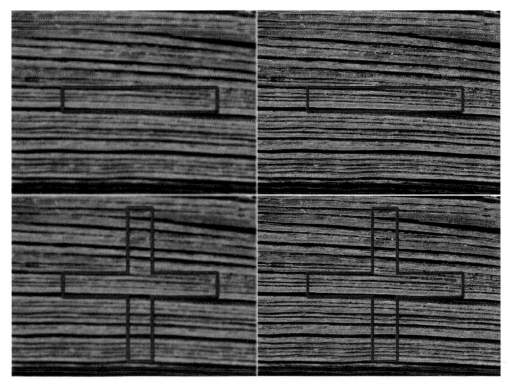

right. In this example, both the horizontal and cross-type sensors were able to produce an equally sharp focus (upper and lower right), but the cross-type sensor probably focused the image a tad faster. And, in lower light levels, with subjects that were moving, or with subjects that have no pattern and less contrast to begin with, the cross-type sensor not only works faster but can focus subjects that a horizontal- or vertical-only sensor can't handle at all.

So, you can see that having a center cross-type focus sensor that is extra-sensitive with faster lenses is a definite advantage.

Focus Modes

The XS has three AF modes: One Shot AF (also known as Single Autofocus), AI Servo (Continuous Autofocus), and AI Focus AF (which switches between the two as appropriate). I'll explain all of these in more detail later in this section.

Focus Pocus

Although Canon added autofocus capabilities in the 1980s, back in the day of film cameras, prior to that focusing was always done manually. Honest. Even though viewfinders were bigger and brighter than they are today, special focusing screens, magnifiers, and other gadgets were often used to help the photographer achieve correct focus. Imagine what it must have been like to focus manually under demanding, fast-moving conditions such as sports photography.

MANUAL FOCUS

With Manual focus activated by sliding the switch on the lens, your XS lets you set the focus yourself. There are some advantages and disadvantages to this approach. While your batteries will last slightly longer in Manual focus mode, it will take you longer to focus the camera for each photo, a process that can be tricky. Modern digital cameras, even dSLRs, depend so much on autofocus that the viewfinders of models that have less than full-frame-sized sensors are no longer designed for optimum manual focus. Pick up any film camera and you'll see a bigger, brighter viewfinder with a focusing screen that's a joy to focus on manually. Of course, the Rebel XS has a viewfinder that is slightly smaller than its more costly sibling, the Rebel XSi. It provides .81 magnification, compared with .87 magnification with the XSi. (That means that with a 50mm focal length, the image appears to be 81 percent of life size.) The XS viewfinder seems even smaller than that of the EOS 50D, which also has a brighter image because it uses an efficient *pentaprism* to conduct light to your eye, while the Rebel XS has a less-expensive system of mirrors (called a *pentamirror*). Of course, these differences are what make the more advanced cameras cost as much as twice as much! (But despite their image size differences, the 50D, XSi, and XS all show you 95 percent of the frame.)

Focusing was problematic because our eyes and brains have poor memory for correct focus, which is why your eye doctor must shift back and forth between sets of lenses and ask "Does that look sharper—or was it sharper before?" in determining your correct prescription. Similarly, manual focusing involves jogging the focus ring back and forth as you go from almost in focus, to sharp focus, to almost focused again. The little clockwise and counterclockwise arcs decrease in size until you've zeroed in on the point of correct focus. As I mentioned earlier in this chapter, what you're looking for is the image with the most contrast between the edges of elements in the image.

The XS's autofocus mechanism, like all such systems found in SLR cameras, also evaluates these increases and decreases in sharpness, but it is able to remember the progression perfectly, so that autofocus can lock in much more quickly and, with an image that has sufficient contrast, more precisely. Unfortunately, while the XS's focus system finds it easy to measure degrees of apparent focus at each of the focus points in the viewfinder, it doesn't really know with any certainty *which* object should be in sharpest focus. Is it the closest object? The subject in the center? Something lurking *behind* the closest subject? A person standing over at the side of the picture? Many of the techniques for using autofocus effectively involve telling the Rebel XS exactly what it should be focusing on, as described later in this chapter.

Adding Circles of Confusion

But there are other factors in play, as well. You know that increased depth of-field brings more of your subject into focus. But more depth-of-field also makes autofocusing (or manual focusing) more difficult because the contrast is lower between objects at different distances. So, autofocus with a 200mm lens (or zoom setting) may be easier than at a 28mm focal length (or zoom setting) because the longer lens has less apparent depth-of-field. By the same token, a lens with a maximum aperture of f/1.8 will be easier to autofocus (or manually focus) than one of the same focal length with an f/4 maximum aperture, because the f/4 lens has more depth-of-field *and* a dimmer view. That's why lenses with a maximum aperture smaller than f/5.6 can give your XS's autofocus system fits.

To make things even more complicated, many subjects aren't polite enough to remain still. They move around in the frame, so that even if the XS is sharply focused on your main subject, it may change position and require refocusing. An intervening subject may pop into the frame and pass between you and the subject you meant to photograph. You (or the XS) have to decide whether to lock focus on this new subject, or remain focused on the original subject. Finally, there are some kinds of subjects that are difficult to bring into sharp focus because they lack enough contrast to allow the XS's AF system (or our eyes) to lock in. Blank walls, a clear blue sky, or other subject matter may make focusing difficult.

If you find all these focus factors confusing, you're on the right track. Focus is, in fact, measured using something called a *circle of confusion.* An ideal image consists of zillions of tiny little points, which, like all points, theoretically have no height or width. There is perfect contrast between the point and its surroundings. You can think of each point as a pinpoint of light in a darkened room. When a given point is out of focus, its edges decrease in contrast and it changes from a perfect point to a tiny disc with blurry edges (remember, blur is the lack of contrast between boundaries in an image). (See Figure 5.12.)

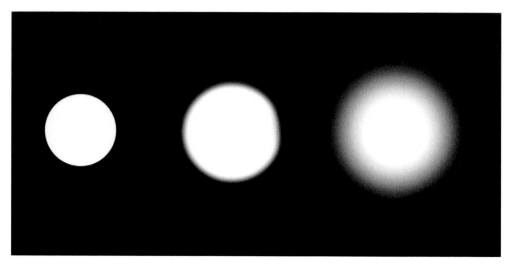

Figure 5.12
When a pinpoint of light (left) goes out of focus, its blurry edges form a circle of confusion (center and right).

If this blurry disc—the circle of confusion—is small enough, our eye still perceives it as a point. It's only when the disc grows large enough that we can see it as a blur rather than a sharp point that a given point is viewed as out of focus. You can see, then, that enlarging an image, either by displaying it larger on your computer monitor or by making a large print, also enlarges the size of each circle of confusion. Moving closer to the image does the same thing. So, parts of an image that may look perfectly sharp in a 5 × 7-inch print viewed at arm's length, might appear blurry when blown up to 11 × 14 and examined at the same distance. Take a few steps back, however, and it may look sharp again.

To a lesser extent, the viewer also affects the apparent size of these circles of confusion. Some people see details better at a given distance and may perceive smaller circles of confusion than someone standing next to them. For the most part, however, such differences are small. Truly blurry images will look blurry to just about everyone under the same conditions.

Technically, there is just one plane within your picture area, parallel to the back of the camera (or sensor, in the case of a digital camera), that is in sharp focus. That's the plane in which the points of the image are rendered as precise points. At every other plane in front of or behind the focus plane, the points show up as discs that range from slightly blurry to extremely blurry. In practice, the discs in many of these planes will still be so small that we see them as points, and that's where we get depth-of-field. Depth-of-field is just the range of planes that include discs that we perceive as points rather than blurred splotches. The size of this range increases as the aperture is reduced in size and is allocated roughly one-third in front of the plane of sharpest focus, and two-thirds behind it. The range of sharp focus is always greater behind your subject than in front of it. (See Figure 5.13.)

Figure 5.13
Faced with an ugly background, a large f/stop focused attention on this nautical chain, with everything beyond it blurry and out of focus because of the limited depth-of-field.

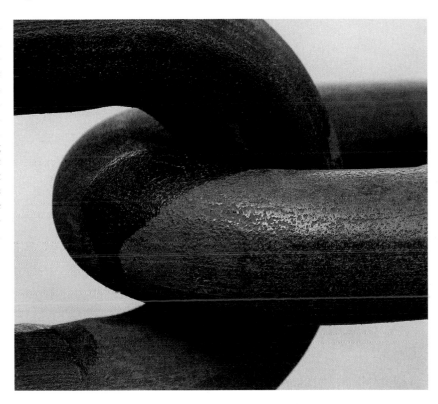

Making Sense of Sensors

The number and type of autofocus sensors can affect how well the system operates. As I mentioned, the Canon EOS Rebel XS has seven AF points, like the original Digital Rebel and Digital Rebel XT, and only two fewer than the Rebel XSi. Canon's high-end camera, like the 21MP Canon EOS-1Ds Mark III, has a whopping 45 autofocus points. These focus sensors can consist of vertical or horizontal lines of pixels, cross-shapes, and often a mixture of these types within a single camera, although, as I mentioned, the Rebel XS includes a cross-type sensor at the center position. The more AF points available, the more easily the camera can differentiate among areas of the frame, and the more precisely you can specify the area you want to be in focus if you're manually choosing a focus spot.

As the camera collects contrast information from the sensors, it then evaluates it to determine whether the desired sharp focus has been achieved. The calculations may include whether the subject is moving, and whether the camera needs to "predict" where the subject will be when the shutter release button is fully depressed and the picture is taken. The speed with which the camera is able to evaluate focus and then move the lens elements into the proper position to achieve the sharpest focus determines how fast the autofocus mechanism is. Although your XS will almost always focus more quickly than a human, there are types of shooting situations where that's not fast enough. For example, if you're having problems shooting sports because the XS's autofocus system manically follows each moving subject, a better choice might be to switch autofocus modes or shift into Manual and prefocus on a spot where you anticipate the action will be, such as a goal line or soccer net. At night football games, for example, when I am shooting with a telephoto lens almost wide open, I often focus manually on one of the referees who happens to be standing where I expect the action to be taking place (say, a halfback run or a pass reception). When I am less sure about what is going to happen, I may switch to AI Servo autofocus and let the camera decide.

Your Autofocus Mode Options

Choosing the right autofocus mode and the way in which focus points are selected is your key to success. Using the wrong mode for a particular type of photography can lead to a series of pictures that are all sharply focused—on the wrong subject. When I first started shooting sports with an autofocus SLR (back in the film camera days), I covered one game alternating between shots of base runners and outfielders with pictures of a promising young pitcher, all from a position next to the third base dugout. The base runner and outfielder photos were great, because their backgrounds didn't distract the autofocus mechanism. But all my photos of the pitcher had the focus tightly zeroed in on the fans in the stands behind him. Because I was shooting film instead of a digital camera, I didn't know about my gaffe until the film was developed. A simple change, such as locking in focus or focus zone manually, or even manually focusing, would have done the trick.

To save battery power, your XS doesn't start to focus the lens until you partially depress the shutter release. But, autofocus isn't some mindless beast out there snapping your pictures in and out of focus with no feedback from you after you press that button. There are several settings you can modify that return at least a modicum of control to you. Your first decision should be whether you set the XS to One Shot, AI Servo AF, or AI Focus AF. With the camera set for one of the Creative Zone modes, press the AF button (the right cross key) and use the left/right cross keys to select the focus mode you want (see Figure 5.14). Press Set to confirm your choice. (The AF/M switch on the lens must be set to AF before you can change autofocus mode.)

Figure 5.14

Press the
left/right cross
keys until the
AF choice you
want is
selected.

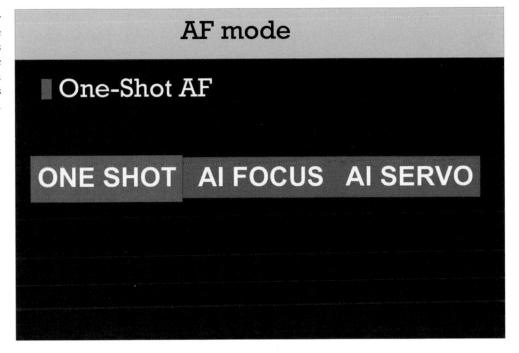

One Shot AF

In this mode, also called *Single Autofocus*, focus is set once and remains at that setting until the button is fully depressed, taking the picture, or until you release the shutter button without taking a shot. For non-action photography, this setting is usually your best choice, as it minimizes out-of-focus pictures (at the expense of spontaneity). The drawback here is that you might not be able to take a picture at all while the camera is seeking focus; you're locked out until the autofocus mechanism is happy with the current setting. One Shot AF/Single Autofocus is sometimes referred to as *focus priority* for that reason. Because of the small delay while the camera zeroes in on correct focus, you might experience slightly more shutter lag. This mode uses less battery power.

When sharp focus is achieved, the selected focus point will flash red in the viewfinder, and the focus confirmation light at the lower right will flash green. If you're using Evaluative metering, the exposure will be locked at the same time. By keeping the shutter button depressed halfway, you'll find you can reframe the image while retaining the focus (and exposure) that's been set.

AI Servo AF

This mode, also known as *Continuous Autofocus*, is the mode to use for sports and other fast-moving subjects. In this mode, once the shutter release is partially depressed, the camera sets the focus but continues to monitor the subject, so that if it moves or you move, the lens will be refocused to suit. Focus and exposure aren't really locked until you press the shutter release down all the way to take the picture. You'll often see Continuous Autofocus referred to as *Release Priority*. If you press the shutter release down all the way while the system is refining focus, the camera will go ahead and take a picture, even if the image is slightly out of focus. You'll find that AI Servo AF produces the least amount of shutter lag of any autofocus mode: press the button and the camera fires. It also uses the most battery power, because the autofocus system operates as long as the shutter release button is partially depressed.

AI Servo AF uses a technology called *predictive AF*, which allows the XS to calculate the correct focus if the subject is moving toward or away from the camera at a constant rate. It uses either the automatically selected AF point or the point you select manually to set focus.

AI Focus AF

This setting is actually a combination of the first two. When selected, the camera focuses using One Shot AF and locks in the focus setting. But, if the subject begins moving, it will switch automatically to AI Servo AF and change the focus to keep the subject sharp. AI Focus AF is a good choice when you're shooting a mixture of action pictures and less dynamic shots and want to use One-Shot AF when possible. The camera will default to that mode, yet switch automatically to AI Servo AF when it would be useful for subjects that might begin moving unexpectedly.

Setting AF Point

You can change which of the seven focus points the Canon EOS Rebel XS uses to calculate correct focus, or allow the camera to select the point for you. As I mentioned in Chapter 1, in A-DEP, or any of the Basic Zone shooting modes, the focus point is always selected automatically by the camera. In the other Creative Zone modes, you can allow the camera to select the focus point automatically, or you can specify which focus point should be used.

To review, there are several methods to set the focus point manually. You can press the AF point selection button on the back of the camera, look through the viewfinder, and use the cross keys to move the focus point to the zone you want to use. It is not necessary to *hold* the AF point selection button down. Just press it once, and the cross keys become active for about four seconds, or until you stop moving the focus point around. For example, press the cross keys straight up or down, and the top or bottom focus points are selected. To the left or right, and the side points are selected. Press the Set button, and the center focus point becomes active.

You can also choose a focus point by pressing the AF point selection button and then rotating the Main dial. The focus point will cycle among the edge points counter-clockwise (if you turn the Main dial to the left) or clockwise (if you spin the Main dial to the right). At each end of the cycle, the center focus point and then all seven focus points will be active. When all seven are "live," auto point selection will be switched back on.

Continuous Shooting

The Canon EOS Rebel XS's pair of Continuous Shooting modes remind me how far digital photography has brought us. The first accessory I purchased when I worked as a sports photographer some years ago was a motor drive for my film SLR. It enabled me to snap off a series of shots in rapid succession, which came in very handy when a fullback broke through the line and headed for the end zone. Even a seasoned action photographer can miss the decisive instant when a crucial block is made, or a baseball superstar's bat shatters and pieces of cork fly out. Continuous shooting simplifies taking a series of pictures, either to ensure that one has more or less the exact moment you want to capture or to capture a sequence that is interesting as a collection of successive images.

The XS's "motor drive" capabilities are, in many ways, much superior to what you get with a film camera. For one thing, a motor-driven film camera can eat up film at an incredible pace, which is why many of them are used with cassettes that hold hundreds of feet of film stock. At three frames per second (typical of film cameras), a short burst of a few seconds can burn up as much as half of an ordinary 36 exposure roll of film. Digital cameras, in contrast, have reusable "film," so if you waste a few dozen shots on non-decisive moments, you can erase them and shoot more.

The increased capacity of digital film cards gives you a prodigious number of frames to work with. At a baseball game I covered earlier this year, I took more than 1,000 images in a couple hours. Yet, even shooting RAW+JPEG Fine I could fit more than 200 images on a single 4GB Compact Flash card. If I'd switched to JPEG, I could have taken about 900 different images without switching cards. Even at the top speed of 3.0 frames per second that the XS is capable of, that's a lot of shooting. Given an average burst of about eight frames per sequence (nobody really takes 15-20 shots or more of one play in a baseball game), I was able to capture 32 different sequences before I needed to swap cards. Figure 5.15 shows a typical short burst of three shots taken at a basketball game as a player drove in for a layup.

On the other hand, for some sports (such as football) the longer bursts came in handy, because running and passing plays often last 5 to 10 seconds, and change in character as the action switches from the quarterback dropping back to pass or hand off the ball, then the receiver or running back trying to gain as much yardage as possible.

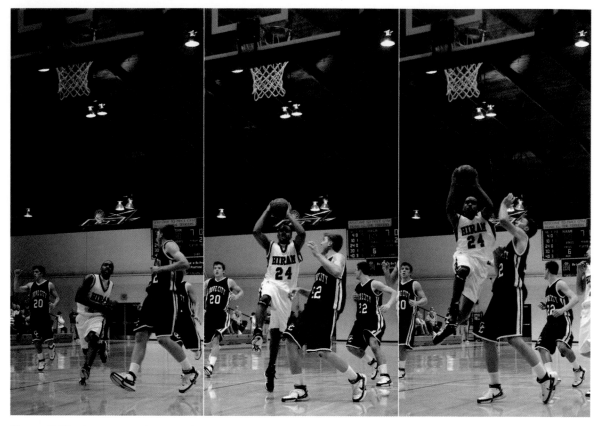

Figure 5.15 Continuous shooting allows you to capture an entire sequence of exciting moments as they unfold.

To use the XS's Continuous Shooting modes, press the Drive button (left cross key). Use the left/right cross keys to select Continuous Shooting (3.0 frames per second). (See Figure 5.16.) Press the Set button to confirm your choice. When you partially depress the shutter button, the viewfinder will display a number representing the maximum number of shots you can take at the current quality settings. If your battery is low, this figure will be lower. A "buSY" indicator will appear if your camera's internal buffer fills up with shots; you must then wait for this indicator to disappear before you can resume shooting.

The Rebel XS will continually refocus during a sequence if the camera is set to AI Servo AF mode. If One-Shot AF is selected, focus will be set for the first picture in the sequence, and all subsequent shots will use the same focus. You'll want to select the appropriate focus mode before you begin shooting. You'll find that the highest frame rates are attained when using One-Shot AF, because the XS isn't taking time to refocus between shots. So, even with action photos, that may be your best choice if your subject is moving across the frame, or is standing in one place. If the subject is approaching the camera, you'll want to use AI Servo AF, even if that means a slower frame rate.

Figure 5.16
Press the Drive
button and use
the left/right
cross keys to
select
Continuous
Shooting.

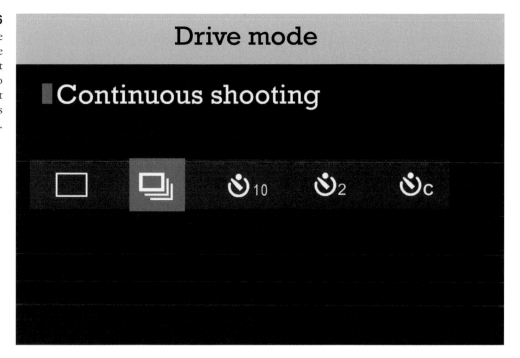

If you use flash while in Continuous Shooting mode, your frame rate will slow down significantly as the Rebel XS waits for the flash to recycle between shots. (Take heart, many digital cameras can't shoot continuously at all when flash is used.) The larger buffer in the XS will generally allow you to take as many as 50 JPEG Fine shots in a single burst at 3 fps, or 5 RAW photos and just 4 RAW+JPEG images (both at a slower frame rate of about 1.5 fps, because of the extra time needed to store the files to your memory card). The number of shots you can take in one burst will vary, depending on the file size, speed of your memory card, ISO setting, and Custom Functions (such as noise reduction) you may be using. So, don't count on getting specific bursts; let your own experience be your guide.

To increase this number, reduce the image-quality setting by switching to JPEG only (from JPEG+RAW), to a lower JPEG quality setting, or by reducing the XS's resolution from L to M or S. The reason the size of your bursts is limited is that continuous images are first shuttled into the XS's internal memory buffer, then doled out to the memory card as quickly as they can be written to the card. Technically, the XS takes the RAW data received from the digital image processor and converts it to the output format you've selected—either .jpg or .cr2 (raw)—and deposits it in the buffer ready to store on the card.

This internal "smart" buffer can suck up photos much more quickly than the memory card and, indeed, some memory cards are significantly faster or slower than others.

When the buffer fills, you can't take any more continuous shots (a buSY indicator appears in the viewfinder and LCD status panel) until the XS has written some of them to the card, making more room in the buffer. (You should keep in mind that faster memory cards write images more quickly, freeing up buffer space faster. You can read more about memory cards in Chapter 9.)

Setting Image Parameters

You can fine-tune the images that you take in several different ways. For example, if you don't want to choose a predefined white balance or use white balance bracketing (both discussed earlier in this book), you can set a custom white balance based on the illumination of the site where you'll be taking photos, or choose a white balance based on color temperature. With the Picture Style options, you can set up customized sharpening, tone, color, saturation, and hue for various types of pictures, plus three personal sets of settings that you can recall at any time. This section shows you how to use the available image parameters.

Customizing White Balance

Back in the film days, color films were standardized, or balanced, for a particular "color" of light. Digital cameras like the Rebel XS use a particular "white balance" matched to the color of light used to expose your photograph. The right white balance is measured using a scale called *color temperature*. Color temperatures were assigned by heating a mythical "black body radiator" and recording the spectrum of light it emitted at a given temperature in degrees Kelvin. So, daylight at noon has a color temperature in the 5,500 to 6,000 degree range. Indoor illumination is around 3,400 degrees. Hotter temperatures produce bluer images (think blue-white hot) while cooler temperatures produce redder images (think of a dull-red glowing ember). Because of human nature, though, bluer images are actually called "cool" (think wintry day) and redder images are called "warm" (think ruddy sunset), even though their color temperatures are reversed.

If a photograph is exposed indoors under warm illumination with a digital camera sensor balanced for cooler daylight, the image will appear much too reddish. An image exposed outdoors with the white balance set for incandescent illumination will seem much too blue. These color casts may be too strong to remove in an image editor from JPEG files, although if you shoot RAW you can change the WB setting to the correct value when you import the image into your editor.

Mismatched white balance settings are easier to achieve accidentally than you might think, even for experienced photographers. I'd just finished shooting some backstage photos at a concert using electronic flash and had manually set WB for flash. Then, I began taking more pictures using the incandescent interior stage lighting and ended up with a few shots like Figure 5.17. Another time, I was shooting outdoors on a farm, with the camera white balance still set for incandescent illumination. The excessively blue image shown in Figure 5.18 resulted. (I suppose I should salvage my reputation as a photo guru by admitting that both these images were taken "incorrectly" deliberately, as illustrations for this book; in real life, I'm excessively attentive to how my white balance is set.)

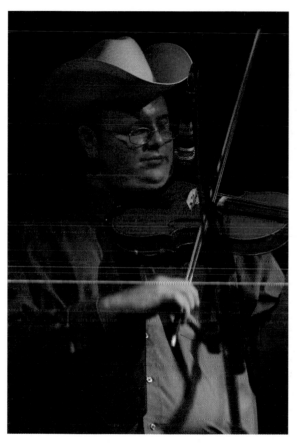

Figure 5.17 An image exposed indoors with the WB set for daylight or electronic flash will appear too reddish.

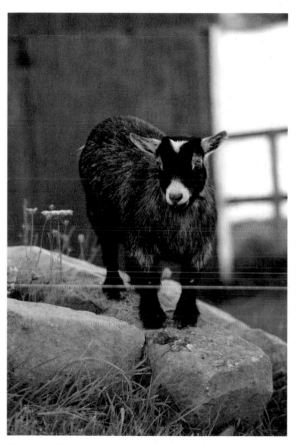

Figure 5.18 An image exposed under daylight illumination with the WB set for tungsten illumination will appear too blue.

The Auto White Balance (AWB) setting (see Figure 5.19), available by pressing the WB button and using the left/right cross keys to choose AWB, examines your scene and chooses an appropriate value based on your scene and the colors it contains. However, the XS's selection process is far from foolproof. Under bright lighting conditions, it may evaluate the colors in the image and still assume the light source is daylight and balance the picture accordingly, even though, in fact, you may be shooting under extremely

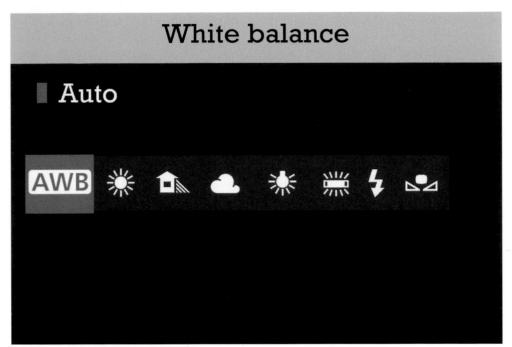

Figure 5.19

Your white balance selections include (left to right): automatic, daylight, shade, cloudy, incandescent, fluorescent, flash, and custom.

bright incandescent illumination. In dimmer light, the camera's electronics may assume that the illumination is tungsten, and if there are lots of reddish colors present, set color balance for that. Fortunately, some electronic flash units, such as the Canon Speedlite 580EX II, can report to the camera the particular white balance that they are outputting, since a flash's color temperature can vary depending on how brief the flash exposure is.

The other presets in the WB list apply specific color temperatures. For example, the Daylight setting sets WB to 5,200K, while the Shade setting uses a much bluer 7,000K. The chief difference between direct daylight and shade or even tungsten light sources is nothing more than the proportion of red and blue light. The spectrum of colors is continuous, but it is biased toward one end or the other.

However, some types of fluorescent lights produce illumination that has a severe deficit in certain colors, such as only *particular* shades of red. If you looked at the spectrum or rainbow of colors encompassed by such a light source, it would have black bands in it, representing particular wavelengths of light that are absent. You can't compensate for this deficiency by adding all tones of red. That's why the fluorescent setting of your XS may provide less than satisfactory results with some kinds of fluorescent bulbs. If you take many photographs under a particular kind of non-compatible fluorescent light, you might want to investigate specialized fluorescent light filters for your lenses, available from camera stores, or learn how to adjust for various sources in your image editor.

However, you might also get acceptable results using the choice on the WB list. Custom allows you to use specific white balances you've set yourself using the Custom WB and WB SHIFT/BKT options in the Shooting 2 menu, as described with step-by-step instructions in Chapter 3.

Finally, as I described in Chapter 3, in the section on white balance bracketing, you can *shift* the XS's standard color temperature that is used as a basis for all its corrections, changing the default temperature to a new value with a bias towards the green, magenta, blue, or amber directions, which correspond to movements along the central axes of the chart shown in Figure 5.20 in the up (green), down (magenta), blue (left), or amber/yellow (right) directions. You can also combine biases of adjacent hues by moving the cursor diagonally towards the upper left (more blue and more green), upper right (more green and more amber), lower right (more amber and more magenta), and lower left (more magenta and more blue).

Figure 5.20
The standard white balance setting can be biased in a direction of your choosing.

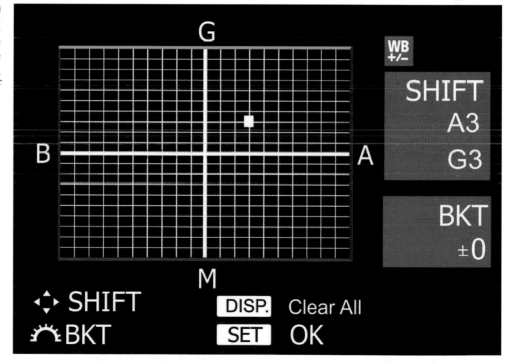

Image Parameters in Picture Styles

As I outlined in Chapter 3, you can redefine the amount of sharpening, contrast, color saturation, and color tone for any of the five preset Picture Styles (Standard, Portrait, Landscape, Neutral, and Faithful) or create your own styles in User Def 1, User Def 2, and User Def 3 (see Figure 5.21). In addition, you can modify the Filter Effect and Toning Effect options in the Monochrome Picture Style. You can learn how to make

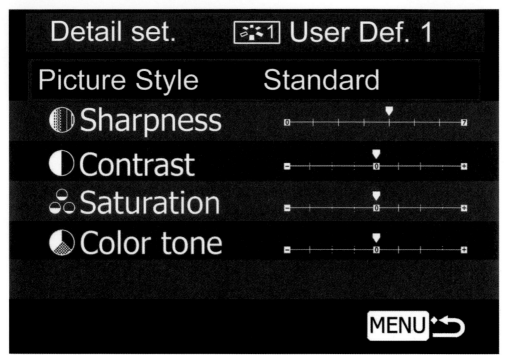

Figure 5.21
You can customize the sharpness, contrast, color saturation, or tone of the standard Picture Styles, as well as any of the three User Def styles.

these changes in Chapter 3, but here is a summary of how the key parameters affect your images.

- **Sharpness.** Increases or decreases the contrast of the edge outlines in your image, making the photo appear more or less sharp, depending on whether you've selected 0 (no sharpening) to +7 (extreme sharpening). Remember that boosting sharpness also increases the overall contrast of an image, so you'll want to use this parameter in conjunction with the contrast parameter with caution.

- **Contrast.** Compresses the range of tones in an image (increase contrast from 0 to +4) or expands the range of tones (from 0 to −4) to decrease contrast. Higher contrast images tend to lose detail in both shadows and highlights, while lower contrast images retain the detail but appear more flat and have less snap.

- **Color saturation.** You can adjust the richness of the color from low saturation (0 to −4) to high saturation (0 to +4). Lower saturation produces a muted look that can be more realistic for certain kinds of subjects, such as humans. Higher saturation produces a more vibrant appearance, but can be garish and unrealistic if carried too far. Boost your saturation if you want a vivid image, or to brighten up pictures taken on overcast days.

- **Color tone.** This parameter changes the bias of the image toward the red or yellow ends of the scale, with settings from 0 to −4 producing ruddier skin tones, and 0 to +4 creating more yellowish skin tones.

Working with Live View

Live View is one of those features that experienced SLR users (especially those dating from the film era) sometimes think they don't need—until they try it. It's also one of those features (like truly "silent" shooting, without any shutter click) that point-and-shoot refugees are surprised that digital SLRs (until recently) have lacked. As I noted earlier, SLRs have actual, mechanical shutters that can't be completely silenced, as can be done with point-and-shoot cameras. I've fielded almost as many queries from those who want to know how to preview their images on the LCD—just as they did with their point-and-shoot cameras. Indeed, many P & S models don't even *have* optical viewfinders, engendering a whole generation of amateur photographers who think the only way to frame and compose an image is to hold the camera out at arm's length so the back panel LCD can be viewed more easily.

While dSLR veterans didn't really miss what we've come to know as Live View, it was at least, in part, because they didn't have it and couldn't miss what they never had. After all, why would you eschew a big, bright, magnified through-the-lens optical view that showed depth-of-field fairly well, and which was easily visible under virtually all ambient light conditions? LCD displays, after all, were small, tended to wash out in bright light, and didn't really provide you with an accurate view of what your picture was going to look like.

There were technical problems, as well. Real-time previews theoretically disabled a dSLR's autofocus system, as focus was achieved by measuring contrast through the optical viewfinder, which is blocked when the mirror is flipped up for a live view. Extensive previewing had the same effect on the sensor as long exposures: the sensor heated up, producing excess noise. Pointing the camera at a bright light source when using a real-time view could damage the sensor. The list of potential problems goes on and on.

That was then. This is now.

The Canon EOS Rebel XS has a gorgeous 2.5-inch LCD that can be viewed under a variety of lighting conditions and from wide-ranging angles, so you don't have to be exactly behind the display to see it clearly. (See Figure 5.22.) It offers a 100-percent view of the sensor's capture area (the optical viewfinder shows just 95 percent of the sensor's field of view). It's large enough to allow manual focusing—but if you want to use automatic focus, there's an option that allows briefly flipping the mirror back down for autofocusing, interrupting Live View, and then restoring the sensor preview image after focus is achieved. You still have to avoid pointing your XS at bright light sources (especially the Sun) when using Live View, but the real-time preview can be used for fairly long periods without frying the sensor. (Image quality can degrade, but the camera issues a warning when the sensor starts to overheat.)

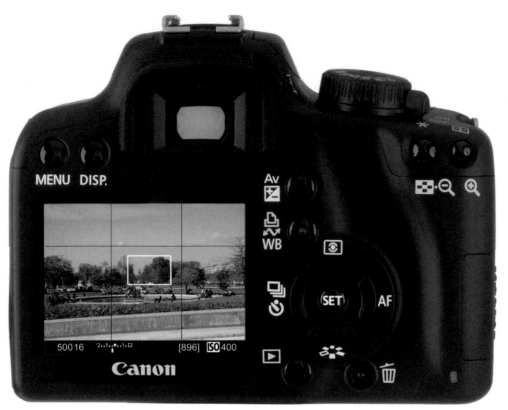

Figure 5.22
Live View
really shines on
the Canon
EOS Rebel
XS's large 2.5-
inch LCD.

Unlike some of the previous attempts at a Live View-type mode by other sensors (and including Canon with its EOS 20Da), the XS's Live View works. No beam-splitting prisms that divert some light to the sensor, no grainy black-and-white real-time preview, no need for a spare sensor to provide a simulated Live View. Canon's system works just like you'd want it to: the mirror flips up, the shutter opens, and what the sensor sees is displayed in full color on the LCD on the back of the camera. You can adjust the brightness of the LCD with the Main dial.

What You Can/Cannot Do with Live View

You may not have considered just what you can do with Live View, because the capability is so novel. But once you've played with it, you'll discover dozens of applications for this capability, as well as a few things that you can't do. Here's a list of Live View Do's/Don'ts/Cans/Can'ts.

- **Preview your images on a TV.** Connect your Rebel XS to a television using the video cable, and you can preview your image on a large screen.

- **Preview remotely.** Extend the cable between the camera and TV screen, and you can preview your images some distance away from the camera.

- **Shoot from your computer.** Canon gives you the software you need to control your camera from your computer, so you can preview images and take pictures without physically touching the Rebel XS.

- **Continuous shooting.** You can shoot bursts of images using Live View, but all shots will use the focus and exposure setting established for the first picture in the series.

- **Shoot from tripod or handheld.** Of course, holding the camera out at arm's length to preview an image is poor technique, and will introduce a lot of camera shake. If you want to use Live View for handheld images, use an image-stabilized lens and/or a high shutter speed. A tripod is a better choice if you can use one.

- **Watch your power.** Live View uses a lot of juice and will deplete your battery rapidly. Canon estimates that you can get 130-170 shots per battery when using Live View, depending on the temperature. The optional AC adapter is a useful accessory.

- **Watch for the warning icon.** A "thermometer" icon appears in the viewfinder when the camera starts to overheat. Image quality will begin degrading at this time (expect increased noise in your images). However, the Rebel XS will turn itself off automatically before the sensor temperature reaches the danger point and will keep the camera shut down until the high temperature subsides.

Enabling Live View

You need to take some steps before using Live View, and then you can jump right in. This workflow prevents you from accidentally using Live View when you don't mean to, thus potentially losing a shot, and it also helps ensure that you've made all the settings necessary to successfully use the feature efficiently. Here are the steps to follow:

1. **Set focus to Manual.** For most precise focus, it's a good idea to set the lens focus switch to the MF position, because most Live View pictures are taken using Manual focus (even though an autofocus option, described below, is available). Take this step now so you won't forget that you'll be doing the focusing yourself.

2. **Choose a shooting mode.** Select a Creative Zone shooting mode. Live View doesn't work with any of the Basic Zone modes. You can choose A-DEP, but the XS will behave as if you selected P, instead, and A-DEP's automatic focus point selection (like all autofocus features) will be disabled.

3. **Enable Live View.** You'll need to activate Live View by choosing Live View function settings from the Set-Up 2 menu. Select Live view shoot, choose Enable and press the Set button to confirm your choice, and the Menu button to exit.

Tip

Two other Live View functions can be set from the Shooting 2 menu. You can choose Grid Display (On or Off) to enable or disable a Rule of Thirds grid display that can help you compose and align your images on the LCD. You can also set a Metering Timer, which determines how long the XS continues to measure exposure when you switch to Live View mode.

4. **Activate Live View.** You can continue taking pictures normally through the XS's viewfinder. When you're ready to activate Live View, press the Set button. The mirror will flip up, and the sensor image will appear on the LCD.

5. **Adjust brightness.** If the image is too bright, rotate the Main dial to the right; if it is too dark, rotate the dial to the left.

6. **View the information display.** You can press the DISP button to change the amount and type of information displayed on the screen during Live View. Cycle among a basic display of information shown at the bottom of the LCD; to a display that shows current Drive mode, white balance setting, Picture Style, Image Quality, and an "Exposure simulation" icon overlaid on the left side of the screen; to a display that shows a live histogram.

Tip

The live histogram display in the upper right of the LCD, accessed by pressing the DISP button during Live View, shows you valuable exposure information. I explained about histograms in Chapter 4. You should know that this live histogram may not display correctly under very bright or dim light conditions.

UNDERSTANDING EXPOSURE SIMULATION

When the ExpSIM icon is shown in white (use the DISP button to cycle to either of the two full information displays), that shows you that the Live View image approximates the actual image that will be produced. If the icon is blinking, that doesn't mean that the exposure is wrong; only that the current LCD display is darker or lighter than the actual image will be. If flash or a Bulb exposure is being set, the ExpSIM icon will be grayed out.

7. **Focus and take your photo.** I'll describe both Manual and Autofocus with Live View in a section that follows.

8. **Exit Live View.** To exit Live View, press the Set button again. The XS will automatically exit Live View if you haven't performed any operations with the camera for the time set using the Auto power off option in Set-Up Menu 1.

Activating Live View

As I noted, once you've enabled Live View, you can continue taking pictures normally through the XS's viewfinder. When you're ready to activate Live View, press the Set button.

Here are some things you should keep in mind when Live View is active:

- **Some functions don't work as expected.** Custom Functions for mirror lockup (C.Fn.III-08), Shutter/AE lock button (C.Fn.IV-09), and the definition of the Set button (C.Fn.IV-10) are disabled. Auto Lighting, if enabled in the Custom Functions menu, may produce a picture that is darker than normal. Changing the light source while viewing with Live View can cause the LCD screen to flicker. Bright objects on the LCD may be blacked out, but will photograph correctly (for the exposure used). If you've selected A-DEP mode, the XS will use Programmed exposure instead.

- **Manual focus.** You can focus manually, unless you use the optional Live View interrupt/autofocus feature. Later in this section, I'll provide instructions for using MF with Live View.

- **Limited settings available.** You can change ISO, WB, and exposure compensation during Live View, but not Picture Style, Drive mode, AF mode, or AF point.

- **Exposure fixed in Continuous Shooting mode.** The exposure for the first shot will be used for subsequent pictures in the sequence.

- **Exposure lag.** If you reframe your photo, there is a lag before the exposure is set properly for the new composition. If you take a picture before the exposure has been recalculated, you may get an under- or overexposed photo.

- **Metering mode cannot be changed.** Evaluative metering linked to the focus frame is used. You cannot change to Partial, Spot, or Center-Weighted metering when Live View is active.

- **Press DOF button to check focus.** If you press the Depth-of-Field button while using Live View, the lens will stop down to the taking aperture and you'll see the effective depth-of-field.

■ **Flash OK.** You can use flash when working with Live View, but you'll hear two clicks. Rest easy: only one photo will actually be taken. You may also see a "Busy" message on the LCD if the flash isn't fully charged and ready for firing.

■ **Live View continues.** When you press the shutter release, the XS will take a photo, then display the image you just shot for review, as normal. When picture review is finished, the camera returns to Live View mode. You can take as many consecutive shots using Live View as you like, barring sensor overheating. To exit Live View entirely, press the Set button.

■ **Shooting functions interrupt.** If you change shooting functions, such as EV compensation, white balance, or ISO settings while using Live View, then Live View will quit. Continue making your changes, then press the Set button to activate Live View once more.

■ **Information display.** During Live View, useful information is shown on the screen, such as battery status, Picture Style, and most of the shooting information (shutter speed, f/stop, ISO setting, number of exposures remaining) you'd see through the viewfinder. Press the Info. button to change the amount of information shown. Figure 5.23 shows a typical display as seen on the LCD, including the optional Rule of Thirds grid.

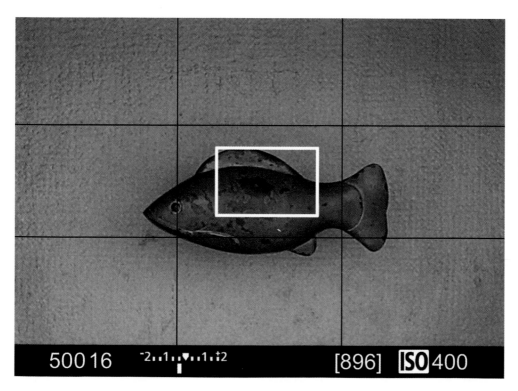

Figure 5.23
The information display includes the focus frame that's in the center of the screen, but which can be moved using the cross keys.

Manual Focusing

Focusing manually on an LCD screen isn't as difficult as you might think, particularly if you have the XS mounted on a tripod, but Canon has made the process even easier by providing a magnified view. Just follow these steps to focus manually.

1. Make sure the focus switch on the lens is set to MF.

2. Use the left/right/up/down cross keys to move the white focus frame that's super-imposed on the screen to the location where you want to focus.

3. Press the Zoom button. The area of the image inside the focus frame will be magnified 5X. (See Figure 5.24.) Press the Zoom button again to increase the magnification to 10X. A third press will return you to the full-frame view. The enlarged area is artificially sharpened to make it easier for you to see the contrast changes, and simplify focusing. When zoomed in, the current shutter speed and aperture are shown in orange.

4. Use the focus ring on the lens to focus the image. When you're satisfied, you can zoom back out.

Figure 5.24

You can manually focus the center area, which can be zoomed in 5X or 10X.

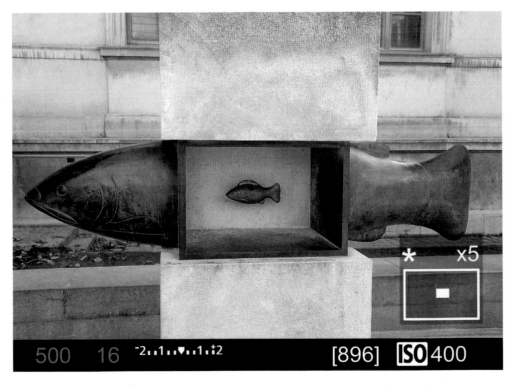

Using Autofocus with Live View

You can temporarily interrupt Live View mode to allow the Rebel XS to use autofocus. Because the step takes a few seconds, you're better off using autofocus when the camera is mounted on a tripod. If you handhold the XS, you may displace the point of focus achieved by the autofocus system. Canon also recommends that you use One-Shot focus and center the focus point. You can use AI-Servo and automatic or manual focus point selection, but if the focus point doesn't coincide with the subject you want to focus on, you'll end up with an out-of-focus image.

There are two different autofocus methods possible with Live View: Quick Mode and Live Mode. To choose the mode you want, access C.Fn.III-07 AF During Live View Shooting. Choose 1 to enable this feature's Quick mode, or 2 to use Live mode.

Quick Mode uses the XS's standard *phase detection* autofocus system to focus. It's very fast, but requires flipping down the mirror and blanking out Live View during the focus process. To autofocus using Quick Mode:

1. Make sure the focus switch on the lens is set to AF and the AF mode is set to One-Shot.

2. Select the autofocus point you want to use *before* activating Live View. Press the AF point selection button and navigate with the left/right/up/down cross keys to chose your focus point.

3. Press the shutter release button to lock in that focus point.

4. Press Set to activate Live View. The Live View image with the selected AF point will be shown.

5. With the chosen AF point centered on the subject you want to focus on, press and hold the * button on the back of the camera.

6. The XS will flip the mirror back down (canceling Live View temporarily), calculate focus, and beep when finished. Because you're using One-Shot, the camera focuses *once*, even if you are handholding the camera and moving the framing slightly.

7. Let go of the * button to reestablish the Live View image.

8. If focus and exposure are satisfactory, press the shutter button down to take the picture.

You can also focus using Live Mode. This procedure uses a process called *contrast detection,* which evaluates the sharpness of the image on the sensor to achieve focus. It is slower and is more difficult. To focus using Live Mode:

1. Set the lens focus mode switch to AF.

2. Press Set to activate Live View. An AF focus point will be displayed on the screen.

3. You can move this point around anywhere on the visible screen using the left/right/up/down cross keys. To center the AF point, press the Trash button. Press the Zoom button to magnify the image, centered around the current AF point.

4. Place the focus point on the subject and press the * button.

5. The XS will attempt to focus the image on the sensor, and will beep and change the focus point indicator to green if successful.

6. If the camera is unable to focus automatically, the AF point turns white. Low contrast subjects, subjects illuminated only by dim light, confusing horizontal patterns, small objects, moving subjects, and some filters can cause this contrast detection autofocus mode to fail. If that happens, switch to Quick Mode and try again.

7. When satisfied with focus and exposure, press the shutter release to take the photo.

Phase Detection vs. Contrast Detection

This discussion of phase detection versus contrast detection, which I hinted at earlier in the chapter, may be a little too techie for some readers, but if you really want to understand how autofocus works in Live View, it's a worthwhile topic to consider. Extra details like this are why you bought this fat book instead of a pocket-sized guide to the Rebel XS.

■ **Phase detection.** In this mode, the autofocus sampling area is divided into two halves by a lens in the sensor. The two halves are compared, much like (actually, exactly like) a two-window rangefinder used in surveying, weaponry, and non-SLR cameras like the venerable Leica M film models. The contrast between the two images changes as focus is moved in or out, until sharp focus is achieved when the images are "in phase," or lined up. Phase detection is the normal mode used by the Rebel XS in Quick Mode. As with any rangefinder-like function, accuracy is better when the "base length" between the two images is larger. (Think back to your high school trigonometry; you could calculate a distance more accurately when the separation between the two points where the angles were measured was greater.) For that reason, phase detection autofocus is more accurate with larger (wider) lens openings than with smaller lens openings, and may not work at all when the f/stop is smaller than f/5.6. The XS is able to perform these comparisons very quickly. The chief drawback of Quick Mode is that your Live View blanks out during autofocus.

■ **Contrast detection.** This is a slower mode, suitable for static subjects, and used by the Rebel XS with Live View in Live Mode. It's a bit easier to understand. When an image is out of focus (as at left in the image of the leaves in Figure 5.10 earlier in this chapter), the transitions between pixels are soft and blurred. Even the boundary between the leaf tips and the foliage behind is smudged. When the image is brought into focus (right in the earlier figure), the transitions are sharp and clear. Although this example is a bit exaggerated so you can see the results on the printed page, it's easy. The advantage of Live Mode is that you can move the focus point *anywhere* on the XS's screen, but just among the seven focus points used in Quick Mode.

6

Working with Lenses

In April 2008, Canon announced that it had produced its 40 millionth EF-series lens, a mere 21 years after the company's current autofocus mount was introduced (back in the film era). Considering that it took 11 years for Canon to sell its first 10 million copies of its EF lens line, but only two years and three months to peddle its most recent 10 million lenses, it's easy to see that the digital photography revolution can take credit for the most recent explosion.

With more than five dozen lenses in its current lineup, Canon is catering to the wide-ranging needs of a broad user base, from novice photo enthusiasts to advanced amateur and professional photographers. It's this mind-bending assortment of high quality lenses that is available to enhance the capabilities of cameras like the Canon EOS Rebel XS. Thousands of current and older lenses introduced by Canon and third party vendors since 1987 can be used to give you a wider view, bring distant subjects closer, let you focus closer, shoot under lower light conditions, or provide a more detailed, sharper image for critical work. Other than the sensor itself, the lens you choose for your dSLR is the most important component in determining image quality and perspective of your images.

This chapter explains how to select the best lenses for the kinds of photography you want to do.

But Don't Forget the Crop Factor

From time to time you've heard the term *crop factor*, and you've probably also heard the term *lens multiplier factor*. Both are misleading and inaccurate terms used to describe the same phenomenon: the fact that cameras like the Rebel XS (and most other affordable digital SLRs) provide a field of view that's smaller and narrower than that produced by certain other (usually much more expensive) cameras, when fitted with exactly the same lens.

Figure 6.1 quite clearly shows the phenomenon at work. The outer rectangle, marked 1X, shows the field of view you might expect with a 28mm lens mounted on a Canon 1Ds Mark III camera, a so-called "full-frame" model. The rectangle marked 1.3X shows the effective field of view from the same vantage point with the exact same lens mounted on a Canon 1D Mark III camera, while the area marked 1.6X shows the field of view you'd get with that 28mm lens installed on a Rebel XS. It's easy to see from the illustration that the 1X rendition provides a wider, more expansive view, while the other two are, in comparison, *cropped.*

The cropping effect is produced because the sensors of the latter two cameras are smaller than the sensors of the 1Ds Mark III. The "full-frame" camera has a sensor that's the size of the standard 35mm film frame, 24mm × 36mm. Your Rebel XS's sensor does *not* measure 24mm × 36mm; instead, it specs out at 22.2mm × 14.8mm, or about 62.5 percent of the area of a full-frame sensor, as shown by the yellow boxes in the figure. You can calculate the relative field of view by dividing the focal length of the lens by

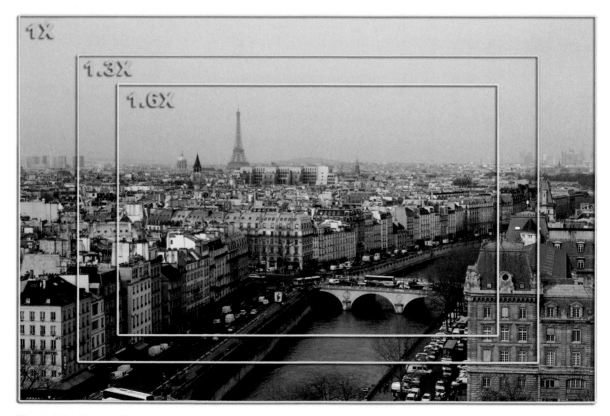

Figure 6.1 Canon offers digital SLRs with full-frame (1X) crops, as well as 1.3X and 1.6X crops.

.625. Thus, a 100mm lens mounted on a Rebel XS has the same field of view as a 160mm lens on the 1Ds Mark III. We humans tend to perform multiplication operations in our heads more easily than division, so such field of view comparisons are usually calculated using the reciprocal of .625—1.6—so we can multiply instead. (100 / .625=160; 100 × 1.6=160.)

This translation is generally useful only if you're accustomed to using full-frame cameras (usually of the film variety) and want to know how a familiar lens will perform on a digital camera. I strongly prefer *crop factor* over *lens multiplier*, because nothing is being multiplied; a 100mm lens doesn't "become" a 160mm lens—the depth-of-field and lens aperture remain the same. (I'll explain more about these later in this chapter.) Only the field of view is cropped. But *crop factor* isn't much better, as it implies that the 24 × 36mm frame is "full" and anything else is "less." I get e-mails all the time from photographers who point out that they own full-frame cameras with 36mm × 48mm sensors (like the Mamiya 645ZD or Hasselblad H3D-39 medium format digitals). By their reckoning, the "half size" sensors found in cameras like the 1Ds Mark III are "cropped."

If you're accustomed to using full-frame film cameras, you might find it helpful to use the crop factor "multiplier" to translate a lens's real focal length into the full-frame equivalent, even though, as I said, nothing is actually being multiplied. Throughout most of this book, I've been using actual focal lengths and not equivalents, except when referring to specific wide-angle or telephoto focal length ranges and their fields of view.

Your First Lens

The Canon EOS Rebel XS is frequently purchased with a lens, often the Canon EF-S 18-55mm f/3.5-5.6 IS autofocus lens, which adds only about $100 to the price tag of the body alone, and is thus an irresistible bargain. You can also buy the XS body alone if you already have some lenses. Other Canon models, including the EOS 1D Mark III, EOS 1Ds Mark III, and EOS 40D, are generally purchased without a lens by veteran Canon photographers who already have a complement of optics to use with their cameras.

I bought my EOS 40D as a body-only, because I already had a collection of lenses, but when it came time to pick up my XS, I went with the kit that included the 18-55 image-stabilized lens. Who can turn down an IS lens for only $100? However, you'll also find many purchasers who fall into one of the following categories: Those who are upgrading from the Digital Rebel models or an EOS 10D/20D/30D; from a Canon film camera; or who are buying the XS as a second camera body to complement their other Canon camera. These owners, too, generally already have lenses they can use with their new XS.

So, depending on which category you fall into, you'll need to make a decision about what kit lens to buy, or decide what other kind of lenses you need to fill out your complement of Canon optics. This section will cover "first lens" concerns, while later in the chapter we'll look at "add-on lens" considerations.

When deciding on a first lens, there are several factors you'll want to consider:

- **Cost.** You might have stretched your budget a bit to purchase your Rebel XS, so you might want to keep the cost of your first lens fairly low. Fortunately, there are excellent lenses available that will add from $100 to $300 to the price of your camera if purchased at the same time.

- **Zoom range.** If you have only one lens, you'll want a fairly long zoom range to provide as much flexibility as possible. Fortunately, the two most popular basic lenses for the XS (the 18-55mm and 17-85mm zooms) have 3X to 5X zoom ranges, extending from moderate wide-angle/normal out to medium telephoto. Either is fine for everyday shooting, portraits, and some types of sports.

- **Adequate maximum aperture.** You'll want an f/stop of at least f/3.5 to f/4 for shooting under fairly low light conditions. The thing to watch for is the maximum aperture when the lens is zoomed to its telephoto end. You may end up with no better than an f/5.6 maximum aperture. That's not great, but you can often live with it.

- **Image quality.** Your starter lens should have good image quality, because that's one of the primary factors that will be used to judge your photos. Even at a low price, the several different lenses sold with the XS as a kit include extra-low dispersion glass and aspherical elements that minimize distortion and chromatic aberration; they are sharp enough for most applications. If you read the user evaluations in the online photography forums, you know that owners of the kit lenses have been very pleased with their image quality.

- **Size matters.** A good walking-around lens is compact in size and light in weight.

- **Fast/close focusing.** Your first lens should have a speedy autofocus system (which is where the ultrasonic motor/USM found in all but the bargain basement lenses is an advantage). Close focusing (to 12 inches or closer) will let you use your basic lens for some types of macro photography.

You can find comparisons of the lenses discussed in the next section, as well as third-party lenses from Sigma, Tokina, Tamron, and other vendors, in online groups and websites. I'll provide my recommendations, but more information is always helpful.

Buy Now, Expand Later

The XS is commonly available with several good, basic lenses that can serve you well as a "walk-around" lens (one you keep on the camera most of the time, especially when you're out and about without your camera bag). The number of options available to you is actually quite amazing, even if your budget is limited to about $100-$350 for your first lens. One other vendor, for example, offers only 18mm-70mm and 18mm-55mm kit lenses in that price range, plus a 24mm-85mm zoom. The most popular starter lens Canon offers for the XS is shown in Figure 6.2. Canon's best-bet first lenses are as follows:

- **Canon EF-S 18-55mm f/3.5-5.6 Autofocus lens.** This discontinued lens is the least expensive option as long as it continues to be available, as it's often offered with a body for less than $100. This medium-wide to short telephoto lens (29mm-88mm full-frame equivalent) has been the standard lens found on earlier Digital Rebel models, and it is sometimes sold as the basic kit lens for the Rebel XS for those on a budget. It is designed exclusively for Canon dSLRs with a 1.6X crop factor, and it shouldn't be used on full-frame cameras (more on this later). A maximum aperture of f/5.6 at 55mm makes this a relatively slow lens that's not great for low-light shooting.

- **Canon EF-S 18-55mm f/3.5-5.6 IS Autofocus lens.** This new lens, introduced at the same time as the Rebel XS, is worth the slight extra premium (still in the $100 range), because it adds image stabilization that can counter camera shake by providing the vibration-stopping capabilities of a shutter speed four stops faster than the one you've dialed it. That is, with image stabilization activated, you can shoot at 1/30th second and eliminate camera shake as if you were using a shutter speed of 1/250th second. (At least, that's what Canon claims; I usually have slightly less impressive results.) Of course, IS doesn't freeze subject motion—that basketball player driving for a layup will still be blurry at 1/30th second, even though the effects of camera shake will be effectively nullified. But this lens is an all-around good choice.

- **Canon EF-S 17-85mm f/4-5.6 IS USM Autofocus lens.** This lens smashes through the arbitrary $350 price barrier I set earlier, but I'm making an exception because the 17-85mm lens is a very popular "basic" lens sold for the XS, despite its $500-plus price tag. The allure here is the longer telephoto range, coupled with the built-in image stabilization, which allows you to shoot rock-solid photos at shutter speeds that are at least two or three notches slower than you'd need normally (say, 1/8th second instead of 1/30th or 1/60th second), as long as your subject isn't moving. It also has a quiet, fast, reliable ultrasonic motor (more on that later, too). This is another lens designed for the 1.6X crop factor; all but one of the remaining lenses in this list can also be used on full-frame cameras. (I'll tell you why later in this chapter.) This lens is shown in Figure 6.3.

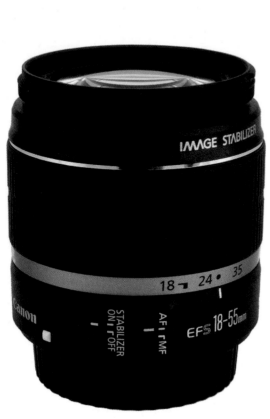

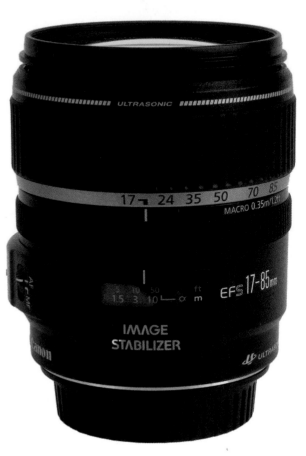

Figure 6.2 The Canon EF-S 18-55mm f/3.5-5.6 IS Autofocus lens ships as a basic kit lens for the Rebel XS.

Figure 6.3 The Canon EF-S 17-85mm f/4-5.6 IS USM Autofocus lens is another popular starter lens for the Rebel XS.

- **Canon EF 55-200mm f/4.5/5.6 II USM Autofocus Lightweight Compact Telephoto Zoom lens.** If you bought the 18-55mm kit lens, this one picks up where that one leaves off, going from short telephoto to medium long (88mm-320mm full-frame equivalent). It's actually faster at 55mm than the basic kit lens and features a desirable ultrasonic motor. Best of all, it's very affordable at around $225. If you can afford only two lenses, the 18-55mm and this one make a good basic set.

- **EF-S 55-250mm f/4-5.6 IS Telephoto Zoom lens.** This is an image-stabilized EF-S lens (which means it can't be used with Canon's 1.3X and 1.0X crop-factor pro cameras), providing the longest focal range in the EF-S range to date, and that 4-stop Image Stabilizer. Again, it's more money than the older, non-stabilized EF version, but it's worth the extra cost.

- **Canon EF 24-85mm f/3.5-4.5 USM Autofocus Wide-Angle Telephoto Zoom lens.** If you can get by with normal focal length to medium telephoto range, Canon offers four affordable lenses, plus one more expensive killer lens that's worth the extra expenditure. All of them can be used on full-frame or cropped-frame digital Canons, which is why they include "wide angle" in their product names. They're really wide-angle lenses only when mounted on a full-frame camera. This one, priced in the $300 range, and an older lens that might be hard to find, offers a useful range of focal lengths, extending from the equivalent of 38mm to 136mm.

- **Canon EF 28-105mm f/3.5-4.5 II USM Autofocus Wide-Angle Telephoto Zoom lens.** If you want to save about $100 and gain a little reach, this 45mm-168mm (equivalent lens) might be what you are looking for.

- **Canon EF 28-135mm f/3.5-5.6 IS USM Image-Stabilized Autofocus Wide-Angle Telephoto Zoom lens.** Image stabilization is especially useful at longer focal lengths, which makes this 45mm-216mm (equivalent) lens worth its $400-plus price tag. Several retailers are packing this lens with the XS as a kit.

- **Canon EF 28-200mm f/3.5-5.6 USM Autofocus Wide-Angle Telephoto Zoom lens.** If you want one lens to do everything except wide-angle photography, this 7X zoom lens costs less than $400 and takes you from the equivalent of 45mm out to a long 320mm.

- **Canon Zoom Wide-Angle-Telephoto EF 24-70mm f/2.8L USM Autofocus lens.** I couldn't leave this premium lens out of the mix, even though it costs well over $1,000. As part of Canon's L-series (Luxury) lens line, it offers the best sharpness over its focal range than any of the other lenses in this list. Best of all, it's fast (for a zoom), with an f/2.8 maximum aperture that *doesn't change* as you zoom out. Unlike the other lenses, which may offer only an f/5.6 maximum f/stop at their longest zoom setting, this is a *constant aperture* lens, which retains its maximum f/stop. The added sharpness, constant aperture, and ultra-smooth USM motor are what you're paying for with this lens.

What Lenses Can You Use?

The previous section helped you sort out what lens you need to buy with your XS (assuming you already didn't own any Canon lenses). Now, you're probably wondering what lenses can be added to your growing collection (trust me, it will grow). You need to know which lenses are suitable and, most importantly, which lenses are fully compatible with your Rebel XS.

With the Canon XS, the compatibility issue is a simple one: It accepts any lens with the EF or EF-S designation, with full availability of all autofocus, autoaperture, autoexposure, and image-stabilization features (if present). It's comforting to know that any EF (for full-frame or cropped sensors) or EF-S (for cropped sensor cameras only) will work as designed with your camera. As I noted at the beginning of the chapter, that's more than 40 million lenses!

But wait, there's more. You can also attach Nikon F mount, Leica R, Olympus OM, and M42 ("Pentax screw mount") lenses with a simple adapter, if you don't mind losing automatic focus and aperture control. If you use one of these lenses, you'll need to focus manually (even if the lens operates in Autofocus mode on the camera it was designed for), and adjust the f/stop to the aperture you want to use to take the picture. That means that lenses that don't have an aperture ring (such as Nikon G-series lenses) must be used only at their maximum aperture. Because of these limitations, you probably won't want to make extensive use of "foreign" lenses on your XS, but an adapter can help you when you really, really need to use a particular focal length but don't have a suitable Canon-compatible lens. For example, I occasionally use an older 400mm lens that was originally designed for the Nikon line on my XS. The lens needs to be mounted on a tripod for steadiness, anyway, so its slower operation isn't a major pain. Another good match is the 105mm Micro-Nikkor I sometimes use with my Canon XS. Macro photos, too, are most often taken with the camera mounted on a tripod, and manual focus makes a lot of sense for fine-tuning focus and depth-of-field. Because of the contemplative nature of close-up photography, it's not much of an inconvenience to stop down to the taking aperture just before exposure.

The limitations on use of lenses within Canon's own product line (as well as lenses produced for earlier Canon SLRs by third-party vendors) are fairly clear-cut. The Rebel XS cannot be used with any of Canon's earlier lens mounting schemes for its film cameras, including the immediate predecessor to the EF mount, the FD mount (introduced with

WHY SO MANY LENS MOUNTS?

Four different lens mounts in 40-plus years might seem like a lot of different mounting systems, especially when compared to the Nikon F mount of 1959, which retained quite a bit of compatibility with that company's film and digital camera bodies during that same span. However, in digital photography terms, the EF mount itself is positively ancient, having remained reasonably stable for almost two decades. Lenses designed for the EF system work reliably with every EOS film and digital camera ever produced.

However, at the time, yet another lens mount switch, especially a change from the traditional breech system to a more conventional bayonet-type mount, was indeed a daring move by Canon. One of the reasons for staying with a particular lens type is to "lock" current users into a specific camera system. By introducing the EF mount, Canon in effect cut loose every photographer in its existing user base. If they chose to upgrade, they were free to choose another vendor's products and lenses. Only satisfaction with the previous Canon product line and the promise of the new system would keep them in the fold.

the Canon F1 in 1964 and used until the Canon T60 in 1990), FL (1964-1971), or the original Canon R mount (1959-1964). That's really all you need to know. While you'll find FD-to-EF adapters for about $40, you'll lose so many functions that it's rarely worth the bother.

In retrospect, the switch to the EF mount seems like a very good idea, as the initial EOS film cameras can now be seen as the beginning of Canon's rise to eventually become the leader in film and (later) digital SLR cameras. By completely revamping its lens mounting system, the company was able to take advantage of the latest advances in technology without compromise.

For example, when the original EF bayonet mount was introduced in 1987, the system incorporated new autofocus technology (EF actually stands for "electro focus") in a more rugged and less complicated form. A tiny motor was built into the lens itself, eliminating the need for mechanical linkages with the camera. Instead, electrical contacts are used to send power and the required focusing information to the motor. That's a much more robust and resilient system that made it easier for Canon to design faster and more accurate autofocus mechanisms just by redesigning the lenses.

EF vs. EF-S

Today, in addition to its EF lenses, Canon offers lenses that use the EF-S (the S stands for "short back focus") mount, with the chief difference being (as you might expect) lens components that extend farther back into the camera body of some of Canon's latest digital cameras (specifically those with smaller than full-frame sensors), such as the XS and Rebels. As I'll explain next, this refinement allows designing more compact, less-expensive lenses especially for those cameras, but not for models like the EOS 5D, 1Ds Mark III, or 1D Mark III (even though the latter camera does have a sensor that is smaller than full frame).

Canon's EF-S lens mount variation was born in 2003, when the company virtually invented the consumer-oriented digital SLR category by introducing the original EOS 300D/Digital Rebel, a dSLR that cost less than $1,000 *with lens* at a time when all other interchangeable lens digital cameras (including the XS's "grandparent," the original EOS 10D) were priced closer to $2,000 with a basic lens. Like the EOS 10D introduced earlier that same year, the Rebel featured a smaller than full-frame sensor with a 1.6X crop factor (Canon calls this format APS-C). But the Rebel accepted lenses that took advantage of the shorter mirror found in APS-C cameras, with elements of shorter focal length lenses (wide angles) that extended *into* the camera, space that was off limits in other models because the mirror passed through that territory as it flipped up to expose the shutter and sensor. (Canon even calls its flip-up reflector a "half mirror.")

In short (so to speak), the EF-S mount made it easier to design less-expensive wide-angle lenses that could be used *only* with 1.6X-crop cameras, and featured a simpler design and reduced coverage area suitable for those non-full-frame models. The new mount made it possible to produce lenses like the ultra-wide EF-S 10-22mm f/3.5-4.5 USM lens, which has the equivalent field of view as a 16mm-35mm zoom on a full-frame camera. (See Figure 6.4.)

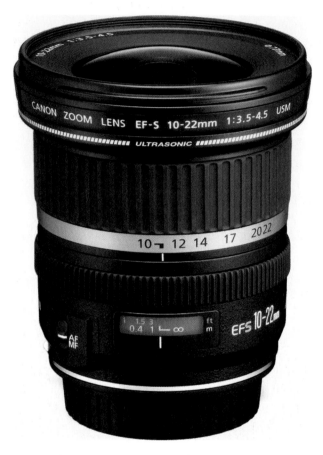

Figure 6.4
The EF-S 10-22mm ultra-wide lens was made possible by the shorter back focus difference offered by the original Digital Rebel and subsequent Canon 1.6X "cropped sensor" models.

Suitable cameras for EF-S lenses include the Digital Rebel, the newer Canon EOS 300D/350D/Digital Rebel XT/XTi, the Canon EOS 20D/30D/40D/50D, and, today, the Rebel XSi and XS. The EF-S lenses cannot be used on the EOS 10D, the 1D Mark II N/Mark III (which have a 28.7mm × 19.1mm APS-H sensor with a 1.3X crop factor), or any of the full-frame digital or film EOS models, such as the EOS 1Ds Mark III or EOS 5D Mark II. It's easy to tell an EF lens from an EF-S lens: The latter incorporate EF-S into their name! Plus, EF lenses have a raised red dot on the barrel that is used to align the lens with a matching dot on the camera when attaching the lens. EF-S lenses and compatible bodies use a white square instead. EF-S lenses also have a rubber ring at the attachment end that provides a bit of weather/dust sealing and protects the back components of the lens if a user attempts to mount it on a camera that is not EF-S compatible.

Ingredients of Canon's Alphanumeric Soup

The actual product names of individual Canon lenses are fairly easy to decipher; they'll include either the EF or EF-S designation, the focal length or focal length range of the lens, its maximum aperture, and some other information. Additional data may be engraved or painted on the barrel or ring surrounding the front element of the lens, as shown in Figure 6.5. Here's a decoding of what the individual designations mean:

- **EF/EF-S.** If the lens is marked EF, it can safely be used on any Canon EOS camera, film or digital. If it is an EF-S lens, it should be used only on an EF-S compatible camera, such as the Rebels, EOS 20D/30D/40D, and any newer APS-C cameras introduced after the publication of this book.

- **Focal length.** Given in millimeters or a millimeter range, such as *60mm* in the case of a popular Canon macro lens, or *17-55mm*, used to describe a medium-wide to short-telephoto zoom.

Figure 6.5
Most of the key specifications of the lens are marked on the ring around the front element.

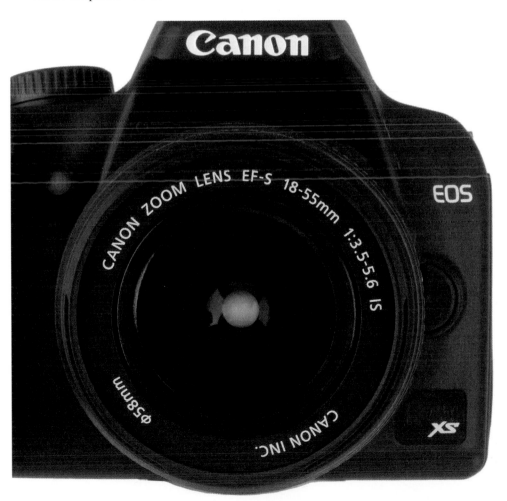

- **Maximum aperture.** The largest f/stop available with a particular lens is given in a string of numbers that might seem confusing at first glance. For example, you might see *1:1.8* for a fixed-focal length (prime) lens, and *1:4.5-5.6* for a zoom. The initial 1: signifies that the f/stop given is actually a ratio or fraction (in regular notation, f/ replaces the 1:), which is why a 1:2 (or f/2) aperture is larger than an 1:4 (or f/4) aperture—just as 1/2 is larger than 1/4. With most zoom lenses, the maximum aperture changes as the lens is zoomed to the telephoto position, so a range is given instead: 1:4.5-5.6. (Some zooms, called *constant aperture* lenses, keep the same maximum aperture throughout their range.)

- **Autofocus type.** Most newer Canon lenses that aren't of the bargain-basement type use Canon's *ultrasonic motor* autofocus system (more on that later) and are given the USM designation. If USM does not appear on the lens or its model name, the lens uses the less sophisticated AFD (arc-form drive) autofocus system or the micro-motor (MM) drive mechanism.

- **Series.** Canon adds a Roman numeral to many of its products to represent an updated model with the same focal length or focal length range, so some lenses will have a II or III added to their name.

- **Pro quality.** Canon's more expensive lenses with more rugged construction and higher optical quality, intended for professional use, include the letter L (for "luxury") in their product name. You can further differentiate these lenses visually by a red ring around the lens barrel and the off-white color of the metal barrel itself in virtually all telephoto L-series lenses. (Some L-series lenses have shiny or textured black plastic exterior barrels.) Internally, every L lens includes at least one lens element that is built of ultra-low dispersion glass, is constructed of expensive fluorite crystal, or uses an expensive ground (not molded) aspheric (non-spherical) lens component. You can usually identify an L lens by its upscale price, too.

- **Filter size.** You'll find the front lens filter thread diameter in millimeters included on the lens, preceded by a Ø symbol, as in Ø67 or Ø72.

- **Special-purpose lenses.** Some Canon lenses are designed for specific types of work, and they include appropriate designations in their names. For example, close-focusing lenses such as the Canon EF-S 60mm f/2.8 Macro USM lens incorporate the word *Macro* into their name. Lenses with perspective control features preface the lens name with T-S (for tilt-shift). Lenses with built-in image-stabilization features, such as the nifty EF 28-300mm f/3.5-5.6L IS USM Telephoto Zoom include *IS* in their product names.

SORTING THE MOTOR DRIVES

Incorporating the autofocus motor inside the lens was an innovative move by Canon, and this allowed the company to produce better and more sophisticated lenses as technology became available to upgrade the focusing system. As a result, you'll find four different types of motors in Canon-designed lenses, each with cost and practical considerations.

- **AFD (Arc-form drive)** and **Micromotor (MM)** drives are built around tiny versions of electromagnetic motors, which generally use gear trains to produce the motion needed to adjust the focus of the lens. Both are slow, noisy, and not particularly effective with larger lenses. Manual focus adjustments are possible only when the motor drive is disengaged.

- **Micromotor ultrasonic motor (USM)** drives use high-frequency vibration to produce the motion used to drive the gear train, resulting in a quieter operating system at a cost that's not much more than that of electromagnetic motor drives. With the exception of a couple lenses that have a slipping clutch mechanism, manual focus with this kind of system is possible only when the lens's motor is switched off and the lens is set in Manual mode. This is the kind of USM system you'll find in lower cost lenses.

- **Ring ultrasonic motor (USM)** drives, available in two different types (*electronic focus ring USM* and *ring USM*), also use high-frequency movement, but generate motion using a pair of vibrating metal rings to adjust focus. Both variations allow a feature called Full Time Manual (FTM) focus, which lets you make manual adjustments to the lens's focus even when the autofocus mechanism is engaged. With electronic focus ring USM, manual focus is possible only when the lens is mounted on the camera and the camera is turned on; the focus ring of lenses with ring USM can be turned at any time.

Your Second (and Third...) Lens

There are really only two advantages to owning just a single lens. One of them is creative. Keeping one set of optics mounted on your XS all the time forces you to be especially imaginative in your approach to your subjects. I once visited Europe with only a single camera body and a 35mm f/2 lens. The experience was actually quite exciting, because I had to use a variety of techniques to allow that one lens to serve for landscapes, available light photos, action, close-ups, portraits, and other kinds of images. Canon makes an excellent 35mm f/2 lens (which focuses down to 9.6 inches) that's perfect for that kind of experiment; although, today, my personal choice would be the sublime (and expensive) Canon Wide-Angle EF 35mm f/1.4L USM Autofocus lens.

Of course, it's more likely that your "single" lens is actually a zoom, which is, in truth, many lenses in one, taking you from, say, 17mm to 85mm (or some other range) with a rapid twist of the zoom ring. You'll still find some creative challenges when you stick to a single zoom lens's focal lengths.

The second advantage of the unilens camera is only a marginal technical benefit since the introduction of the Rebel XS. If you don't exchange lenses, the chances of dust and dirt getting inside your XS and settling on the sensor is reduced (but *not* eliminated entirely). Although I've known some photographers who minimized the number of lens changes they made for this very reason, reducing the number of lenses you work with is not a productive or rewarding approach for most of us. The XS's automatic sensor cleaning feature has made this "advantage" much less significant than it was in the past.

It's more likely that you'll succumb to the malady known as *Lens Lust,* which is defined as an incurable disease marked by a significant yen for newer, better, longer, faster, sharper, anything-er optics for your camera. (And, it must be noted, this disease can *cost* you significant yen—or dollars, or whatever currency you use.) In its worst manifestations, sufferers find themselves with lenses that have overlapping zoom ranges or capabilities, because one or the other offers a slight margin in performance or suitability for specific tasks. When you find yourself already lusting after a new lens before you've really had a chance to put your latest purchase to the test, you'll know the disease has reached the terminal phase.

What Lenses Can Do for You

A saner approach to expanding your lens collection is to consider what each of your options can do for you and then choosing the type of lens that will really boost your creative opportunities. Here's a general guide to the sort of capabilities you can gain by adding a lens to your repertoire.

- **Wider perspective.** Your 18-55mm f/3.5-5.6 or 17-85mm f/4-5.6 lens has served you well for moderate wide-angle shots. Now you find your back is up against a wall and you *can't* take a step backwards to take in more subject matter. Perhaps you're standing on the rim of the Grand Canyon, and you want to take in as much of the breathtaking view as you can. You might find yourself just behind the baseline at a high school basketball game and want an interesting shot with a little perspective distortion tossed in the mix. There's a lens out there that will provide you with what you need, such as the EF-S 10-22mm f/3.5-4.5 USM Zoom. If you want to stay in the sub-$600 price category, you'll need something like the Sigma Super Wide-Angle 10-20mm f/4-5.6 EX DC HSM Autofocus lens. The two lenses provide the equivalent of a 16mm to 32/35mm wide-angle view. For a distorted view, there is the Canon Fisheye EF 15mm f/2.8 Autofocus, with a similar lens available from Sigma, which offers an extra-wide circular fisheye, and the Sigma Fisheye 8mm f/3.5 EX DG Circular Fisheye. Your extra-wide choices may not be abundant, but they are there. Figure 6.6 shows the perspective you get from an ultra-wide-angle lens.

■ **Bring objects closer.** A long lens brings distant subjects closer to you, offers better control over depth-of-field, and avoids the perspective distortion that wide-angle lenses provide. They compress the apparent distance between objects in your frame. In the telephoto realm, Canon is second to none, with a dozen or more offerings in the sub-$600 range, including the Canon EF 100-300mm f/4.5-5.6 USM Autofocus and Canon EF 70-300mm f/4-5.6 IS USM Autofocus Telephoto Zoom lenses, and a broad array of zooms and fixed-focal length optics if you're willing to spend up to $1,000 or a bit more. Don't forget that the Rebel XS's crop factor narrows the field of view of all these lenses, so your 70-300mm lens looks more like a 112mm-480mm zoom through the viewfinder. Figures 6.7 and 6.8 were taken from the same position as Figure 6.6, but with an 85mm and 500mm lens, respectively.

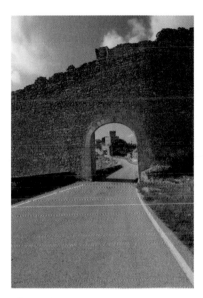

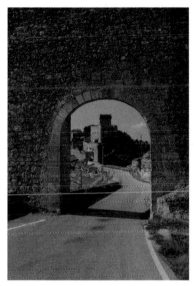

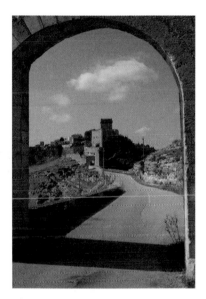

Figure 6.6 An ultra-wide-angle lens provided this view of a castle in Spain.

Figure 6.7 This photo, taken from roughly the same distance, shows the view using a short telephoto lens.

Figure 6.8 A longer telephoto lens captured this closer view of the castle from approximately the same shooting position.

■ **Bring your camera closer.** Macro lenses allow you to focus to within an inch or two of your subject. Canon's best close-up lenses are all fixed focal length optics in the 50mm to 180mm range (including the well-regarded Canon EF-S 60mm f/2.8 Compact and Canon EF 100mm f/2.8 USM Macro Autofocus lenses). But you'll find macro zooms available from Sigma and others. They don't tend to focus quite as close, but they provide a bit of flexibility when you want to vary your subject distance (say, to avoid spooking a skittish creature).

- **Look sharp.** Many lenses, particularly Canon's luxury "L" line, are prized for their sharpness and overall image quality. While your run-of-the-mill lens is likely to be plenty sharp for most applications, the very best optics are even better over their entire field of view (which means no fuzzy corners), are sharper at a wider range of focal lengths (in the case of zooms), and have better correction for various types of distortion. That's why the Canon EF 28-105mm f/3.5-4.5 II USM Zoom lens costs a couple hundred dollars, while the "similar" (in zoom range only) Canon EF 24-105mm f/4L IS USM Zoom is priced $1,000 higher.

- **More speed.** Your Canon EF 100-300mm f/4.5-5.6 Telephoto Zoom lens might have the perfect focal length and sharpness for sports photography, but the maximum aperture won't cut it for night baseball or football games, or, even, any sports shooting in daylight if the weather is cloudy or you need to use some ungodly fast shutter speed, such as 1/4,000th second. You might be happier with the Canon EF 100mm f/2 Medium Telephoto for close-range stuff, or even the pricier Canon EF 135mm f/2L. If money is no object, you can spring for Canon's 400mm f/2.8 and 600mm f/4 L-series lenses (both with image stabilization and priced in the $6,500-and-up stratosphere). Or, maybe you just need the speed and can benefit from an f/1.8 or f/1.4 lens in the 20mm-85mm range. They're all available in Canon mounts (there's even an 85mm f/1.2 and 50mm f/1.2 for the real speed demons). With any of these lenses you can continue photographing under the dimmest of lighting conditions without the need for a tripod or flash.

- **Special features.** Accessory lenses give you special features, such as tilt/shift capabilities to correct for perspective distortion in architectural shots. Canon offers three of these TS-E lenses in 24mm, 45mm, and 90mm focal lengths, at a little over $1,000 each. You'll also find macro lenses, including the MP-E 65mm f/2.8 1-5x macro photo lens, which shoots *only* in the 1X to 5X life-size range. If you want diffused images, check out the EF 135mm f/2.8 with two soft-focus settings. The fisheye lenses mentioned earlier, and all IS (image-stabilized) lenses also count as special-feature optics.

Zoom or Prime?

Zoom lenses have changed the way serious photographers take pictures. One of the reasons that I own 12 SLR film bodies is that in ancient times it was common to mount a different fixed focal length prime lens on various cameras and take pictures with two or three cameras around your neck (or tucked in a camera case) so you'd be ready to take a long shot or an intimate close-up or wide-angle view on a moment's notice, without the need to switch lenses. It made sense (at the time) to have a half dozen or so bodies (two to use, one in the shop, one in transit, and a couple backups). Zoom lenses of the time had a limited zoom range, were heavy, and not very sharp (especially when you tried to wield one of those monsters handheld).

That's all changed today. Lenses like the razor-sharp Canon EF 28-300mm f/3.5-5.6L IS USM can boast 10X or longer zoom ranges, in a package that's about 7 inches long, and while not petite at 3.7 pounds, quite usable handheld (especially with IS switched on). Although such a lens might seem expensive at $2,200-plus, it's actually much less costly than the six or so lenses it replaces.

When selecting between zoom and prime lenses, there are several considerations to ponder. Here's a checklist of the most important factors. I already mentioned image quality and maximum aperture earlier, but those aspects take on additional meaning when comparing zooms and primes.

- **Logistics.** As prime lenses offer just a single focal length, you'll need more of them to encompass the full range offered by a single zoom. More lenses mean additional slots in your camera bag, and extra weight to carry. Just within Canon's line alone you can select from about a dozen general purpose prime lenses in 28mm, 35mm, 50mm, 85mm, 100mm, 135mm, 200mm, and 300mm focal lengths, all of which are overlapped by the 28-300mm zoom I mentioned earlier. Even so, you might be willing to carry an extra prime lens or two in order to gain the speed or image quality that lens offers.

- **Image quality.** Prime lenses usually produce better image quality at their focal length than even the most sophisticated zoom lenses at the same magnification. Zoom lenses, with their shifting elements and f/stops that can vary from zoom position to zoom position, are in general more complex to design than fixed focal length lenses. That's not to say that the very best prime lenses can't be complicated as well. However, the exotic designs, aspheric elements, low-dispersion glass, and Canon's new diffraction optics (DO) technology (a three-layer diffraction grating to better control how light is captured by a lens) can be applied to improving the quality of the lens, rather than wasting a lot of it on compensating for problems caused by the zoom process itself.

- **Maximum aperture.** Because of the same design constraints, zoom lenses usually have smaller maximum apertures than prime lenses, and the most affordable zooms have a lens opening that grows effectively smaller as you zoom in. The difference in lens speed verges on the ridiculous at some focal lengths. For example, the 18mm-55mm basic zoom gives you a 55mm f/5.6 lens when zoomed all the way out, while prime lenses in that focal length commonly have f/1.8 or faster maximum apertures. Indeed, the fastest f/2, f/1.8, f/1.4, and f/1.2 lenses are all primes, and if you require speed, a fixed focal length lens is what you should rely on. Figure 6.9 shows an image taken with a Canon 85mm f/1.8 Series EF USM Telephoto lens.

■ **Speed.** Using prime lenses takes time and slows you down. It takes a few seconds to remove your current lens and mount a new one, and the more often you need to do that, the more time is wasted. If you choose not to swap lenses, when using a fixed focal length lens you'll still have to move closer or farther away from your subject to get the field of view you want. A zoom lens allows you to change magnifications and focal lengths with the twist of a ring and generally saves a great deal of time.

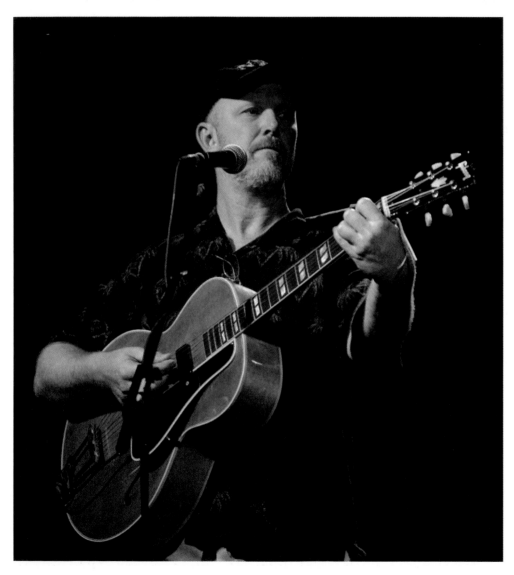

Figure 6.9
An 85mm f/1.8 lens was perfect for this hand-held photo of a musician.

Categories of Lenses

Lenses can be categorized by their intended purpose—general photography, macro photography, and so forth—or by their focal length. The range of available focal lengths is usually divided into three main groups: wide-angle, normal, and telephoto. Prime lenses fall neatly into one of these classifications. Zooms can overlap designations, with a significant number falling into the catch-all wide-to-telephoto zoom range. This section provides more information about focal length ranges, and how they are used.

Any lens with an equivalent focal length of 10mm to 20mm is said to be an *ultra-wide-angle lens*; from about 20mm to 40mm (equivalent) is said to be a *wide-angle lens*. *Normal lenses* have a focal length roughly equivalent to the diagonal of the film or sensor, in millimeters, and so fall into the range of about 45mm to 60mm (on a full-frame camera). *Telephoto lenses* usually fall into the 75mm and longer focal lengths, while those from about 300mm-400mm and longer often are referred to as *super-telephotos*.

Using Wide-Angle and Wide-Zoom Lenses

To use wide-angle prime lenses and wide zooms, you need to understand how they affect your photography. Here's a quick summary of the things you need to know.

- **More depth-of-field.** Practically speaking, wide-angle lenses offer more depth-of-field at a particular subject distance and aperture. (But see the sidebar below for an important note.) You'll find that helpful when you want to maximize sharpness of a large zone, but not very useful when you'd rather isolate your subject using selective focus (telephoto lenses are better for that).

- **Stepping back.** Wide-angle lenses have the effect of making it seem that you are standing farther from your subject than you really are. They're helpful when you don't want to back up, or can't because there are impediments in your way.

- **Wider field of view.** While making your subject seem farther away, as implied above, a wide-angle lens also provides a larger field of view, including more of the subject in your photos. Table 6.1 shows the diagonal field of view offered by an assortment of lenses, taking into account the crop factor introduced by the Rebel XS's smaller-than-full-frame sensor.

- **More foreground.** As background objects retreat, more of the foreground is brought into view by a wide-angle lens. That gives you extra emphasis on the area that's closest to the camera. Photograph your home with a normal lens/normal zoom setting, and the front yard probably looks fairly conventional in your photo (that's why they're called "normal" lenses). Switch to a wider lens and you'll discover that your lawn now makes up much more of the photo. So, wide-angle lenses are great when you want to emphasize that lake in the foreground, but problematic when your intended subject is located farther in the distance.

Table 6.1 Field of View at Various Focal Lengths

Diagonal Field of View	Focal Length at 1X Crop	Focal Length Needed to Produce Same Field of View at 1.6X Crop
107 degrees	16mm	10mm
94 degrees	20mm	12mm
84 degrees	24mm	15mm
75 degrees	28mm	18mm
63 degrees	35mm	22mm
47 degrees	50mm	31mm
28 degrees	85mm	53mm
18 degrees	135mm	85mm
12 degrees	200mm	125mm
8.2 degrees	300mm	188mm

■ **Super-sized subjects.** The tendency of a wide-angle lens to emphasize objects in the foreground, while de-emphasizing objects in the background can lead to a kind of size distortion that may be more objectionable for some types of subjects than others. Shoot a bed of flowers up close with a wide angle, and you might like the distorted effect of the larger blossoms nearer the lens. Take a photo of a family member with the same lens from the same distance, and you're likely to get some complaints about that gigantic nose in the foreground.

■ **Perspective distortion.** When you tilt the camera so the plane of the sensor is no longer perpendicular to the vertical plane of your subject, some parts of the subject are now closer to the sensor than they were before, while other parts are farther away. So, buildings, flagpoles, or NBA players appear to be falling backwards, as you can see in Figure 6.10. While this kind of apparent distortion (it's not caused by a defect in the lens) can happen with any lens, it's most apparent when a wide angle is used.

■ **Steady cam.** You'll find that it's easier to handhold a wide-angle lens at slower shutter speeds, without need for image stabilization, than it is to handhold a telephoto lens. The reduced magnification of the wide-lens or wide-zoom setting doesn't emphasize camera shake like a telephoto lens does.

Figure 6.10
Tilting the camera back produces this "falling back" look in architectural photos.

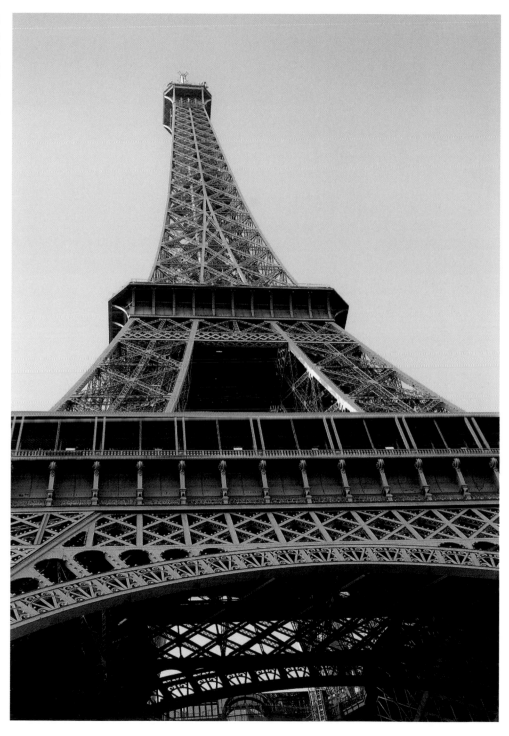

■ **Interesting angles.** Many of the factors already listed combine to produce more interesting angles when shooting with wide-angle lenses. Raising or lowering a telephoto lens a few feet probably will have little effect on the appearance of the distant subjects you're shooting. The same change in elevation can produce a dramatic effect for the much-closer subjects typically captured with a wide-angle lens or wide-zoom setting.

You can see from Table 6.1 that wide-angle lenses provide a broader field of view, and that, because of the XS's 1.6 crop factor, lenses must have a shorter focal length to provide the same field of view. If you like working with a 28mm lens with your full-frame camera, you'll need an 18mm lens for your Rebel XS to get the same field of view. (Some focal lengths have been rounded slightly for simplification.)

DOF IN DEPTH

The depth-of-field (DOF)advantage of wide-angle lenses is diminished when you enlarge your picture; believe it or not, a wide-angle image enlarged and cropped to provide the same subject size as a telephoto shot would have the *same* depth-of-field. Try it: take a wide-angle photo of a friend from a fair distance, and then zoom in to duplicate the picture in a telephoto image. Then, enlarge the wide shot so your friend is the same size in both. The wide photo will have the same DOF (and will have much less detail, too).

Avoiding Potential Wide-Angle Problems

Wide-angle lenses have a few quirks that you'll want to keep in mind when shooting so you can avoid falling into some common traps. Here's a checklist of tips for avoiding common problems:

■ **Symptom: converging lines.** Unless you want to use wildly diverging lines as a creative effect, it's a good idea to keep horizontal and vertical lines in landscapes, architecture, and other subjects carefully aligned with the sides, top, and bottom of the frame. That will help you avoid undesired perspective distortion. Sometimes it helps to shoot from a slightly elevated position so you don't have to tilt the camera up or down.

■ **Symptom: color fringes around objects.** Lenses are often plagued with fringes of color around backlit objects, produced by *chromatic aberration*, which comes in two forms: *longitudinal/axial*, in which all the colors of light don't focus in the same plane; and *lateral/transverse*, in which the colors are shifted to one side. Axial chromatic aberration can be reduced by stopping down the lens, but transverse CA cannot. Both can be reduced by using lenses with low diffraction index glass (or UD elements, in Canon nomenclature) and by incorporating elements that cancel the chromatic aberration of other glass in the lens. For example, a strong positive lens made of low dispersion crown glass (made of a soda-lime-silica composite) may be mated with a weaker negative lens made of high-dispersion flint glass, which contains lead.

■ **Symptom: lines that bow outward.** Some wide-angle lenses cause straight lines to bow outwards, with the strongest effect at the edges. In fisheye (or *curvilinear*) lenses, this defect is a feature, as you can see in Figure 6.11, which was an experimental shot where I set the white balance on tungsten, and used flash for the foreground, producing a mixed-color look. When distortion is not desired, you'll need to use a lens that has corrected barrel distortion. Manufacturers like Canon do their best to minimize or eliminate it (producing a *rectilinear* lens), often using *aspherical* lens elements (which are not cross-sections of a sphere). You can also minimize barrel distortion simply by framing your photo with some extra space all around, so the edges where the defect is most obvious can be cropped out of the picture.

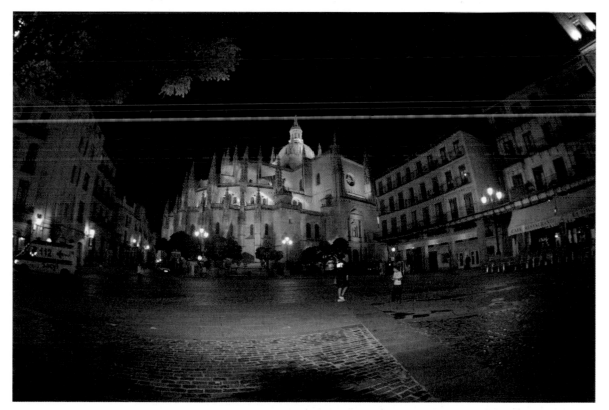

Figure 6.11 Many wide-angle lenses cause lines to bow outwards towards the edges of the image; with a fisheye lens, this tendency is especially useful for creating special effects, as in this shot.

- **Symptom: dark corners and shadows in flash photos.** The Canon EOS Rebel XS's built-in electronic flash is designed to provide even coverage for lenses as wide as 17mm. If you use a wider lens, you can expect darkening, or *vignetting*, in the corners of the frame. At wider focal lengths, the lens hood of some lenses (my 17mm-85mm lens is a prime offender) can cast a semi-circular shadow in the lower portion of the frame when using the built-in flash. Sometimes removing the lens hood or zooming in a bit can eliminate the shadow. Mounting an external flash unit, such as the mighty Canon 580EX can solve both problems, as it has zoomable coverage up to 114 degrees with the included adapter, sufficient for a 9mm recti-linear lens (14mm equivalent). Its higher vantage point eliminates the problem of lens-hood shadow, too.

- **Symptom: light and dark areas when using polarizing filter.** If you know that polarizers work best when the camera is pointed 90 degrees away from the sun and have the least effect when the camera is oriented 180 degrees from the sun, you know only half the story. With lenses having a focal length of 10mm to 18mm (the equivalent of 16mm-28mm), the angle of view (107 to 75 degrees diagonally, or 97 to 44 degrees horizontally) is extensive enough to cause problems. Think about it: when a 10mm lens is pointed at the proper 90-degree angle from the sun, objects at the edges of the frame will be oriented at 135 to 41 degrees, with only the center at exactly 90 degrees. Either edge will have much less of a polarized effect. The solution is to avoid using a polarizing filter with lenses having an actual focal length of less than 18mm (or 28mm equivalent).

Using Telephoto and Tele-Zoom Lenses

Telephoto lenses also can have a dramatic effect on your photography, and Canon is especially strong in the long-lens arena, with lots of choices in many focal lengths and zoom ranges. You should be able to find an affordable telephoto or tele-zoom to enhance your photography in several different ways. Here are the most important things you need to know. In the next section, I'll concentrate on telephoto considerations that can be problematic—and how to avoid those problems.

- **Selective focus.** Long lenses have reduced depth-of-field within the frame, allow-ing you to use selective focus to isolate your subject. You can open the lens up wide to create shallow depth-of-field, or close it down a bit to allow more to be in focus. The flip side of the coin is that when you *want* to make a range of objects sharp, you'll need to use a smaller f/stop to get the depth-of-field you need. Like fire, the depth-of-field of a telephoto lens can be friend or foe. Figure 6.12 shows a photo of a piece of antique glassware that couldn't be removed from its display shelf, so I photographed it using a short telephoto lens and wider f/stop to de-emphasize the other glassware in the background.

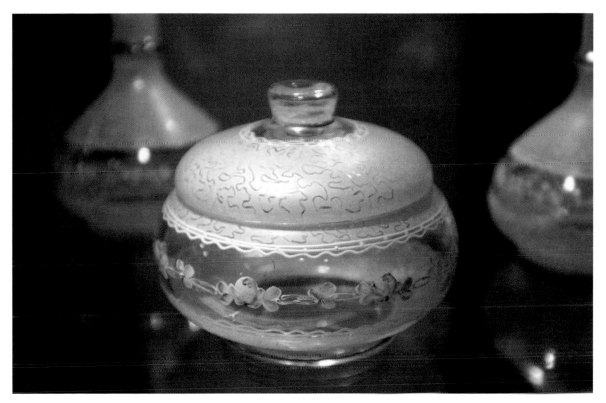

Figure 6.12 A wide f/stop helped isolate this antique glassware from the other items on the display shelf.

■ **Getting closer.** Telephoto lenses bring you closer to wildlife, sports action, and candid subjects. No one wants to get a reputation as a surreptitious or "sneaky" photographer (except for paparazzi), but when applied to candids in an open and honest way, a long lens can help you capture memorable moments while retaining enough distance to stay out of the way of events as they transpire.

■ **Reduced foreground/increased compression.** Telephoto lenses have the opposite effect of wide angles: they reduce the importance of things in the foreground by squeezing everything together. This compression even makes distant objects appear to be closer to subjects in the foreground and middle ranges. You can use this effect as a creative tool.

■ **Accentuates camera shakiness.** Telephoto focal lengths hit you with a double-whammy in terms of camera/photographer shake. The lenses themselves are bulkier, more difficult to hold steady, and may even produce a barely perceptible see-saw rocking effect when you support them with one hand halfway down the lens barrel. Telephotos also magnify any camera shake. It's no wonder that image stabilization is popular in longer lenses.

- **Interesting angles require creativity.** Telephoto lenses require more imagination in selecting interesting angles, because the "angle" you do get on your subjects is so narrow. Moving from side to side or a bit higher or lower can make a dramatic difference in a wide-angle shot, but raising or lowering a telephoto lens a few feet probably will have little effect on the appearance of the distant subjects you're shooting.

Avoiding Telephoto Lens Problems

Many of the "problems" that telephoto lenses pose are really just challenges and not that difficult to overcome. Here is a list of the seven most common picture maladies and suggested solutions.

- **Symptom: flat faces in portraits.** Head-and-shoulders portraits of humans tend to be more flattering when a focal length of 50mm to 85mm is used. Longer focal lengths compress the distance between features like noses and ears, making the face look wider and flat. A wide-angle might make noses look huge and ears tiny when you fill the frame with a face. So stick with 50mm to 85mm focal lengths, going longer only when you're forced to shoot from a greater distance, and wider only when shooting three-quarters/full-length portraits, or group shots.

- **Symptom: blur due to camera shake.** Use a higher shutter speed (boosting ISO if necessary), consider an image-stabilized lens, or mount your camera on a tripod, monopod, or brace it with some other support. Of those three solutions, only the first will reduce blur caused by *subject* motion; an IS lens or tripod won't help you freeze a racecar in mid-lap.

- **Symptom: color fringes.** Chromatic aberration is the most pernicious optical problem found in telephoto lenses. There are others, including spherical aberration, astigmatism, coma, curvature of field, and similarly scary-sounding phenomena. The best solution for any of these is to use a better lens that offers the proper degree of correction, or stop down the lens to minimize the problem. But that's not always possible. Your second-best choice may be to correct the fringing in your favorite RAW conversion tool or image editor. Photoshop's Lens Correction filter (found in the Filter > Distort menu) offers sliders that minimize both red/cyan and blue/yellow fringing.

- **Symptom: lines that curve inwards.** Pincushion distortion is found in many telephoto lenses. You might find after a bit of testing that it is worse at certain focal lengths with your particular zoom lens. Like chromatic aberration, it can be partially corrected using tools like Photoshop's Lens Correction filter.

- **Symptom: low contrast from haze or fog.** When you're photographing distant objects, a long lens shoots through a lot more atmosphere, which generally is muddied up with extra haze and fog. That dirt or moisture in the atmosphere can reduce contrast and mute colors. Some feel that a skylight or UV filter can help, but this practice is mostly a holdover from the film days. Digital sensors are not sensitive enough to UV light for a UV filter to have much effect. So you should be prepared to boost contrast and color saturation in your Picture Styles menu or image editor if necessary.

- **Symptom: low contrast from flare.** Lenses are furnished with lens hoods for a good reason: to reduce flare from bright light sources at the periphery of the picture area, or completely outside it. Because telephoto lenses often create images that are lower in contrast in the first place, you'll want to be especially careful to use a lens hood to prevent further effects on your image (or shade the front of the lens with your hand).

- **Symptom: dark flash photos.** Edge-to-edge flash coverage isn't a problem with telephoto lenses as it is with wide angles. The shooting distance is. A long lens might make a subject that's 50 feet away look as if it's right next to you, but your camera's flash isn't fooled. You'll need extra power for distant flash shots, and probably more power than your XS's built-in flash provides. The shoe-mount Canon 580EX II Speedlite, for example, can automatically zoom its coverage down to that of a medium telephoto lens, providing a theoretical full-power shooting aperture of about f/8 at 50 feet and ISO 400. (Try *that* with the built-in flash!)

Telephotos and Bokeh

Bokeh describes the aesthetic qualities of the out-of-focus parts of an image and whether out-of-focus points of light   circles of confusion—are rendered as distracting fuzzy discs or smoothly fade into the background. *Boke* is a Japanese word for "blur," and the h was added to keep English speakers from rendering it monosyllabically to rhyme with *broke*. Although bokeh is visible in blurry portions of any image, it's of particular concern with telephoto lenses, which, thanks to the magic of reduced depth-of-field, produce more obviously out-of-focus areas.

Bokeh can vary from lens to lens, or even within a given lens depending on the f/stop in use. Bokeh becomes objectionable when the circles of confusion are evenly illuminated, making them stand out as distinct discs, or, worse, when these circles are darker in the center, producing an ugly "doughnut" effect. A lens defect called spherical aberration may produce out-of-focus discs that are brighter on the edges and darker in the center, because the lens doesn't focus light passing through the edges of the lens exactly as it does light going through the center. (Mirror or *catadioptric* lenses also produce this effect.)

Other kinds of spherical aberration generate circles of confusion that are brightest in the center and fade out at the edges, producing a smooth blending effect, as you can see at right in Figure 6.13. Ironically, when no spherical aberration is present at all, the discs are a uniform shade, which, while better than the doughnut effect, is not as pleasing as the bright center/dark edge rendition. The shape of the disc also comes into play, with

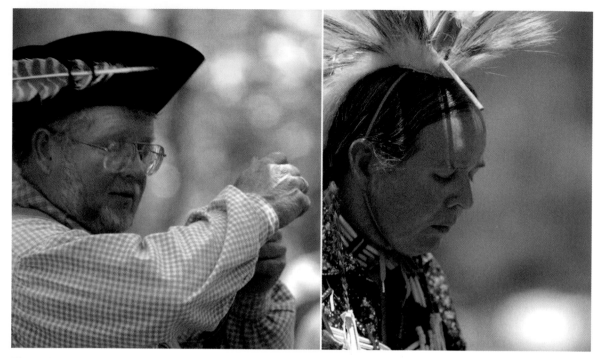

Figure 6.13 Bokeh is less pleasing when the discs are prominent (left), and less obtrusive when they blend into the background (right).

round smooth circles considered the best, and nonagonal or some other polygon (determined by the shape of the lens diaphragm) considered less desirable.

If you plan to use selective focus a lot, you should investigate the bokeh characteristics of a particular lens before you buy. Canon user groups and forums will usually be full of comments and questions about bokeh, so the research is fairly easy.

Add-ons and Special Features

Once you've purchased your telephoto lens, you'll want to think about some appropriate accessories for it. There are some handy add-ons available that can be valuable. Here are a couple of them to think about.

Lens Hoods

Lens hoods are an important accessory for all lenses, but they're especially valuable with telephotos. As I mentioned earlier, lens hoods do a good job of preserving image contrast by keeping bright light sources outside the field of view from striking the lens and, potentially, bouncing around inside that long tube to generate flare that, when coupled with atmospheric haze, can rob your image of detail and snap. In addition, lens hoods serve as valuable protection for that large, vulnerable, front lens element. It's easy to forget that you've got that long tube sticking out in front of your camera and accidentally whack the front of your lens into something. It's cheaper to replace a lens hood than it is to have a lens repaired, so you might find that a good hood is valuable protection for your prized optics.

When choosing a lens hood, it's important to have the right hood for the lens, usually the one offered for that lens by Canon or the third-party manufacturer. You want a hood that blocks precisely the right amount of light: neither too much light nor too little. A hood with a front diameter that is too small can show up in your pictures as vignetting. A hood that has a front diameter that's too large isn't stopping all the light it should. Generic lens hoods may not do the job.

When your telephoto is a zoom lens, it's even more important to get the right hood, because you need one that does what it is supposed to at both the wide-angle and telephoto ends of the zoom range. Lens hoods may be cylindrical, rectangular (shaped like the image frame), or petal shaped (that is, cylindrical, but with cut-out areas at the corners which correspond to the actual image area). Lens hoods should be mounted in the correct orientation (a bayonet mount for the hood usually takes care of this).

Telephoto Extenders

Telephoto extenders (often called teleconverters outside the Canon world) multiply the actual focal length of your lens, giving you a longer telephoto for much less than the price of a lens with that actual focal length. These extenders fit between the lens and your camera and contain optical elements that magnify the image produced by the lens. Available in 1.4X and 2.0X configurations from Canon, an extender transforms, say, a 200mm lens into a 280mm or 400mm optic, respectively. Given the XS's crop factor, your 200mm lens now has the same field of view as a 448mm or 640mm lens on a full-frame camera. At around $300 each, they're quite a bargain, aren't they?

Actually, there are some downsides. While extenders retain the closest focusing distance of your original lens, autofocus is maintained only if the lens's original maximum aperture is f/4 or larger (for the 1.4X extender) or f/2.8 or larger (for the 2X extender). The components reduce the effective aperture of any lens they are used with, by one f/stop with the 1.4X extender, and 2 f/stops with the 2X extender. So, your EF 200mm f/2.8L II USM becomes a 280mm f/4 or 400mm f/5.6 lens. Although Canon extenders are precision optical devices, they do cost you a little sharpness, but that improves when you reduce the aperture by a stop or two. Each of the extenders is compatible only with a particular set of lenses of 135mm focal length or greater, so you'll want to check Canon's compatibility chart to see if the component can be used with the lens you want to attach to it.

If your lenses are compatible and you're shooting under bright lighting conditions, the Canon Extender EF 1.4x II, and Canon Extender EF 2x II make handy accessories.

Macro Focusing

Some telephotos and telephoto zooms available for the Rebel XS have particularly close focusing capabilities, making them *macro* lenses. Of course, the object is not necessarily to get close (get too close and you'll find it difficult to light your subject). What you're really looking for in a macro lens is to magnify the apparent size of the subject in the final image. Camera-to-subject distance is most important when you want to back up farther from your subject (say, to avoid spooking skittish insects or small animals). In that case, you'll want a macro lens with a longer focal length to allow that distance while retaining the desired magnification.

Canon makes 50mm, 60mm, 65mm, 100mm, and 180mm lenses with official macro designations. You'll also find macro lenses, macro zooms, and other close-focusing lenses available from Sigma, Tamron, and Tokina. If you want to focus closer with a macro lens, or any other lens, you can add an accessory called an *extension tube*, like the one shown in Figure 6.14. These add-ons move the lens farther from the focal plane, allowing it to focus more closely. Canon also sells add-on close-up lenses, which look like filters, and allow lenses to focus more closely.

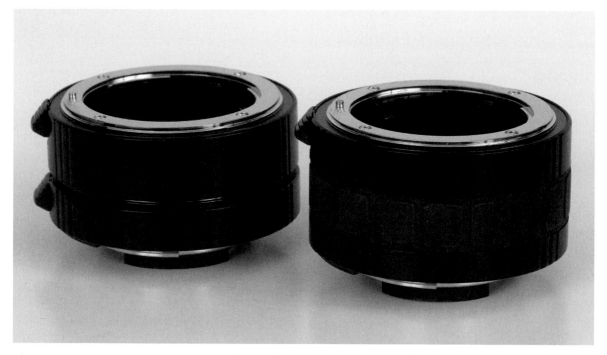

Figure 6.14 Extension tubes enable any lens to focus more closely to the subject.

Image Stabilization

Canon has a burgeoning line of more than a dozen lenses with built-in image stabilization (IS) capabilities. This feature uses lens elements that are shifted internally in response to the motion of the lens during handheld photography, countering the shakiness the camera and photographer produce and which telephoto lenses magnify. However, IS is not limited to long lenses; the feature works like a champ at the 17mm zoom position of Canon's EF-S 17-85mm f/4-5.6 IS USM and EF-S 17-55 f/2.8 IS USM lenses. Other Canon IS lenses provide stabilization with zooms that are as wide as 24-28mm.

Image stabilization provides you with camera steadiness that's the equivalent of at least two or three shutter speed increments. (Canon claims four, which I feel may be optimistic.) This extra margin can be invaluable when you're shooting under dim lighting conditions or handholding a long lens for, say, wildlife photography. Perhaps that shot of a foraging deer calls for a shutter speed of 1/1,000 second at f/5.6 with your EF 100-400mm f/4.5-5.6L IS USM lens. Relax. You can shoot at 1/250 second at f/11 and get virtually the same results, as long as the deer doesn't decide to bound off.

Or, maybe you're shooting a high school play without a tripod or monopod, and you'd really, really like to use 1/15 second at f/4. Assuming the actors aren't flitting around the stage at high speed, your 17mm-85mm IS lens can grab the shot for you at its wide-angle position. However, keep these facts in mind:

- **IS doesn't stop action.** Unfortunately, no IS lens is a panacea to replace the action-stopping capabilities of a higher shutter speed. Image stabilization applies only to camera shake. You still need a fast shutter speed to freeze action. IS works great in low light, when you're using long lenses, and for macro photography. It's not always the best choice for action photography, unless there's enough light to allow a sufficiently high shutter speed. If so, IS can make your shot even sharper.

- **IS slows you down.** The process of adjusting the lens elements takes time, just as autofocus does, so you might find that IS adds to the lag between when you press the shutter and when the picture is actually taken. That's another reason why image stabilization might not be a good choice for sports.

- **Use when appropriate.** Some IS lenses produce worse results if you use them while you're panning, although newer Canon IS lenses have a mode that works fine when the camera is deliberately moved from side to side during exposure. Older lenses can confuse the motion with camera shake and overcompensate. You might want to switch off IS when panning or when your camera is mounted on a tripod.

- **Do you need IS at all?** Remember that an inexpensive monopod might be able to provide the same additional steadiness as an IS lens, at a much lower cost. If you're out in the field shooting wild animals or flowers and think a tripod isn't practical, try a monopod first.

IMAGE STABILIZATION: IN THE CAMERA OR IN THE LENS?

Sony's acquisition of Konica Minolta's dSLR assets and the introduction of an improved in-camera image-stabilization system has revised an old debate about whether IS belongs in the camera or in the lens. Perhaps it's my Canon bias showing, but I am quite happy not to have image stabilization available in the body itself. Here are some reasons:

- Should in-camera IS fail, you have to send the whole camera in for repair, and camera repairs are generally more expensive than lens repairs. I like being able to simply switch to another lens if I have an IS problem.

- IS in the camera doesn't steady your view in the viewfinder, whereas an IS lens shows you a steadied image as you shoot.

- You're stuck with the IS system built into your camera. If an improved system is incorporated into a lens and the improvements are important to you, just trade in your old lens for the new one.

- Optimized stabilization. Canon claims that it is able to produce the best possible image stabilization for each lens it introduces, something that would not be possible if a "one size fits all lenses" stabilization scheme had to be built into the camera.

7

Making Light Work for You

Successful photographers and artists have an intimate understanding of the importance of light in shaping an image. Rembrandt was a master of using light to create moods and reveal the character of his subjects. Artist Thomas Kinkade's official tagline is "Painter of Light." The late Dean Collins, co-founder of Finelight Studios, revolutionized how a whole generation of photographers learned and used lighting. While writing this book, I attended a seminar called "Captivated by the Light," run by photo guru Ed Pierce. It's impossible to underestimate how the use of light adds to—and how misuse can detract from—your photographs.

All forms of visual art use light to shape the finished product. Sculptors don't have control over the light used to illuminate their finished work, so they must create shapes using planes and curved surfaces so that the form envisioned by the artist comes to life from a variety of viewing and lighting angles. Painters, in contrast, have absolute control over both shape and light in their work, as well as the viewing angle, so they can use both the contours of their two-dimensional subjects and the qualities of the "light" they use to illuminate those subjects to evoke the image they want to produce.

Photography is a third form of art. The photographer may have little or no control over the subject (other than posing human subjects) but can often adjust both viewing angle *and* the nature of the light source to create a particular compelling image. The direction and intensity of the light sources create the shapes and textures that we see. The distribution and proportions determine the contrast and tonal values: whether the image is stark or high key, or muted and low in contrast. The colors of the light (because even "white" light has a color balance that the sensor can detect), and how much of those colors the subject reflects or absorbs, paint the hues visible in the image.

As a Rebel XS photographer, you must learn to be a painter and sculptor of light if you want to move from *taking* a picture to *making* a photograph. This chapter provides an introduction to using the two main types of illumination: *continuous* lighting (such as daylight, incandescent, or fluorescent sources) and the brief, but brilliant snippets of light we call *electronic flash*.

Continuous Illumination versus Electronic Flash

Continuous lighting is exactly what you might think: uninterrupted illumination that is available all the time during a shooting session. Daylight, moonlight, and the artificial lighting encountered both indoors and outdoors count as continuous light sources (although all of them can be "interrupted" by passing clouds, solar eclipses, a blown fuse, or simply by switching a lamp off). Indoor continuous illumination includes both the lights that are there already (such as incandescent lamps or overhead fluorescent lights indoors) and fixtures you supply yourself, including photoflood lamps or reflectors used to bounce existing light onto your subject.

The surge of light we call electronic flash is produced by a burst of photons generated by an electrical charge that is accumulated in a component called a *capacitor* and then directed through a glass tube containing xenon gas, which absorbs the energy and emits the brief flash. Electronic flash is notable because it can be much more intense than continuous lighting, lasts only a brief moment, and can be much more portable than supplementary incandescent sources. It's a light source you can carry with you and use anywhere.

Indeed, your Rebel XS has a flip-up electronic flash unit built in. But you can also use an external flash, either mounted on the XS's accessory shoe or used off-camera and linked with a cable or triggered by a slave light (which sets off a flash when it senses the firing of another unit). Studio flash units are electronic flash, too, and aren't limited to "professional" shooters, as there are economical "monolight" (one-piece flash/power supply) units available in the $200 price range. Anyone can buy a couple to store in a closet and use to set up a home studio, or use as supplementary lighting when traveling away from home.

There are advantages and disadvantages to each type of illumination. Here's a quick checklist of pros and cons:

- **Lighting preview—Pro: continuous lighting.** With continuous lighting, you always know exactly what kind of lighting effect you're going to get and, if multiple lights are used, how they will interact with each other, as shown in Figure 7.1. With electronic flash, the general effect you're going to see may be a mystery until you've built some experience, and you may need to review a shot on the LCD, make some adjustments, and then reshoot to get the look you want. (In this sense, a digital camera's review capabilities replace the Polaroid test shots pro photographers relied on in decades past.)

Figure 7.1
You always
know how
the lighting
will look
when using
continuous
illumination.

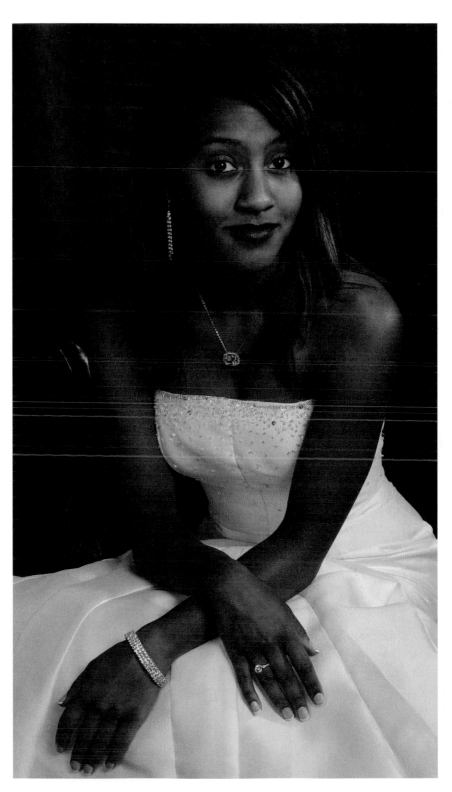

- **Lighting preview—Con: electronic flash.** While some external flash have a modeling light function (consisting of a series of low-powered bursts that flash for a period of time), your XS lacks such a capability in its internal flash, and, in any case, this feature is no substitute for continuous illumination, or an always-on modeling lamp like that found in studio flash. As the number of flash units increases, lighting previews, especially if you want to see the proportions of illumination provided by each flash, grow more complex.

- **Exposure calculation—Pro: continuous lighting.** Your XS has no problem calculating exposure for continuous lighting, because it remains constant and can be measured through a sensor that interprets the light reaching the viewfinder. The amount of light available just before the exposure will, in almost all cases, be the same amount of light present when the shutter is released. The XS's Partial metering mode can be used to measure and compare the proportions of light in the highlights and shadows, so you can make an adjustment (such as using more or less fill light) if necessary. You can even use a handheld light meter to measure the light yourself and set the exposure in Manual mode.

- **Exposure calculation—Con: electronic flash.** Electronic flash illumination doesn't exist until the flash fires, and so can't be measured by the XS's exposure sensor when the mirror is flipped up during the exposure. Instead, the light must be measured by interpreting the intensity of a preflash triggered an instant before the main flash, as it is reflected back to the camera and through the lens. An alternative is to use a sensor built into the external flash itself and measure reflected light that has not traveled through the lens. If you have a do-it-yourself bent, there are handheld flash meters, too, including models that measure both flash and continuous light.

- **Evenness of illumination—Pro/Con: continuous lighting.** Of continuous light sources, daylight, in particular, provides illumination that tends to fill an image completely, lighting up the foreground, background, and your subject almost equally. Shadows do come into play, of course, so you might need to use reflectors or fill-in light sources to even out the illumination further, but barring objects that block large sections of your image from daylight, the light is spread fairly evenly. Indoors, however, continuous lighting is commonly less evenly distributed. The average living room, for example, has hot spots and dark corners. But on the plus side, you can *see* this uneven illumination and compensate with additional lamps.

- **Evenness of illumination—Con: electronic flash.** Electronic flash units (like continuous light sources such as lamps that don't have the advantage of being located 93 million miles from the subject) suffer from the effects of their proximity, because of the *inverse square law*, which I'll describe in the next section.

- **Action stopping—Con: continuous lighting.** Action stopping with continuous light sources is completely dependent on the shutter speed you've dialed in on the camera. And the speeds available are dependent on the amount of light available and your ISO sensitivity setting. Outdoors in daylight, there will probably be enough sunlight to let you shoot at 1/2,000th second and f/6.3 with a non-grainy sensitivity setting of ISO 400. That's a fairly useful combination of settings if you're not using a super-telephoto with a small maximum aperture. But inside, the reduced illumination quickly has you pushing your Rebel XS to its limits. For example, if you're shooting indoor sports, there probably won't be enough available light to allow you to use a 1/2,000th second shutter speed (although I routinely shoot indoor basketball with my XS at ISO 1600 and 1/500th second at f/4). In many indoor sports situations, you may find yourself limited to 1/500th second or slower.

■ **Action stopping—Pro: electronic flash.** When it comes to the ability to freeze moving objects in their tracks, the advantage goes to electronic flash. The brief duration of electronic flash serves as a very high "shutter speed" when the flash is the main or only source of illumination for the photo. Your Rebel XS's shutter speed may be set for 1/200th second during a flash exposure, but if the flash illumination predominates, the *effective* exposure time will be the 1/1,000th to 1/50,000th second or less duration of the flash, as you can see in Figure 7.2, because the flash unit

Figure 7.2
Electronic flash can freeze almost any action.

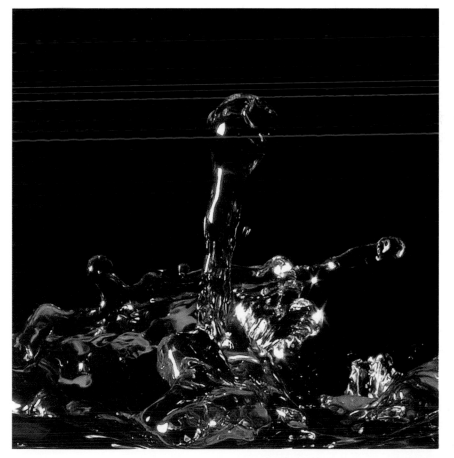

reduces the amount of light released by cutting short the duration of the flash. The only fly in the ointment is that, if the ambient light is strong enough, it may produce a secondary, "ghost" exposure, as I'll explain later in this chapter.

■ **Cost—Pro: continuous lighting.** Incandescent or fluorescent lamps are generally much less expensive than electronic flash units, which can easily cost several hundred dollars. I've used everything from desktop hi-intensity lamps to reflector flood-lights for continuous illumination at very little cost. There are lamps made especially for photographic purposes, too, priced up to $50 or so. Maintenance is economical, too; many incandescent or fluorescents use bulbs that cost only a few dollars.

■ **Cost—Con: electronic flash.** Electronic flash units aren't particularly cheap. The lowest-cost dedicated flash designed specifically for the Canon dSLRs is about $110. Such units are limited in features, however, and intended for those with entry-level cameras. Plan to spend some money to get the features that a sophisticated electronic flash offers.

■ **Flexibility—Con: continuous lighting.** Because incandescent and fluorescent lamps are not as bright as electronic flash, the slower shutter speeds required (see Action stopping, above) mean that you may have to use a tripod more often, especially when shooting portraits. The incandescent variety of continuous lighting gets hot, especially in the studio, and the side effects range from discomfort (for your human models) to disintegration (if you happen to be shooting perishable foods like ice cream). The heat also makes it more difficult to add filtration to incandescent sources.

■ **Flexibility—Pro: electronic flash.** Electronic flash's action-freezing power allows you to work without a tripod in the studio (and elsewhere), adding flexibility and speed when choosing angles and positions. Flash units can be easily filtered, and, because the filtration is placed over the light source rather than the lens, you don't need to use high quality filter material. For example, a couple sheets of unexposed, processed Ektachrome film can make a dandy infrared-pass filter for your flash unit. Roscoe or Lee lighting gels, which may be too flimsy to use in front of the lens, can be mounted or taped in front of your flash with ease.

Continuous Lighting Basics

While continuous lighting and its effects are generally much easier to visualize and use than electronic flash, there are some factors you need to take into account, particularly the color temperature of the light. (Color temperature concerns aren't exclusive to continuous light sources, of course, but the variations tend to be more extreme and less predictable than those of electronic flash.)

Color temperature, in practical terms, is how "bluish" or how "reddish" the light appears to be to the digital camera's sensor. Indoor illumination is quite warm, comparatively, and appears reddish to the sensor. Daylight, in contrast, seems much bluer to the sensor. Our eyes (our brains, actually) are quite adaptable to these variations, so white objects don't appear to have an orange tinge when viewed indoors, nor do they seem excessively blue outdoors in full daylight. Yet, these color temperature variations are real and the sensor is not fooled. To capture the most accurate colors, we need to take the color temperature into account in setting the color balance (or *white balance*) of the XS—either automatically using the camera's smarts, or manually, using our own knowledge and experience.

Color temperature can be confusing, because of a seeming contradiction in how color temperatures are named: warmer (more reddish) color temperatures (measured in degrees Kelvin) are the *lower* numbers, while cooler (bluer) color temperatures are *higher* numbers. It might not make sense to say that 3,400K is warmer than 6,000K, but that's the way it is. If it helps, think of a glowing red ember contrasted with a white-hot welder's torch, rather than fire and ice.

The confusion comes from physics. Scientists calculate color temperature from the light emitted by a mythical object called a black body radiator, which absorbs all the radiant energy that strikes it, and reflects none at all. Such a black body not only *absorbs* light perfectly, but it *emits* it perfectly when heated (and since nothing in the universe is perfect, that makes it mythical).

At a particular physical temperature, this imaginary object always emits light of the same wavelength or color. That makes it possible to define color temperature in terms of actual temperature in degrees on the Kelvin scale that scientists use. Incandescent light, for example, typically has a color temperature of 3,200K to 3,400K. Daylight might range from 5,500K to 6,000K. Each type of illumination we use for photography has its own color temperature range—with some cautions. The next sections will summarize everything you need to know about the qualities of these light sources.

Daylight

Daylight is produced by the sun, and so is moonlight (which is just reflected sunlight). Daylight is present, of course, even when you can't see the sun. When sunlight is direct, it can be bright and harsh. If daylight is diffused by clouds, softened by bouncing off objects such as walls or your photo reflectors, or filtered by shade, it can be much dimmer and less contrasty.

Daylight's color temperature can vary quite widely. It is highest (most blue) at noon when the sun is directly overhead because the light is traveling through a minimum amount of the filtering layer we call the atmosphere. The color temperature at high noon may be 6,000K. At other times of day, the sun is lower in the sky and the particles in

INVERSE SQUARE LAW

The inverse square law affects all light sources—even the sun, but is most noticeable when the illumination is located fairly close to your subject. That's because this effect is most dramatic when the distance between the light source and the subject is changed by a significant fraction. It was first applied to both gravity and light by Sir Isaac Newton, and dictates that as a light source's distance increases from the subject, the amount of light reaching the subject falls off proportionately to the square of the distance. In plain English, that means that a flash or lamp that's 12 feet away from a subject provides only one-quarter as much illumination as a source that's 6 feet away (rather than half as much). (See Figure 7.3.) This translates into relatively shallow "depth-of-light."

While the inverse square law applies to all types of light, both continuous and electronic flash, some kinds of illumination—such as the sun—are so far away that we never see a significant change in the relative distance. But, if you were able to move the sun an additional 93 million miles from our planet, its illumination would indeed be one-quarter as intense (not half as bright). Of course, in that case, calculating the correct exposure in daylight would not be on the minds of most photographers.

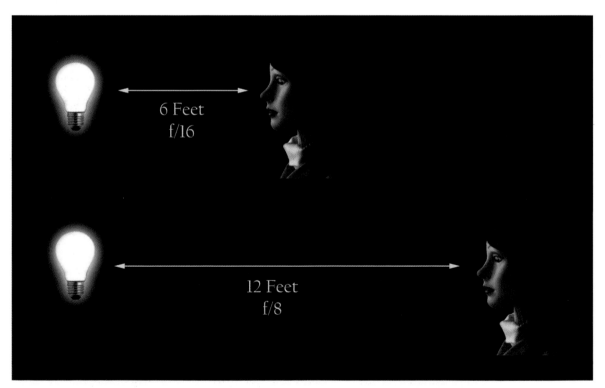

Figure 7.3 A light source that is twice as far away provides only one-quarter as much illumination.

the air provide a filtering effect that warms the illumination to about 5,500K for most of the day. Starting an hour before dusk and for an hour after sunrise, the warm appearance of the sunlight is even visible to our eyes when the color temperature may dip to 5,000–4,500K, as shown in Figure 7.4.

Because you'll be taking so many photos in daylight, you'll want to learn how to use or compensate for the brightness and contrast of sunlight, as well as how to deal with its color temperature. I'll provide some hints later in this chapter.

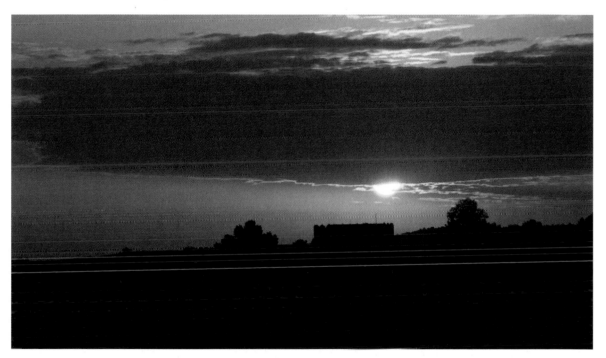

Figure 7.4 At dawn and dusk, the color temperature of daylight may dip as low as 4,500K.

Incandescent/Tungsten Light

The term incandescent or tungsten illumination is usually applied to the direct descendents of Thomas Edison's original electric lamp. Such lights consist of a glass bulb that contains a vacuum, or is filled with a halogen gas, and contains a tungsten filament that is heated by an electrical current, producing photons and heat. Tungsten-halogen lamps are a variation on the basic light bulb, using a more rugged (and longer-lasting) filament that can be heated to a higher temperature, housed in a thicker glass or quartz envelope, and filled with iodine or bromine ("halogen") gases. The higher temperature allows tungsten-halogen (or quartz-halogen/quartz-iodine, depending on their construction) lamps to burn "hotter" and whiter. Although popular for automobile headlamps today, they've also been popular for photographic illumination.

Although incandescent illumination isn't a perfect black body radiator, it's close enough that the color temperature of such lamps can be precisely calculated and used for photography without concerns about color variation (at least, until the very end of the lamp's life).

The other qualities of this type of lighting, such as contrast, are dependent on the distance of the lamp from the subject, type of reflectors used, and other factors that I'll explain later in this chapter.

Fluorescent Light/Other Light Sources

Fluorescent light has some advantages in terms of illumination, but some disadvantages from a photographic standpoint. This type of lamp generates light through an electro-chemical reaction that emits most of its energy as visible light, rather than heat, which is why the bulbs don't get as hot. The type of light produced varies depending on the phosphor coatings and type of gas in the tube. So, the illumination fluorescent bulbs produce can vary widely in its characteristics.

That's not great news for photographers. Different types of lamps have different "color temperatures" that can't be precisely measured in degrees Kelvin, because the light isn't produced by heating. Worse, fluorescent lamps have a discontinuous spectrum of light that can have some colors missing entirely. A particular type of tube can lack certain shades of red or other colors (see Figure 7.5), which is why fluorescent lamps and other alternative technologies such as sodium-vapor illumination can produce ghastly look-ing human skin tones. Their spectra can lack the reddish tones we associate with healthy skin and emphasize the blues and greens popular in horror movies.

Adjusting White Balance

I showed you how to adjust white balance in Chapter 3, using the XS's built-in presets, white balance shift capabilities, and white balance bracketing (there's more on bracket-ing in Chapter 4, too).

In most cases, however, the Rebel XS will do a good job of calculating white balance for you, so Auto can be used as your choice most of the time. Use the preset values or set a custom white balance that matches the current shooting conditions when you need to. The only really problematic light sources are likely to be fluorescents. Vendors, such as GE and Sylvania, may actually provide a figure known as the *color rendering index* (or CRI), which is a measure of how accurately a particular light source represents standard colors, using a scale of 0 (some sodium-vapor lamps) to 100 (daylight and most incandescent lamps). Daylight fluorescents and deluxe cool white fluorescents might have a CRI of about 79 to 95, which is perfectly acceptable for most photographic applications. Warm white fluorescents might have a CRI of 55. White deluxe mercury vapor lights are less suitable with a CRI of 45, while low-pressure sodium lamps can vary from CRI 0-18.

Figure 7.5
The fluorescent lighting in this gym added a distinct greenish cast to the image.

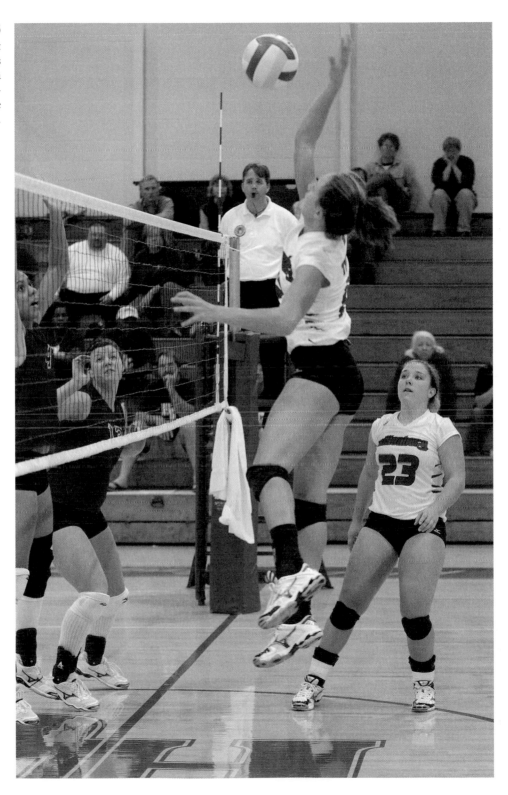

Remember that if you shoot RAW, you can specify the white balance of your image when you import it into Photoshop, Photoshop Elements, or another image editor using your preferred RAW converter. While color-balancing filters that fit on the front of the lens exist, they are primarily useful for film cameras, because film's color balance can't be tweaked as extensively as that of a sensor.

Electronic Flash Basics

Until you delve into the situation deeply enough, it might appear that serious photographers have a love/hate relationship with electronic flash. You'll often hear that flash photography is less natural looking, and that the built-in flash in most cameras should never be used as the primary source of illumination because it provides a harsh, garish look. Indeed, most "pro" cameras like the Canon EOS 1D Mark III and 1Ds Mark III don't have a built-in flash at all. Available ("continuous") lighting is praised, and built-in flash photography seems to be roundly denounced.

In truth, however, the bias is against *bad* flash photography. Indeed, flash has become the studio light source of choice for pro photographers, because it's more intense (and its intensity can be varied to order by the photographer), freezes action, frees you from using a tripod (unless you want to use one to lock down a composition), and has a snappy, consistent light quality that matches daylight. (While color balance changes as the flash duration shortens, some Canon flash units can communicate to the camera the exact white balance provided for that shot.) And even pros will cede that the built-in flash of the Canon EOS Rebel XS has some important uses as an adjunct to existing light, particularly to fill in dark shadows.

But electronic flash isn't as inherently easy to use as continuous lighting. As I noted earlier, electronic flash units are more expensive, don't show you exactly what the lighting effect will be (unless you use a second source called a *modeling light* for a preview), and the exposure of electronic flash units is more difficult to calculate accurately.

How Electronic Flash Works

The bursts of light we call electronic flash are produced by a flash of photons generated by an electrical charge that is accumulated in a component called a *capacitor*, and are then directed through a glass tube containing xenon gas, which absorbs the energy and emits the brief flash. For the pop-up flash built into the Rebel XS, the full burst of light lasts about 1/1,000th second and provides enough illumination to shoot a subject 10 feet away at f/4 using the ISO 100 setting. In a more typical situation, you'd use ISO 200, f/5.6 to f/8 and photograph something 8 to 10 feet away. As you can see, the built-in flash is somewhat limited in range; you'll see why external flash units are often a good idea later in this chapter.

An electronic flash (whether built in or connected to the Rebel XS through a cable plugged into a hot shoe adapter) is triggered at the instant of exposure, during a period when the sensor is fully exposed by the shutter. As I mentioned earlier in this book, the XS has a vertically traveling shutter that consists of two curtains. The first curtain opens and moves to the opposite side of the frame, at which point the shutter is completely open. The flash can be triggered at this point (so-called *first-curtain sync*), making the flash exposure. Then, after a delay that can vary from 30 seconds to 1/200th second (with the Rebel XS; other cameras may sync at a faster or slower speed), a second curtain begins moving across the sensor plane, covering up the sensor again. If the flash is triggered just before the second curtain starts to close, then *second-curtain sync* is used. In both cases, though, a shutter speed of 1/200th second is the maximum that can be used to take a photo.

If you happen to try to set the XS's shutter to a faster speed in Tv or M mode, the camera will automatically adjust the shutter speed down to 1/200th second when using flash. In Av, P, or any of the Basic Zone modes, the XS will never select a shutter speed higher than 1/200th second when using flash. Actually, in P mode, shutter speed is automatically set between 1/60th to 1/200th second when using flash.

Ghost Images

The difference might not seem like much, but whether you use first-curtain sync (the default setting) or second-curtain sync (an optional setting) can make a significant difference to your photograph *if the ambient light in your scene also contributes to the image.* At faster shutter speeds, particularly 1/200th second, there isn't much time for the ambient light to register, unless it is very bright. It's likely that the electronic flash will provide almost all the illumination, so first-curtain sync or second-curtain sync isn't very important.

However, at slower shutter speeds, or with very bright ambient light levels, there is a significant difference, particularly if your subject is moving, or the camera isn't steady. In any of those situations, the ambient light will register as a second image accompanying the flash exposure, and if there is movement (camera or subject), that additional image will not be in the same place as the flash exposure. It will show as a ghost image and, if the movement is significant enough, as a blurred ghost image trailing in front of or behind your subject in the direction of the movement.

When you're using first-curtain sync, the flash goes off the instant the shutter opens, producing an image of the subject on the sensor. Then, the shutter remains open for an additional period (30 seconds to 1/200th second, as I noted). If your subject is moving, say, towards the right side of the frame, the ghost image produced by the ambient light will produce a blur on the right side of the original subject image, making it look as if your sharp (flash-produced) image is chasing the ghost. For those of us who grew up with lightning-fast superheroes that always left a ghost trail *behind them*, that looks unnatural (see Figure 7.6).

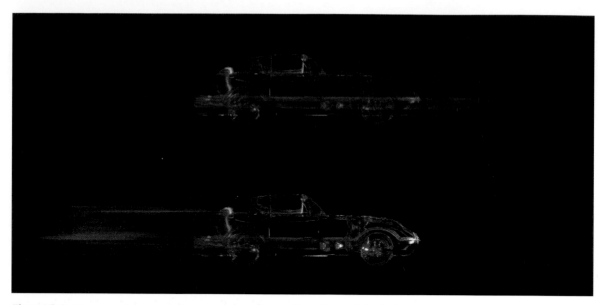

Figure 7.6 First-curtain sync produces an image that trails in front of the flash exposure (top), while second-curtain sync creates a more "natural looking" trail behind the flash image.

So, Canon provides second-curtain sync to remedy the situation. In that mode, the shutter opens, as before. The shutter remains open for its designated duration, and the ghost image forms. If your subject moves from the left side of the frame to the right side, the ghost will move from left to right, too. *Then*, about 1.5 milliseconds before the second shutter curtain closes, the flash is triggered, producing a nice, sharp flash image *ahead* of the ghost image. Voilà! We have monsieur *le Flash* outrunning his own trailing image.

Triggering the electronic flash only when the shutter is completely open makes a lot of sense if you think about what's going on. To obtain shutter speeds faster than 1/200th second, the XS exposes only part of the sensor at one time, by starting the second curtain on its journey before the first curtain has completely opened. That effectively provides a briefer exposure as the open slit between the blades of the shutter passes over the surface of the sensor. If the flash were to fire during the time when the first and second curtains partially obscured the sensor, only the slit that was actually open would be exposed.

Determining Exposure

Calculating the proper exposure for an electronic flash photograph is a bit more complicated than determining the settings by continuous light. The right exposure isn't simply a function of how far away your subject is (which the XS can figure out based on the autofocus distance that's locked in just prior to taking the picture). Various objects reflect more or less light at the same distance so, obviously, the camera needs to measure the amount of light reflected back and through the lens. Yet, as the flash itself isn't available for measuring until it's triggered, the XS has nothing to measure.

The solution is to fire the flash twice. The initial shot is a preflash that can be analyzed, then followed by a main flash that's given exactly the calculated intensity needed to provide a correct exposure. As a result, the primary flash may be longer for distant objects and shorter for closer subjects, depending on the required intensity for exposure. This through-the-lens evaluative flash exposure system is called E-TTL II, and it operates whenever the pop-up internal flash is used, or if you have attached a Canon dedicated flash unit to the XS.

Guide Numbers

Guide numbers, usually abbreviated GN, are a way of specifying the power of an electronic flash in a way that can be used to determine the right f/stop to use at a particular shooting distance and ISO setting. In fact, before automatic flash units became prevalent, the GN was actually used to do just that. A GN is usually given as a pair of numbers for both feet and meters that represent the range at ISO 100. For example, the Rebel XS's built-in flash has a GN of 13/43 (meters/feet) at ISO 100. To calculate the right exposure at that ISO setting, you'd divide the guide number by the distance to arrive at the appropriate f/stop.

Using the XS's built-in flash as an example, at ISO 100 with its GN of 43, if you wanted to shoot a subject at a distance of 10 feet, you'd use f/4.3 (43 divided by 10; round to f/4 for simplicity's sake). At 8 feet, an f/stop of f/5.4 (round up to f/5.6) would be used. Some quick mental calculations with the GN will give you any particular electronic flash's range. You can easily see that the built-in flash would begin to peter out at about 15 feet, where you'd need an aperture of f/2.8 at ISO 100. Of course, in the real world you'd probably bump the sensitivity up to a setting of ISO 400 so you could use a more practical f/5.6 at that distance.

Today, guide numbers are most useful for comparing the power of various flash units. You don't need to be a math genius to see that an electronic flash with a GN of, say, 165 would be *a lot* more powerful than your built-in flash (at ISO 100, you could use f/11 instead of f/2.8 at 15 feet).

Using the Built-In Flash

The Canon EOS Rebel XS's built-in flash is a handy accessory because it is available as required, without the need to carry an external flash around with you constantly. This section explains how to use the flip-up flash in the various Basic Zone and Creative Zone modes.

Basic Zone Flash

When the XS is set to one of the Basic Zone modes (except for Landscape, Sports, or Flash Off modes), the built-in flash will pop up when needed to provide extra illumination in low-light situations, or when your subject matter is backlit and could benefit from some fill flash. The flash doesn't pop up in Landscape mode because the flash doesn't have enough reach to have much effect for pictures of distant vistas in any case; nor does the flash pop up automatically in Sports mode, because you'll often want to use shutter speeds faster than 1/200th second and/or be shooting subjects that are out of flash range. Pop-up flash is disabled in Flash Off mode for obvious reasons.

If you happen to be shooting a landscape photo and do want to use flash (say, to add some illumination to a subject that's closer to the camera), or you want flash with your sports photos, or you *don't* want the flash popping up all the time when using one of the other Basic Zone modes, switch to an appropriate Creative Zone mode and use that instead.

Creative Zone Flash

When you're using a Creative Zone mode, you'll have to judge for yourself when flash might be useful, and flip it up yourself by pressing the Flash button on the side of the pentaprism. The behavior of the internal flash varies, depending on which Creative Zone mode you're using.

- **P/A-DEP.** In these modes, the XS fully automates the exposure process, giving you subtle fill flash effects in daylight, and fully illuminating your subject under dimmer lighting conditions. The camera selects a shutter speed from 1/60th to 1/200th second and sets an appropriate aperture.

- **Av.** In Aperture Priority mode, you set the aperture as always, and the XS chooses a shutter speed from 30 seconds to 1/200th second. Use this mode with care, because if the camera detects a dark background, it will use the flash to expose the main subject in the foreground, and then leave the shutter open long enough to allow the background to be exposed correctly, too. If you're not using an image-stabilized lens, you can end up with blurry ghost images even of non-moving subjects at exposures longer than 1/30th second, and if your camera is not mounted on a tripod, you'll see these blurs at exposures longer than about 1/8th second even if you are using IS.

- **Tv.** When using flash in Tv mode, you set the shutter speed from 30 seconds to 1/200th second, and the XS will choose the correct aperture for the correct flash exposure. If you accidentally set the shutter speed higher than 1/200th second, the camera will reduce it to 1/200th second when you're using the flash.

■ **M.** In Manual mode, you select both shutter speed (30 seconds to 1/200th second) and aperture. The camera will adjust the shutter speed to 1/200th second if you try to use a faster speed with flash. The E-TTL II system will provide the correct amount of exposure for your main subject at the aperture you've chosen (if the subject is within the flash's range, of course).

When using Creative Zone modes (or any Basic Zone mode in which flash is used), if Red-Eye Reduction is turned on in the Shooting menu (as described in Chapter 3), the red-eye reduction lamp will illuminate for about 1.5 seconds when you press down the shutter release halfway, theoretically causing your subjects' irises to contract (if they are looking toward the camera), and thereby reducing the red-eye effect in your photograph. Note that the lamp is located near the camera's hand grip, so you should be careful not to block the beam with your fingers.

Using FE Lock and Flash Exposure Compensation

If you want to lock flash exposure for a subject that is not centered in the frame, you can use the FE Lock button (*) to lock in a specific flash exposure. Just depress and hold the shutter button halfway to lock in focus, then center the viewfinder on the subject you want to correctly expose, and press the * button. The preflash fires and calculates exposure, displaying the FEL (flash exposure lock) message in the viewfinder. Then, recompose your photo and press the shutter down the rest of the way to take the photo.

You can also manually add or subtract exposure to the flash exposure calculated by the XS. Just press the Choose the Flash exp comp entry in Shooting Menu 2, and use the left/right cross keys to enter flash exposure compensation plus or minus two f/stops. The exposure index scale on the LCD and in the viewfinder will indicate the change you've made, and a flash exposure compensation icon will appear to warn you that an adjustment has been made. As with non-flash exposure compensation, the compensation you make remains in effect for the pictures that follow, and even when you've turned the camera off, remember to cancel the flash exposure compensation adjustment by reversing the steps used to set it when you're done using it.

Using External Electronic Flash

Canon offers a broad range of accessory electronic flash units for the Rebel XS. They can be mounted to the flash accessory shoe, or used off-camera with a dedicated cord that plugs into the flash shoe to maintain full communications with the camera for all special features. They range from the Speedlite 580EX, which can correctly expose subjects up to 24 feet away at f/11 and ISO 200, to the 220EX, which is good out to 9 feet at f/11 and ISO 200. (You'll get greater ranges at even higher ISO settings, of course.) There are also two electronic flash units specifically for specialized close-up flash photography.

Speedlite 580EX II

This flagship of the Canon accessory flash line is the most powerful unit the company offers, with a GN of 190, and a manual/automatic zoom flash head that covers the full frame of lenses from 24mm wide angle to 105mm telephoto. (There's a flip-down wide-angle diffuser that spreads the flash to cover a 14mm lens's field of view, too.) All angle specifications given by Canon refer to full-frame sensors, but this flash unit automatically converts its field of view coverage to accommodate the crop factor of the Rebel XS and the other 1.6X crop Canon dSLRs. Compared to the 580 EX it replaces, the Mark II model recycles (inaudibly—no more hum!) 20 percent faster, and has improved dust- and water-resistance so you can use it in harsher environments.

The unit offers full-swivel, 180 degrees in either direction, and has its own built-in AF assist beam and an exposure system that's compatible with the nine focus points of the XS. Powered by economical AA-size batteries, the unit recycles in 0.1 to 6 seconds, and can squeeze 100 to 700 flashes from a set of alkaline batteries.

The 580EX II (see Figure 7.7) automatically communicates white balance information to your camera, allowing it to adjust WB to match the flash output. You can even simulate a modeling light effect: When you press the Depth-of-Field Preview button on the

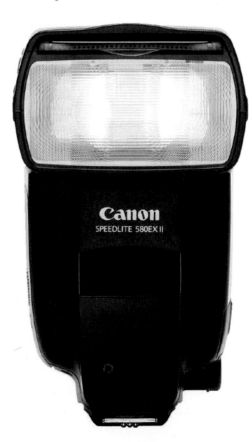

Figure 7.7
The Canon Speedlite 580EX II is the most powerful shoe-mount flash Canon offers.

XS, the 580EX II emits a one-second burst of light that allows you to judge the flash effect. If you're using multiple flash units with Canon's wireless E-TTL system, this model can serve as a master flash that controls the slave units you've set up (more about this later) or function as a slave itself.

It's easy to access all the features of this unit because it has a large backlit LCD panel on the back that provides information about all flash settings. There are 14 Custom Functions that can be controlled from the flash. These functions are (the first setting is the default value) as follows:

C.Fn.-01   Automatic cancellation of Flash Exposure Bracketing (Enable/Disable)

C.Fn.-02   Flash Exposure Bracketing Sequence (Metered > Decreased > Increased Exposure or Decreased > Metered > Increased Exposure)

C.Fn.-03   Flash metering exposure (E-TTL II/E-TTL)

C.Fn.-04   Slave unit's auto power off time (60 minutes/10 minutes)

C.Fn.-05   Cancellation of slave unit auto power off by master unit (Within 1 hour/Within 8 Hours)

C.Fn.-06   Modeling Flash (Enable/Disable)

C.Fn.-07   Flash recycling on external power (Use internal and external power/Use only external power)

C.Fn.-08   Quick Flash with continuous shooting (Disable/Enable)

C.Fn.-09   Test firing with autoflash power level (1/32 power/full power)

C.Fn.-10   Modeling flash triggered by test firing button (Disable/Enable)

C.Fn.-11   Auto setting of flash coverage to match image size (Enable/Disable)

C.Fn.-12   AF-assist beam OFF (Disable/Enable)

C.Fn.-13   Flash Exposure Compensation setting button (Flash unit Select/Set with Select Dial/Select Dial only)

C.Fn.-14   Auto Power Off (On/Off)

Speedlite 430EX II

This less pricey electronic flash has a GN of 141, with automatic and manual zoom coverage from 24mm to 105mm, and the same wide-angle pullout panel found on the 580EX II that covers the area of a 14mm lens on a full-frame camera, and automatic conversion to the cropped frame area of the XS and other 1.6X crop Canon dSLRs. The 430EX II also communicates white balance information with the camera, and has its own AF assist beam. This newer version has faster recycling than the original 430EX model. Compatible with Canon's wireless E-TTL system, it makes a good slave unit, but cannot serve as a master flash. It, too, uses AA batteries, and offers recycle times of 0.1 to 3.7 seconds for 200 to 1,400 flashes, depending on subject distance.

Speedlite 220EX

Unlike the other two units, this one offers automatic operation only, and none of the fancy features of its more expensive siblings. Its 72 guide number is a little beefier than the XS's built-in flash, making it a good choice as a low-power auxiliary flash unit. It lacks a zoomable flash head and offers fixed coverage equivalent to the field of view of a 28mm full-frame lens. Expect 250 to 1,700 flashes from a set of four AA batteries and recycle times of 0.1 to 4.5 seconds. The built-in AF assist beam is linked to the center focusing point of the XS only.

More Advanced Lighting Techniques

As you advance in your Canon EOS Rebel XS photography, you'll want to learn more sophisticated lighting techniques, using more than just straight-on flash, or using just a single flash unit. Entire books have been written on lighting techniques. I recommend *David Busch's Quick Snap Guide to Lighting.* I swear I've read every single word in this book, cover to cover. I'm going to provide a quick introduction to some of the techniques you should be considering.

Diffusing and Softening the Light

Direct light can be harsh and glaring, especially if you're using the flash built into your camera, or an auxiliary flash mounted in the hot shoe and pointed directly at your subject. The first thing you should do is stop using direct light (unless you're looking for a stark, contrasty appearance as a creative effect). There are a number of simple things you can do with both continuous and flash illumination.

- **Use window light.** Light coming in a window can be soft and flattering if it consists of light reflected off the sky or clouds, and a good choice for human subjects. Or, if the light is direct, such as sunlight streaming through the window, it can be strong and dramatic, as you can see in Figure 7.8. Move your subject close enough to the window that its light provides the primary source of illumination. You might want to turn off other lights in the room, particularly to avoid mixing daylight and incandescent light.

- **Use fill light.** Your XS's built-in flash makes a perfect fill-in light for the shadows, brightening inky depths with a kicker of illumination. (See Figure 7.9.)

- **Bounce the light.** External electronic flash units mounted on the XS usually have a swivel that allows them to be pointed up at a ceiling for a bounce light effect. You

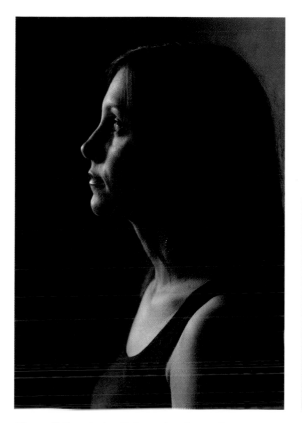

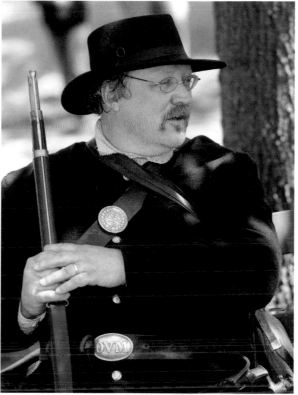

Figure 7.8 Window light makes the perfect illumination for side-lit portraits like this one.

Figure 7.9 The built-in flash filled in the shadows in this photo of a Civil War re-enactor.

can also bounce the light off a wall. You'll want the ceiling or wall to be white or have a neutral gray color to avoid a color cast.

- **Use reflectors.** Another way to bounce the light is to use reflectors or umbrellas that you can position yourself to provide a greater degree of control over the quantity and direction of the bounced light. Good reflectors can be pieces of foamboard, Mylar, or a reflective disk held in place by a clamp and stand. Although some expensive umbrellas and reflectors are available, spending a lot isn't necessary. A simple piece of white foamboard does the job beautifully. Umbrellas have the advantage of being compact and foldable, while providing a soft, even kind of light. They're relatively cheap, too, with a good 40-inch umbrella available for as little as $20.

- **Use diffusers.** Sto-Fen and some other vendors offer clip-on diffusers like the one shown in Figures 7.10 and 7.11, that fit over your electronic flash head and provide a soft, flattering light. These add-ons are more portable than umbrellas and other reflectors, yet provide a nice diffuse lighting effect.

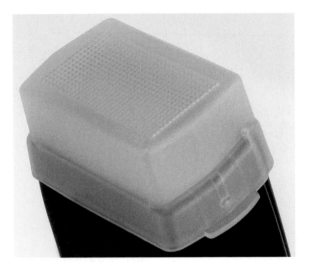

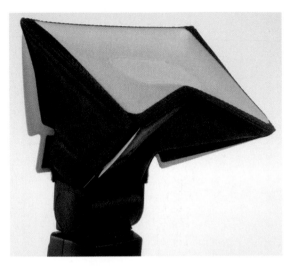

Figure 7.10 The Sto-Fen OmniBounce is a clip-on diffuser that softens the light of an external flash unit.

Figure 7.11 Small softboxes use Velcro strips to attach them to third-party flash units (like the one shown) or any Canon external flash.

Using Multiple Light Sources

Once you gain control over the qualities and effects you get with a single light source, you'll want to graduate to using multiple light sources. Using several lights allows you to shape and mold the illumination of your subjects to provide a variety of effects, from backlighting to side lighting to more formal portrait lighting. You can start simply with several incandescent light sources, bounced off umbrellas or reflectors that you construct. Or you can use more flexible multiple electronic flash setups.

Effective lighting is the one element that differentiates great photography from candid or snapshot shooting. Lighting can make a mundane subject look a little more glamorous—make subjects appear to be soft when you want a soft look, or bright and sparkly when you want a vivid look, or strong and dramatic if that's what you desire. As you might guess, having control over your lighting means that you probably can't use the lights that are already in the room. You'll need separate, discrete lighting fixtures that can be moved, aimed, brightened, and dimmed on command.

Selecting your lighting gear will depend on the type of photography you do, and the budget you have to support it. It's entirely possible for a beginning XS photographer to create a basic, inexpensive lighting system capable of delivering high-quality results for a few hundred dollars, just as you can spend megabucks ($1,000 and up) for a sophisticated lighting system.

Basic Flash Setups

If you want to use multiple electronic flash units, the Canon Speedlites described earlier will serve admirably. The two higher-end models can be used with Canon's wireless E-TTL feature, which allows you to set up to three separate groups of flash units (several flashes can be included in each group) and trigger them using a master flash (such as the 580EX II) and the camera. Just set up one master unit (there's a switch on the unit's foot that sets it for master mode) and arrange the compatible slave units around your subject. You can set the relative power of each unit separately, thereby controlling how much of the scene's illumination comes from the main flash, and how much from the auxiliary flash units, which can be used as fill flash, background lights, or, if you're careful, to illuminate the hair of portrait subjects.

Studio Flash

If you're serious about using multiple flash units, a studio flash setup might be more practical. The traditional studio flash is a multi-part unit, consisting of a flash head that mounts on your light stand, and is tethered to an AC (or sometimes battery) power supply. A single power supply can feed two or more flash heads at a time, with separate control over the output of each head.

When they are operating off AC power, studio flash don't have to be frugal with the juice, and are often powerful enough to illuminate very large subjects or to supply lots and lots of light to smaller subjects. The output of such units is measured in watt seconds (ws), so you could purchase a 200ws, 400ws, or 800ws unit, and a power pack to match.

Their advantages include greater power output, much faster recycling, built-in modeling lamps, multiple power levels, and ruggedness that can stand up to transport, because many photographers pack up these kits and tote them around as location lighting rigs. Studio lighting kits can range in price from a few hundred dollars for a set of lights, stands, and reflectors, to thousands for a high-end lighting system complete with all the necessary accessories.

A more practical choice these days are *monolights* (see Figure 7.12), which are "all-in-one" studio lights that sell for about $200-$400. They have the flash tube, modeling light, and power supply built into a single unit that can be mounted on a light stand. Monolights are available in AC-only and battery-pack versions, although an external battery eliminates some of the advantages of having a flash with everything in one unit. They are very portable, because all you need is a case for the monolight itself, plus the stands and other accessories you want to carry along. Because these units are so popular with photographers who are not full-time professionals, the lower-cost monolights are often designed more for lighter duty than professional studio flash. That doesn't mean they aren't rugged; you'll just need to handle them with a little more care, and, perhaps, not expect them to be used eight hours a day for weeks on end. In most other respects, however, monolights are the equal of traditional studio flash units in terms of fast recycling, built-in modeling lamps, adjustable power, and so forth.

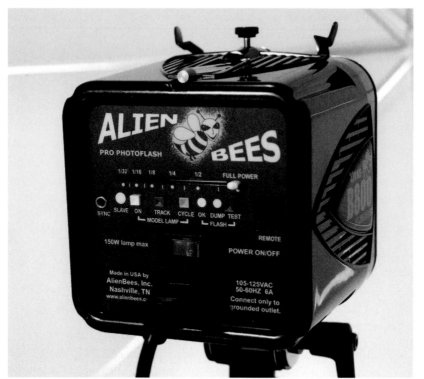

Figure 7.12
All-in-one "monolights" contain flash, power supply, and a modeling light in one compact package (umbrella not included).

Connecting Multiple Units to Your Canon EOS Rebel XS

Non-dedicated electronic flash units can't use the automated E-TTL II features of your Rebel XS; you'll need to calculate exposure manually, through test shots evaluated on your camera's LCD, or by using an electronic flash meter. Moreover, you don't have to connect them to the accessory shoe on top of the camera. Instead, you can use an adapter in the hot shoe to provide a PC/X connector, and use a shutter speed of 1/60th second or slower.

You should be aware that older electronic flash units sometimes use a triggering voltage that is too much for your XS to handle. You can actually damage the camera's electronics if the voltage is too high. You won't need to worry about this if you purchase brand new units from Alien Bees, Adorama, or other vendors. But if you must connect an external flash with an unknown triggering voltage, I recommend using a Wein Safe Sync (see Figure 7.13), which isolates the flash's voltage from the camera triggering circuit, and provides a PC/X adapter for plugging in non-dedicated flash units.

Another safe way to connect external cameras is through a radio-control device, such as the transmitter/receiver set shown in Figure 7.14. It piggybacks onto the PC/X adapter you've fastened to your hot shoe, and plugs into your adaptor's PC/X connector. It transmits a signal to a matching receiver that's connected to your flash unit. The receiver has both a PC connector of its own as well as a "monoplug" connector (it looks like a head-phone plug) that links to a matching port on compatible flash units.

Finally, some flash units have an optical slave trigger built in, or can be fitted with one, so that they fire automatically when another flash, including your camera's built-in unit, fires.

Figure 7.13
A voltage isolator can prevent frying your XS's flash circuits if you use an older electronic flash, and it provides a PC/X connector, which the Rebel XS lacks.

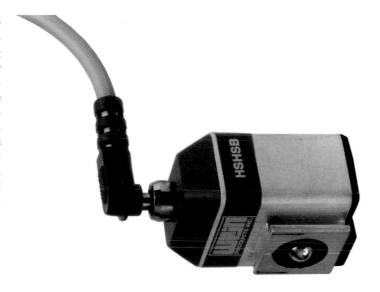

Figure 7.14
A radio-control device frees you from a sync cord tether between your flash and camera.

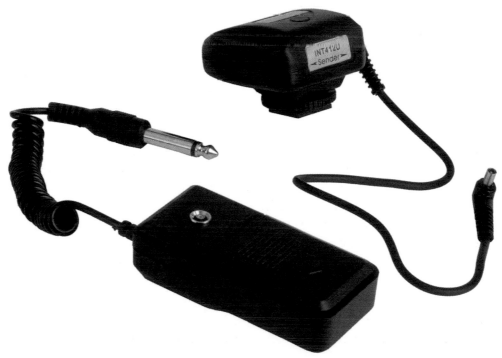

Other Lighting Accessories

Once you start working with light, you'll find there are plenty of useful accessories that can help you. Here are some of the most popular that you might want to consider.

Soft Boxes

Soft boxes are large square or rectangular devices that may resemble a square umbrella with a front cover, and produce a similar lighting effect. They can extend from a few feet square to massive boxes that stand five or six feet tall—virtually a wall of light. With a flash unit or two inside a soft box, you have a large, semi-directional light source that's very diffuse and very flattering for portraiture and other people photography. (See Figure 7.15.)

Soft boxes are also handy for photographing shiny objects. They not only provide a soft light, but if the box itself happens to reflect in the subject (say you're photographing a chromium toaster), the box will provide an interesting highlight that's indistinct and not distracting.

You can buy soft boxes or make your own. Some lengths of friction-fit plastic pipe and a lot of muslin cut and sewed just so may be all that you need.

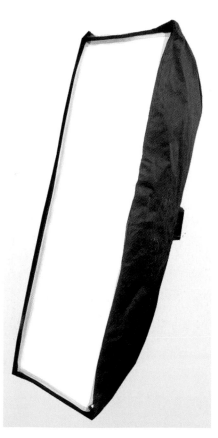

Figure 7.15
Large softboxes provide gentle, diffuse lighting.

Light Stands

Both electronic flash and incandescent lamps can benefit from light stands. These are lightweight, tripod-like devices (but without a swiveling or tilting head) that can be set on the floor, tabletops, or other elevated surfaces and positioned as needed. Light stands should be strong enough to support an external lighting unit, up to and including a relatively heavy flash with soft box or umbrella reflectors. You want the supports to be capable of raising the lights high enough to be effective. Look for light stands capable of extending six to seven feet high. The nine-foot units usually have larger, steadier bases, and extend high enough that you can use them as background supports. You'll be using these stands for a lifetime, so invest in good ones. I bought the light stand shown in Figure 7.16 when I was in college, and I have been using it for decades.

Figure 7.16
Light stands can hold lights, umbrellas, backdrops, and other equipment.

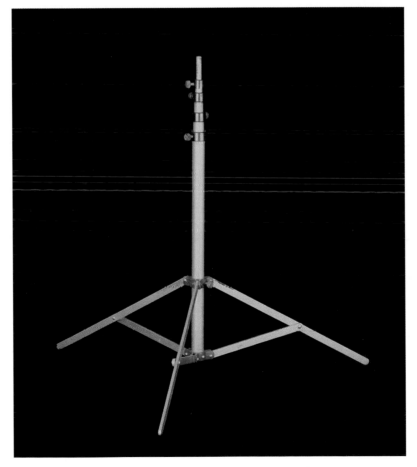

Backgrounds

Backgrounds can be backdrops of cloth, sheets of muslin you've painted yourself using a sponge dipped in paint, rolls of seamless paper, or any other suitable surface your mind can dream up. Backgrounds provide a complementary and non-distracting area behind subjects (especially portraits) and can be lit separately to provide contrast and separation that outlines the subject, or which helps set a mood.

I like to use plain-colored backgrounds for portraits, and white seamless backgrounds for product photography. You can usually construct these yourself from cheap materials and tape them up on the wall behind your subject, or mount them on a pole stretched between a pair of light stands.

Snoots and Barn Doors

These fit over the flash unit and direct the light at your subject. Snoots are excellent for converting a flash unit into a hair light, while barn doors give you enough control over the illumination by opening and closing their flaps that you can use another flash as a background light, with the capability of feathering the light exactly where you want it on the background. Both are shown in Figure 7.17.

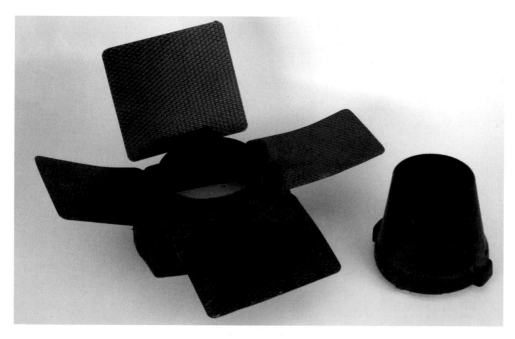

Figure 7.17
Snoots and barn doors allow you to modulate the light from a flash or lamp, and they are especially useful for hair lights and background lights.

8

Downloading and Editing Your Images

Taking the picture is only half the work and, in some cases, only half the fun. After you've captured some great images and have them safely stored on your Canon EOS Rebel XS's memory card, you'll need to transfer them from your camera and memory card to your computer, where they can be organized, fine-tuned in an image editor, and prepared for web display, printing, or some other final destination.

Fortunately, there are lots of software utilities and applications to help you do all these things. This chapter will introduce you to a few of them.

What's in the Box?

Your Canon EOS Rebel XS came with software programs on CD for both Windows PCs and Macs. Pop the CD into your computer and it will self-install a selection of these useful applications and utilities. Manuals for all these programs are included on CD, too, but here's a summary of what you get on the EOS Digital Solutions disk:

Picture Style Editor

The Picture Style Editor, shown in Figure 8.1, allows you to create your own custom Picture Styles, or edit existing styles, including the Standard, Landscape, Faithful, and other predefined settings already present in your Rebel XS. You can change sharpness, contrast, color saturation, and color tone—and a lot more—and then save the modifications as a .PF2 file that can be uploaded to the camera, or used by Digital Photo Professional (described later in this chapter) to modify a RAW image as it is imported.

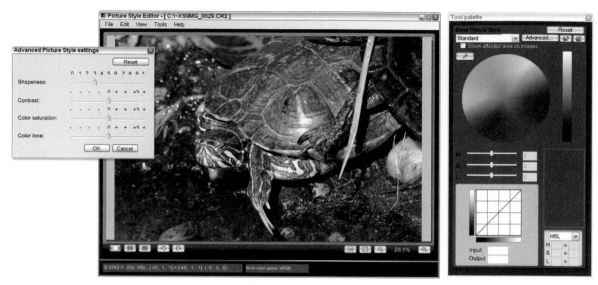

Figure 8.1 The new Picture Style Editor lets you create your own Picture Styles for use by the XS or Digital Photo Professional when importing image files.

You can define your own color response using a color picker in a sample RAW photograph to choose a specific hue, which you can then modify using hue/saturation/luminance adjustments. The range of adjacent colors affected by your new settings can also be specified. Before/after views let you compare the Picture Style settings you've entered with standard settings using a sample image you upload.

Among the most valuable features of the Canon EOS Rebel XS is its compatibility with Canon's Picture Style Editor (PSE, not to be confused with the "other" PSE—Adobe Photoshop Elements) software. With PSE, shooters can actually design the look of their photographs by inputting their own preferred style, color, and tone curves. The Rebel XS also ships with the latest versions of Canon's powerful software applications, including Digital Photo Professional and EOS Utility, which now support the camera's Remote Live View and Dust Delete Data functions, as well as incorporating a broad range of additional improvements designed to enhance image quality and speed up workflow. Also included are ZoomBrowser EX and ImageBrowser for easy browsing, viewing, printing, and archiving with compatible computer operating systems, including Microsoft Windows Vista and Windows XP, as well as Mac OS X.

EOS Utility

Both Windows and Mac versions are provided for this useful program. It serves as command center for several useful functions, all available from the main control panel, shown in Figure 8.2. It includes an image downloading module that previews the images in your XS, and can automatically copy them from the camera to either Digital Photo Professional or ZoomBrowser EX (see Figure 8.3).

Figure 8.2
The EOS Utility has a settings/remote shooting function that allows you to control an XS connected to your computer with the USB cable.

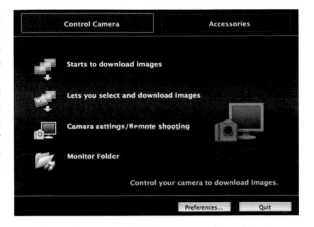

Figure 8.3
The download utility allows transfer of photos from your camera or memory card to Digital Photo Professional or ZoomBrowser EX.

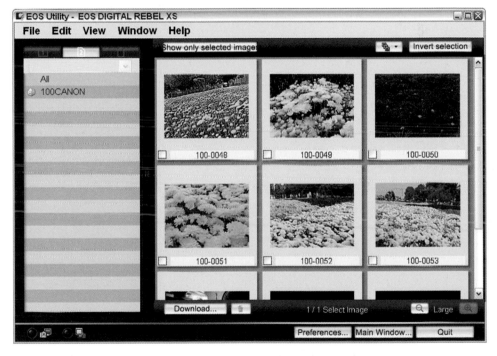

It also includes a camera settings/remote shooting module that allows you to link your computer with the XS and use a dialog box (see Figure 8.4) to change camera settings and to control the camera for remote shooting. You can have access to many of the XS's menus right from the software (see Figure 8.5). The settings feature is especially useful for changing Picture Styles quickly, while you'll find the remote shooting capabilities useful when you want to program a delay before the camera takes a picture, or do some interval (time-lapse) shooting. The updated version of the utility (Version 2.1 and later) supports the XS's Live View and Dust Delete Data functions. It includes many preferences you can use to tailor its operation (see Figure 8.6).

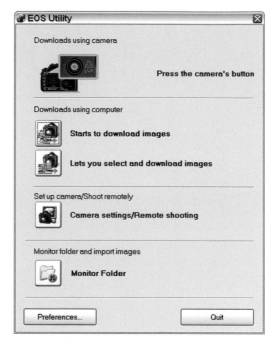

Figure 8.4
The EOS Utility gives you direct control of camera settings for remote shooting.

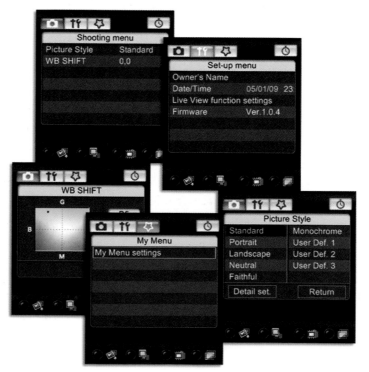

Figure 8.5
You can access many of the Rebel XS's menu settings from your computer.

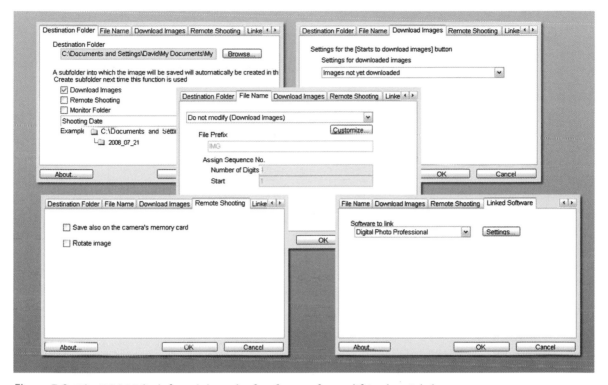

Figure 8.6 The EOS Utility's five tabs' worth of preferences for modifying how it behaves.

ZoomBrowser/ImageBrowser

This is an image viewing and editing application for Windows PCs (the equivalent program for Macs is called ImageBrowser and performs the same functions). You can organize, sort, classify, and rename files, and convert JPEG files in batches. This utility is especially useful for printing index sheets of groups of images (see Figure 8.7). It can also prepare images for e-mailing. It works with RAW Image Task for converting CR2 files to some more widely accepted formats.

The simple image-editing facilities of ZoomBrowser allow red-eye correction, brightness/contrast and color correction, manipulating sharpness, trimming photos, and a few other functions. For more complex editing, you can transfer images directly from this application to Photoshop or another image editor. The ImageBrowser version for Macs has the ability to insert text; can adjust Levels, Sharpness, and Tone Curves; can port the image over to the ArcSoft application; as well as print and e-mail images.

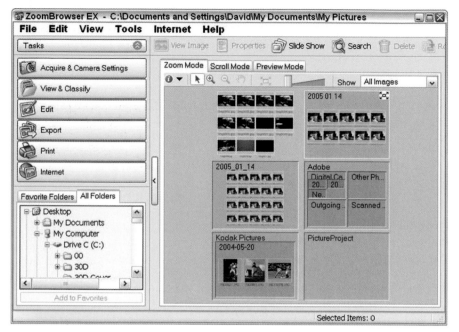

Figure 8.7
ZoomBrowser allows organizing your images and performing common fixes.

PhotoStitch

This Windows/Mac utility allows you to take several JPEG images and combine them to create a panorama in a single new file. You can choose the images to be merged in ZoomBrowser and then transfer them to PhotoStitch, or operate the utility as a stand-alone module and select the images using the standard File > Open commands (see Figure 8.8).

Digital Photo Professional

While far from a Photoshop replacement, Digital Photo Professional is a useful image-editing program that helps you organize, trim, correct, and print images. You can make RAW adjustments, correct tonal curves, color tone, color saturation, sharpness, as well as brightness and contrast. Especially handy are the "recipes" that can be developed and saved so that a given set of corrections can be kept separate from the file itself, and, if desired, applied to other images (see Figure 8.9).

Figure 8.8
Panoramas
are easy to
create with
PhotoStitch.

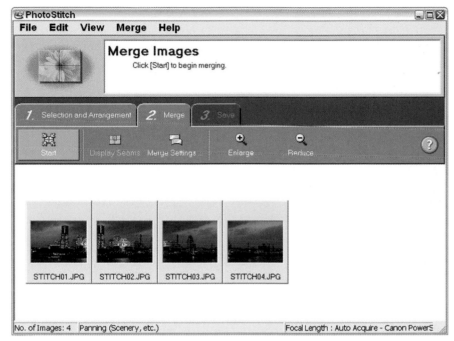

Figure 8.9
Digital Photo
Professional
will never
replace Photo-
shop, but it has
some basic
image editing
features.

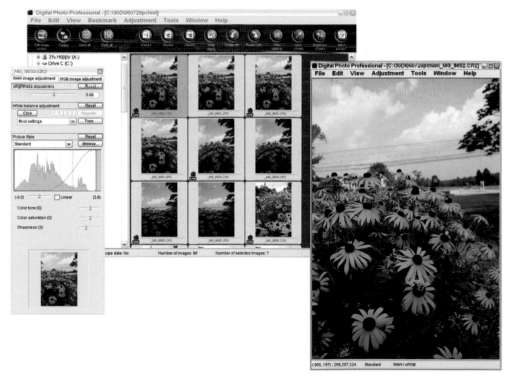

Transferring Your Photos

While it's rewarding to capture some great images and have them ensconced in your camera, eventually you'll be transferring them to your laptop or PC, whether you're using a Windows or Macintosh machine. You have three options for image transfer: direct transfer over a USB cable, automated transfer using a card reader and transfer software such as the EOS Utility or Adobe Photoshop Elements Photo Downloader, or manual transfer using drag and drop from a memory card inserted in a card reader.

Direct-Direct Transfer/Indirect-Direct Transfer

There are some advantages to transferring photos directly from your Rebel XS to a computer. The destination computer doesn't need to have a card reader; all it requires is a USB port. So, if you have the USB cable that came with your camera, you can transfer photos to any computer that has the Canon utility software installed. However, direct transfer uses your XS's internal battery power, while removing the card and transferring the photos with a card reader installed on the destination computer does not.

You can select which images are transferred to the computer, or transfer all the images, both RAW and JPEG, that are on the memory card. Canon gives you two different methods, one using the camera to direct the transfer process (I call this Direct-Direct Transfer), and one using both the camera and software on your computer to manage the transfer (I call this Indirect-Direct Transfer—for no good reason). Both methods require that you install the software furnished with the Rebel XS, including the EOS Utility and Digital Photo Professional. The CD bundled with your camera has versions of each for both Macintosh and Windows.

Direct-Direct Transfer

With this option, you don't have to fiddle with the software on your computer. The camera does all the work (so don't look for options on your computer!). You lose the ability to customize your transfer (say, to rename the files as they are deposited on your computer), but the process is fast and easy. Just follow these steps:

1. Connect the USB cable to the USB terminal on the left side of the Rebel XS (under the rubber cover, as seen from shooting position), and plug the other end into a USB port on the destination computer (which you have cleverly turned on in anticipation of this transfer).

2. Turn on the Rebel XS. The Direct Transfer screen shown in Figure 8.10 will appear on the camera's LCD screen, and the blue transfer LED located to the right of the Print/Share button on the back of the camera will illuminate.

Figure 8.10
You can transfer images directly from your camera to the computer using the Rebel XS as the controller.

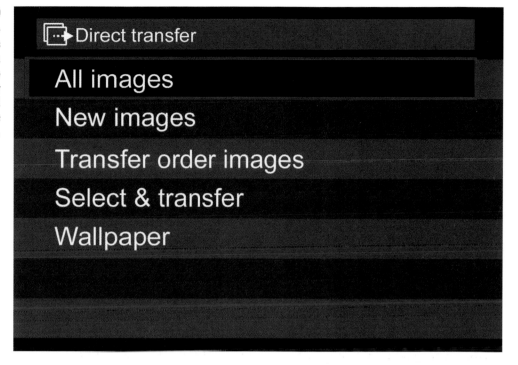

3. Choose one of these options:

   ■ **All Images** to transfer all images on the memory card.

   ■ **New Images** to transfer only images that haven't already been transferred.

   ■ **Transfer Order Images** to transfer images that have already been marked as described in the next section.

   ■ **Select and Transfer** if you'd like to choose specific images to be transferred. (This option is not selectable until you've marked at least some images for transfer, as described in the next section.)

   ■ **Wallpaper** to create a copy of an image that can be used as wallpaper on the desktop of your computer.

4. Press Set or the Print/Share button (illuminated with that blue LED) to start the transfer.

5. Press the Menu button when finished to exit.

Your photos will be transferred automatically, and Digital Photo Professional will open to display thumbnails of the images.

Indirect-Direct Transfer

You can also use a combination of camera selections and the EOS Utility software included with your camera to transfer photos. This option allows you to choose which images to transfer, and to apply various preferences to the process, such as renaming the files to reflect their content.

Follow these steps to transfer your photos using this method:

1. Press the Menu button and select Transfer order selection in the Playback menu. Press Set. You'll see a screen like the one in Figure 8.11.

2. Turn the Main dial to select either All image (if you want to transfer every image) or Sel. Image (if you want to transfer the selected images). Press Set.

3a. If you've chosen All image, choose Mark All and press Set, then press the Menu button to exit this selection screen and store your choice to the memory card. Continue with Step 4.

3b. If you've selected Sel. Image, the transfer image selection screen appears. Use the Main dial to scroll through the available images. Press the Thumbnail/Zoom Out button to toggle between a three-image and single-image view. When an image you want to transfer is highlighted, press the Set button to add a checkmark to the box in the upper-left corner of the image. If you change your mind, press Set again to

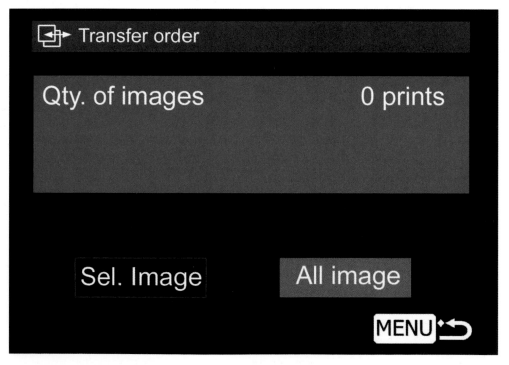

Figure 8.11

Choose to copy a transfer order of selected images, or all images.

unmark the image. Choose all the images you want to transfer, and press Menu to exit this selection screen, and Menu again to store your choices on the memory card.

4. Connect the USB cable to the DIGITAL terminal on the left side of the Rebel XS (under the rubber cover) and plug the other end into a USB port on the destination computer.

5. Turn on the Rebel XS. The EOS Utility will appear, ready to download your photos. (If you have another program installed that also has a transfer utility, such as Adobe Photoshop Elements' Photo Downloader, it may pop up as well. Close that window if you want to use the EOS Utility.)

6. Use the controls within the EOS Utility to activate the transfer process.

Using a Card Reader and Software

You can also use a memory card reader and software to transfer photos and automate the process using the EOS Utility, Photoshop Elements' Photo Downloader, or the downloading program supplied with some other third-party applications. This method is more frugal in its use of your XS's battery and can be faster if you have a speedy USB 2.0 or FireWire card reader attached to an appropriate port.

The installed software automatically remains in memory as you work, and it recognizes when a memory card is inserted in your card reader; you don't have to launch it yourself. With Photoshop Elements' Photo Downloader, you can click Get Photos to begin the transfer of all images immediately or choose Advanced Dialog to produce a dialog box like the one shown in Figure 8.12, and then select which images to download from

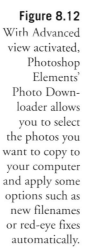

Figure 8.12
With Advanced view activated, Photoshop Elements' Photo Downloader allows you to select the photos you want to copy to your computer and apply some options such as new filenames or red-eye fixes automatically.

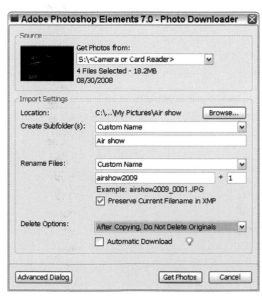

the memory card by marking them with a check. You can select the photos you want to transfer, plus options such as Automatically Fix Red Eyes. Start the download, and a confirmation dialog box like the one in Figure 8.13 shows the progress.

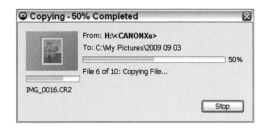

Figure 8.13
The Photo Downloader's confirmation dialog box shows the progress as images are transferred.

Dragging and Dropping

The final way to move photos from your memory card to your computer is the old-fashioned way: manually dragging and dropping the files from one window on your computer to another. The procedure works pretty much the same whether you're using a Mac or a PC.

1. Remove the memory card from the Rebel XS and insert it in your memory card reader.

2. Using Windows Explorer, My Computer, or your Mac desktop, open the icon representing the memory card, which appears on your desktop as just another disk drive.

3. Open a second window representing the folder on your computer that you want to use as the destination for the files you are copying or moving.

4. Drag and drop the files from the memory card window to the folder on your computer. You can select individual files, press Ctrl/Command+A to select all the files, or Ctrl/Command+click to select multiple files.

Editing Your Photos

Image manipulation tasks fall into several categories. You might want to fine-tune your images, retouch them, change color balance, composite several images together, and perform other tasks we know as image editing, with a program like Adobe Photoshop, Photoshop Elements, or Corel Photo Paint.

You might want to play with the settings in RAW files, too, as you import them from their .CR2 state into an image editor. There are specialized tools expressly for tweaking RAW files, ranging from Canon's own Digital Photo Professional to Adobe Camera

Raw, and PhaseOne's Capture One Pro (C1 Pro). A third type of manipulation is the specialized task of noise reduction, which can be performed within Photoshop, Adobe Camera Raw, or tools like Bibble Professional. There are also specialized tools just for noise reduction, such as Noise Ninja (also included with Bibble) and Neat Image.

Each of these utilities and applications deserves a chapter of its own, so I'm simply going to enumerate some of the most popular image-editing and RAW conversion programs here and tell you a little about what they do.

Image Editors

Image editors are general-purpose photo-editing applications that can do color correction, tonal modifications, retouching, combining of several images into one, and usually include tools for working with RAW files and reducing noise. So, you'll find programs like those listed here good for all-around image manipulation. The leading programs are as follows:

Adobe Photoshop/Photoshop Elements. Photoshop is the serious photographer's number one choice for image editing, and Elements is an excellent option for those who need most of Photoshop's power, but not all of its professional-level features. Unfortunately, unlike Photoshop's simultaneous debut of PC/Mac editions, Adobe's releases of Elements for the Macintosh tend to lag behind the Windows versions. While Elements 7 for Windows was introduced about a month after the Rebel XS, the Macintosh edition still isn't available as I write this. Both editors use the latest version of Adobe's Camera Raw plug-in, which makes it easy to adjust things like color space profiles, color depth (either 8 bits or 16 bits per color channel), image resolution, white balance, exposure, shadows, brightness, sharpness, luminance, and noise reduction. One plus with the Adobe products is that they are available in identical versions for both Windows and Macs (eventually!).

Corel Photo Paint. This is the image-editing program that is included in the popular CorelDRAW Graphics suite. Although a Mac version was available in the past, this is primarily a Windows application today. It's a full-featured photo retouching and image-editing program with selection, retouching, and painting tools for manual image manipulations, and it also includes convenient automated commands for a few common tasks, such as red-eye removal. Photo Paint accepts Photoshop plug-ins to expand its assortment of filters and special effects.

Corel Paint Shop Pro. This is a general-purpose Windows-only image editor that has gained a reputation as the "poor man's Photoshop" for providing a substantial portion of Photoshop's capabilities at a fraction of the cost. It includes a nifty set of wizard-like commands that automate common tasks, such as removing red eye and scratches, as well as filters and effects, which can be expanded with other Photoshop plug-ins.

Macromedia Fireworks. This is the image-editing program for Macs and PCs formerly from Macromedia, and now owned by Adobe, and it is most useful when used with web development and animation software like Dreamweaver and Flash. If you're using your Rebel XS images on web pages, you'll like this program's capabilities in the web graphics arena, such as banners, image maps, and rollover buttons.

Corel Painter. Here's another image-editing program from Corel for both Mac and Windows. This one's strength is in mimicking natural media, such as charcoal, pastels, and various kinds of paint. Painter includes a basic assortment of tools that you can use to edit existing images, but the program is really designed for artists to use in creating original illustrations. As a photographer, you might prefer another image editor, but if you like to paint on top of your photographic images, nothing else really does the job of Painter.

Corel PhotoImpact. Corel finally brought one of the last remaining non-Adobe image editors into its fold when it acquired Ulead PhotoImpact. This is a general-purpose photo-editing program for Windows with a huge assortment of brushes for painting, retouching, and cloning, in addition to the usual selection, cropping, and fill tools. If you frequently find yourself performing the same image manipulations on a number of files, you'll appreciate PhotoImpact's batch operations. Using this feature, you can select multiple image files and then apply any one of a long list of filters, enhancements, or auto-process commands to all the selected files.

RAW Utilities

Your software choices for manipulating RAW files are broader than you might think. Camera vendors always supply a utility to read their cameras' own RAW files, but sometimes, particularly with those point-and-shoot cameras that can produce RAW files, the options are fairly limited. Most Canon dSLR users have gone beyond the Canon File View Utility to something better from third parties, such as Capture1. Other vendors, such as Nikon (with its Nikon Capture), offer RAW file handling that is much more flexible and powerful.

Because in the past digital camera vendors offered RAW converters that weren't very good (Canon's File View Utility comes to mind), there is a lively market for third-party RAW utilities available at extra cost. However, the EOS Utility and Digital Photo Professional do a good job and may be all that you need.

The third-party solutions are usually available as standalone applications (often for both Windows and Macintosh platforms), as Photoshop-compatible plug-ins, or both. Because the RAW plug-ins displace Photoshop's own RAW converter, I tend to prefer to use most RAW utilities in standalone mode. That way, if I choose to open a file directly in Photoshop, it automatically opens using Photoshop's fast and easy-to-use Adobe Camera Raw (ACR) plug-in. If I have more time or need the capabilities of another converter, I can load that, open the file, and make my corrections there. Most are able to transfer the processed file directly to Photoshop even if you aren't using plug-in mode.

This section provides a quick overview of the range of RAW file handlers, so you can get a better idea of the kinds of information available with particular applications. I'm going to include both high-end and low-end RAW browsers so you can see just what is available.

Digital Photo Professional

Digital Photo Professional, introduced earlier in this chapter (see Figure 8.9), is preferred by many for Canon dSLR cameras like the Rebel XS.

DPP offers much higher-speed processing of RAW images than was available with the late, not lamented, sluggardly File Viewer Utility (as much as six times faster). Canon says this utility rivals third-party standalone and plug-in RAW converters in speed and features. It supports both Canon's original CRW format and the newer CR2 RAW format used by the XS, along with TIFF, Exif TIFF, and JPEG.

You can save settings that include multiple adjustments and apply them to other images, and use the clever comparison mode to compare your original and edited versions of an image either side by side or within a single split image. The utility allows easy adjustment of color channels, tone curves, exposure compensation, white balance, dynamic range, brightness, contrast, color saturation, ICC Profile embedding, and assignment of monitor profiles. A new feature is the ability to continue editing images while batches of previously adjusted RAW files are rendered and saved in the background.

IrfanView

At the low (free) end of the price scale is IrfanView (see Figure 8.14), a Windows freeware program you can download at www.irfanview.com. It can read many common RAW photo formats. It's a quick way to view RAW files (just drag and drop to the IrfanView window) and make fast changes to the unprocessed file. You can crop, rotate, or correct your image, and do some cool things like swap the colors around (red for blue, blue for green, and so forth) to create false color pictures.

The price is right, and IrfanView has some valuable capabilities. Check out www.irfanview.com.

Phase One Capture One Pro (C1 Pro)

If there is a Cadillac of RAW converters for Nikon and Canon digital SLR cameras, C1 Pro has to be it. This premium-priced program does everything, does it well, and does it quickly. If you can't justify the price tag of this professional-level software, there are "lite" versions for serious amateurs and cash-challenged professionals called Capture One dSLR and Capture One dSLR SE.

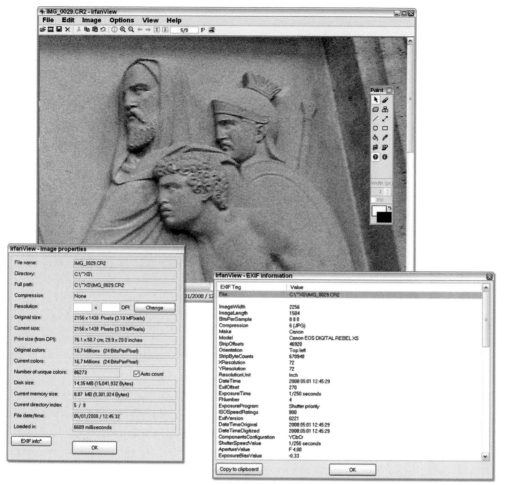

Figure 8.14
IrfanView is a freeware program that can read many RAW file formats, including the XS's CR2 format.

Aimed at photographers with high-volume needs (that would include school and portrait photographers, as well as busy commercial photographers), C1 Pro (shown in Figure 8.15) is available for both Windows and Mac OS X, and supports a broad range of Canon digital cameras. Phase One is a leading supplier of megabucks digital camera backs for medium and larger format cameras, so they really understand the needs of photographers.

The latest features include individual noise reduction controls for each image, automatic levels adjustment, a "quick develop" option that allows speedy conversion from RAW to TIFF or JPEG formats, dual-image side-by-side views for comparison purposes, and helpful grids and guides that can be superimposed over an image. Photographers concerned about copyright protection will appreciate the ability to add watermarks to the output images. See www.phaseone.com.

Figure 8.15

Phase One's C1 Pro is fast and sophisticated.

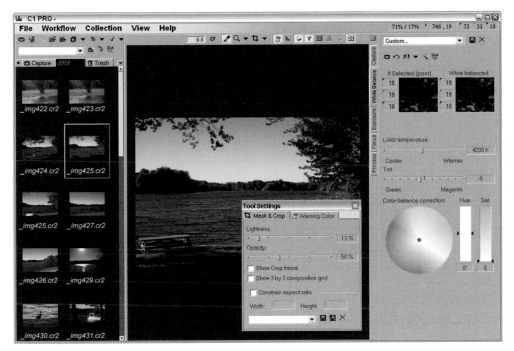

Bibble Pro

One of my personal favorites among third-party RAW converters is Bibble Pro (shown in Figure 8.16), which just came out with a new version as I was writing this book. It supports one of the broadest ranges of RAW file formats available (which can be handy if you find yourself with the need to convert a file from a friend or colleague's non-Canon camera), including NEF files from the Nikon D1,D1x/h, D2H, D100; .CRW files from the Canon C30/D60/10D/300D; .CR2 files from the Canon EOS Rebel XS and other newer models; .ORF files from the Olympus E10/E20/E1/C5050/C5060; .DCR files from the Kodak 720x/760/14n; .RAF files from the Fuji S2Pro; .PEF files from Pentax ISTD; .MRW files from the Minolta Maxxum; and .TIF from Canon 1D/1DS.

The utility supports lots of different platforms, too. It's available for Windows, Mac OS X, and, believe it or not, Linux.

Bibble works fast because it offers instantaneous previews and real-time feedback as changes are made. That's important when you have to convert many images in a short time. Bibble's batch-processing capabilities also let you convert large numbers of files using settings you specify without further intervention.

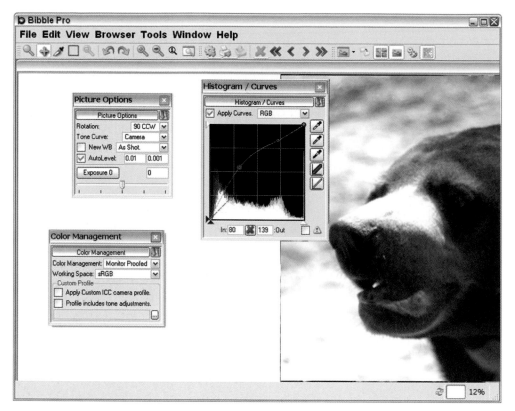

Figure 8.16
Bibble Pro supports a broad range of RAW file formats.

Its customizable interface lets you organize and edit images quickly and then output them in a variety of formats, including 16-bit TIFF and PNG. You can even create a web gallery from within Bibble. I often find myself disliking the generic filenames applied to digital images by cameras, so I really like Bibble's ability to rename batches of files using new names that you specify.

Bibble is fully color managed, which means it can support all the popular color spaces (Adobe sRGB and so forth) and use custom profiles generated by third-party color-management software. There are two editions of Bibble, a Pro version and a Lite version. Because the Pro version is reasonably priced at $129, I don't really see the need to save $60 with the Lite edition, which lacks the top-line's options for tethered shooting, embedding IPTC-compatible captions in images, and can also be used as a Photoshop plug-in (if you prefer not to work with the application in its standalone mode). Bibble Pro now incorporates Noise Ninja technology, so you can get double-duty from this valuable application. See www.bibblelabs.com.

BreezeBrowser

BreezeBrowser, shown in Figure 8.17, was long the RAW converter of choice for Canon dSLR owners who run Windows and who were dissatisfied with Canon's lame antique File Viewer Utility. It works quickly and has lots of options for converting CRW and CR2 files to other formats. You can choose to show highlights that will be blown out in your finished photo as flashing areas (so they can be more easily identified and corrected), use histograms to correct tones, add color profiles, auto rotate images, and adjust all those raw image parameters, such as white balance, color space, saturation, contrast, sharpening, color tone, EV compensation, and other settings.

You can also control noise reduction (choosing from low, normal, or high reduction), evaluate your changes in the live preview, and then save the file as a compressed JPEG or as either an 8-bit or 16-bit TIFF file. BreezeBrowser can also create HTML web galleries directly from your selection of images. See www.breezesys.com.

Figure 8.17
BreezeBrowser makes converting Canon RAW files a breeze.

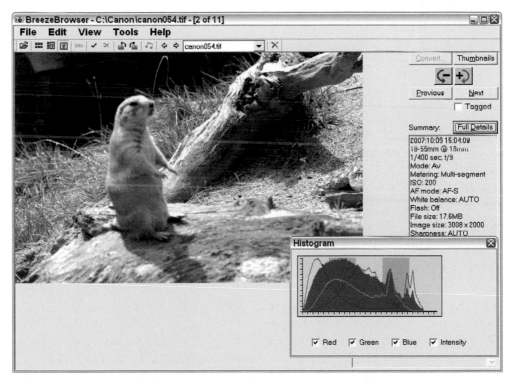

Adobe Photoshop

Adobe Photoshop includes a built-in RAW plug-in that is compatible with the proprietary formats of a growing number of digital cameras, both new and old. This plug-in also works with Photoshop Elements. Note that it's always advisable to visit the Adobe downloads site from time to time, as new versions of Adobe Camera Raw are provided, with support for newer cameras and, sometimes, additional features.

To open a RAW image in Photoshop, just follow these steps (Elements users can use much the same workflow, although fewer settings are available):

1. Transfer the RAW images from your camera to your computer's hard drive.

2. In Photoshop, choose Open from the File menu, or use Bridge.

3. Select a RAW image file. The Adobe Camera Raw plug-in will pop up, showing a preview of the image, like the one shown in Figure 8.18.

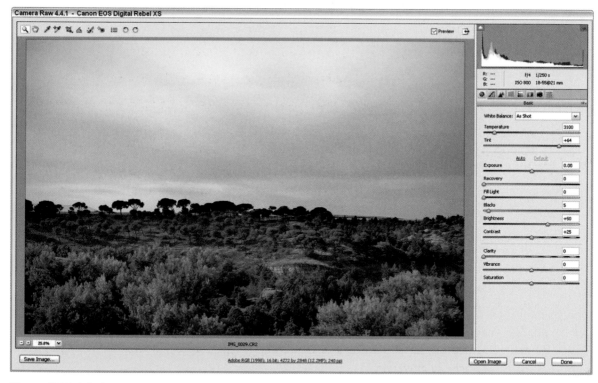

Figure 8.18 The basic ACR dialog box looks like this when processing a single image.

4. If you like, use one of the tools found in the toolbar at the top left of the dialog box. From left to right, they are as follows:

- **Zoom.** Operates just like the Zoom tool in Photoshop.

- **Hand.** Use like the Hand tool in Photoshop.

- **White Balance.** Click an area in the image that should be neutral gray or white to set the white balance quickly.

- **Color Sampler.** Use to determine the RGB values of areas you click with this eyedropper.

- **Crop.** Pre-crops the image so that only the portion you specify is imported into Photoshop. This option saves time when you want to work on a section of a large image, and you don't need the entire file.

- **Straighten.** Drag in the preview image to define what should be a horizontal or vertical line, and ACR will realign the image to straighten it.

- **Retouch.** Used to heal or clone areas you define.

- **Red-Eye Removal.** Quickly zap red pupils in your human subjects.

- **ACR Preferences.** Produces a dialog box of Adobe Camera Raw preferences.

- **Rotate Counterclockwise.** Rotates counterclockwise in 90-degree increments with a click.

- **Rotate Clockwise.** Rotates clockwise in 90-degree increments with a click.

5. Using the Basic tab, you can have ACR show you red and blue highlights in the preview that indicate shadow areas that are clipped (too dark to show detail) and light areas that are blown out (too bright). Click the triangles in the upper-left corner of the histogram display (shadow clipping) and upper-right corner (highlight clipping) to toggle these indicators on or off.

6. Also in the Basic tab you can choose white balance, either from the drop-down list or by setting a color temperature and green/magenta color bias (tint) using the sliders.

7. Other sliders are available to control exposure, recovery, fill light, blacks, brightness, contrast, vibrance, and saturation. A checkbox can be marked to convert the image to grayscale.

8. Make other adjustments (described in more detail below).

9. ACR makes automatic adjustments for you. You can click Default and make the changes for yourself, or click the Auto link (located just above the Exposure slider) to reapply the automatic adjustments after you've made your own modifications.

10. If you've marked more than one image to be opened, the additional images appear in a "filmstrip" at the left side of the screen. You can click on each thumbnail in the filmstrip in turn and apply different settings to each.

11. Click Open Image/Open image(s) into Photoshop using the settings you've made, or click Save Image at the bottom left to save the settings you've made without opening the file.

The Basic tab is displayed by default when the ACR dialog box opens, and it includes most of the sliders and controls you'll need to fine-tune your image as you import it into Photoshop. These include:

- **White Balance.** Leave it As Shot or change to a value such as Daylight, Cloudy, Shade, Tungsten, Fluorescent, or Flash. If you like, you can set a custom white balance using the Temperature and Tint sliders.

- **Exposure.** This slider adjusts the overall brightness and darkness of the image.

- **Recovery.** Restores detail in the red, green, and blue color channels.

- **Fill Light.** Reconstructs detail in shadows.

- **Blacks.** Increases the number of tones represented as black in the final image, emphasizing tones in the shadow areas of the image.

- **Brightness.** This slider adjusts the brightness and darkness of an image.

- **Contrast.** Manipulates the contrast of the midtones of your image.

- **Convert to Grayscale.** Mark this box to convert the image to black and white.

- **Vibrance.** Prevents over-saturation when enriching the colors of an image.

- **Saturation.** Manipulates the richness of all colors equally, from zero saturation (gray/black, no color) at the −100 setting to double the usual saturation at the +100 setting.

Additional controls are available on the Tone Curve, Detail, HSL/Grayscale, Split Toning, Lens Corrections, Camera Calibration, and Presets tabs, shown in Figure 8.19. The Tone Curve tab can change the tonal values of your image. The Detail tab lets you adjust sharpness, luminance smoothing, and apply color noise reduction. The HSL/Grayscale tab offers controls for adjusting hue, saturation, and lightness and converting an image to black and white. Split Toning helps you colorize an image with sepia or cyanotype (blue) shades. The Lens Corrections tab has sliders to adjust for chromatic aberrations and vignetting. The Camera Calibration tab provides a way for calibrating the color corrections made in the Camera Raw plug-in. The Presets tab (not shown) is used to load settings you've stored for reuse.

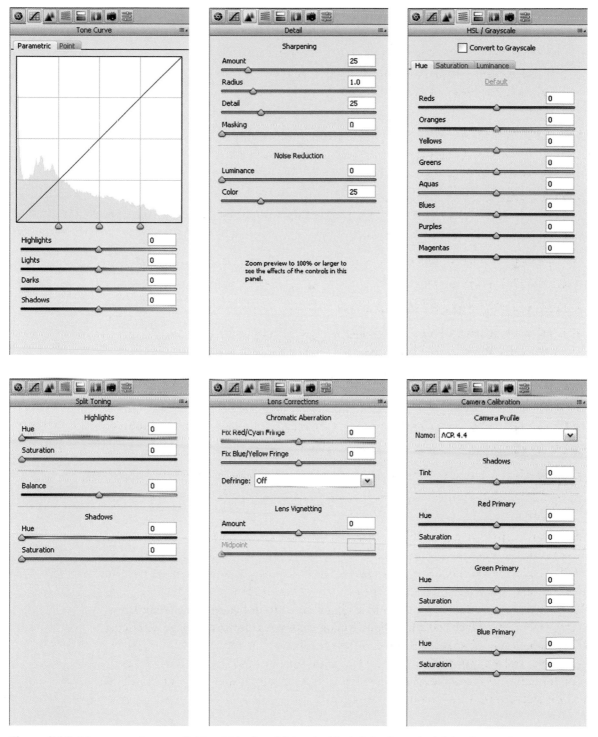

Figure 8.19 More controls are available within the additional tabbed dialog boxes in Adobe Camera Raw.

9

Canon EOS Rebel XS: Troubleshooting and Prevention

One of the nice things about modern electronic cameras like the Canon EOS Rebel XS is that they have fewer mechanical moving parts to fail, so they are less likely to "wear out." No film transport mechanism, no wind lever or motor drive, no complicated mechanical linkages from camera to lens to physically stop down the lens aperture. Instead, tiny, reliable motors are built into each lens (and you lose the use of only that lens should something fail), and one of the few major moving parts in the camera itself is a lightweight mirror (its small size one of the advantages of the XS's 1.6X crop factor) that flips up and down with each shot.

Of course, the camera also has a moving shutter that can fail, but the shutter is built rugged enough that you can expect it to last 100,000 shutter cycles or more. Unless you're shooting sports in Continuous mode day in and day out, the shutter on your XS is likely to last as long as you expect to use the camera.

The only other things on the camera that move are switches, dials, buttons, the flip-up electronic flash, and the door that slides open to allow you to remove and insert the memory card. Unless you're extraordinarily clumsy or unlucky and manage to give your built-in flash a good whack while it is in use, there's not a lot that can go wrong mechanically with your Rebel XS.

On the other hand, one of the chief drawbacks of modern electronic cameras is that they are modern *electronic* cameras. Your XS is fully dependent on two different batteries. Without them, the camera can't be used. There are numerous other electrical and electronic connections in the camera (many connected to those mechanical switches and dials), and components like the color LCD and top-panel status LCD that can potentially fail or suffer damage. The camera also relies on its "operating system," or *firmware*, which can be plagued by bugs that cause unexpected behavior. Luckily, electronic components are generally more reliable and trouble-free, especially when compared to their mechanical counterparts from the pre-electronic film camera days. (Film cameras of the last 10 to 20 years have had almost as many electronic features as digital cameras, but, believe it or not, there were whole generations of film cameras that had *no* electronics or batteries.)

Digital cameras have problems unique to their breed, too; the most troublesome being the need to clean the sensor of dust and grime periodically. This chapter will show you how to diagnose problems, fix some common ills, and, importantly, learn how to avoid them in the future.

Update Your Firmware

As I said, the firmware in your Rebel XS is the camera's operating system, which handles everything from menu display (including fonts, colors, and the actual entries themselves), what languages are available, and even support for specific devices and features. Upgrading the firmware to a new version makes it possible to add new features while fixing some of the bugs that sneak in. For example, one particularly useful firmware update for the 20D several years ago added the ability to use the WFT-E1 wireless file transmitter.

Sometimes firmware updates happen during product development; I received my Rebel XS a few weeks after it was introduced, and it already had firmware Version 1.0.3 installed. Official firmware for your XS is given a version number that you can view by turning the power on, pressing the Menu button, and scrolling to Firmware Ver. x.x.x in the Set-Up 3 menu. As I write this, the current version is 1.0.4, shown in Figure 9.1. The first number in the string represents the major release number, while the second and third represent less significant upgrades and minor tweaks, respectively. Theoretically, a camera should have a firmware version number of 1.0.0 when it is introduced, but vendors have been known to do some minor fixes during testing and unveil a camera with a 1.0.1 firmware designation (or even 1.0.3 in the case of the XS). If a given model is available long enough, as the EOS 20D was, it can evolve into significant upgrades, such as 2.0.3. Of course, camera vendors tend to issue fewer and fewer firmware updates for older products as they age, because, with time, virtually all of the "bugs" have been fixed, and adding new features is no longer practical.

Figure 9.1
You can view
the current
firmware ver-
sion in the Set-
Up 3 menu.

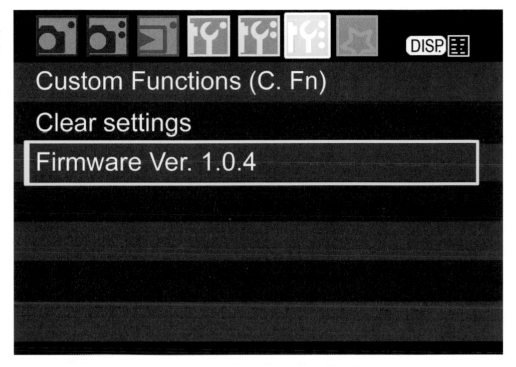

Figure 9.1 You can view the current firmware version in the Set-Up 3 menu.

Oddly enough, sometimes an update is so minor that it doesn't earn an upgraded number. When Canon introduced firmware version 1.0.4 for the EOS 30D, it discovered that some of the characters for Simplified Chinese and Traditional Chinese languages caused problems when displayed on the LCD monitor, and issued a *new* Version 1.0.4. It recommended installing this fixed firmware for anyone experiencing the problem, even if the user had already upgraded to Version 1.0.4.

Firmware upgrades are used most frequently to fix bugs in the software, and much less frequently to add or enhance features. For example, previous firmware upgrades for Canon cameras have mended things like incorrect color temperature reporting when using specific Canon Speedlites, or problems communicating with memory cards under certain conditions. The exact changes made to the firmware are generally spelled out in the firmware release announcement. You can examine the remedies provided and decide if a given firmware patch is important to you. If not, you can usually safely wait a while before going through the bother of upgrading your firmware—at least long enough for the early adopters to report whether the bug fixes have introduced new bugs of their own. Each new firmware release incorporates the changes from previous releases, so if you skip a minor upgrade you should have no problems.

Upgrading Your Firmware

If you're computer savvy, you might wonder how your Rebel XS is able to overwrite its own operating system—that is, how can the existing firmware be used to load the new version on top of itself? It's a little like lifting yourself by reaching down and pulling up on your bootstraps. Not ironically, that's almost exactly what happens: At your command (when you start the upgrade process), the XS shifts into a special mode in which it is no longer operating from its firmware but, rather, from a small piece of software called a *bootstrap loader*—a separate, protected software program that functions only at startup or when upgrading firmware. The loader's function is to look for firmware to

WARNING

Use a fully charged battery or Canon's optional ACK-E5 AC adapter kit to ensure that you'll have enough power to operate the camera for the entire upgrade. Moreover, you should not turn off the camera while your old firmware is being overwritten. Don't open the memory card door or do anything else that might disrupt operation of the XS while the firmware is being installed.

1. Download the firmware from Canon (you'll find it in the Downloads section of the Support portion of Canon's website) and place it on your computer's hard drive. The firmware is contained in a self-extracting file for either Windows or Mac OS. It will have a name such as XS00105.fir.

2. In your camera, format a memory card that's larger than 8MB and smaller than 2GB to ensure that the proper file system has been formatted onto the card. Choose Format from the Set-Up 1 menu, and initialize the card (make sure you don't have images you want to keep before you do this!).

3. You can copy the upgrade software to the card either using a memory card reader or by connecting the camera to your computer with a USB cable and using the EOS Utility application furnished with your camera.

4. Insert the memory card in the camera and then turn the camera on. Press Menu and scroll to Firmware Ver. x.x.x in the Set-Up 3 menu and press the Set button. Choose OK and press the Set button to begin loading the update program.

5. A final confirmation screen will appear. Press Set to confirm. The firmware will be updated.

6. When you see the completion screen, press the Set button to complete the process.

7. Turn off the Rebel XS, remove the AC adapter, if used, and replace the battery. Then turn the camera on to boot up your camera with the new firmware update.

8. Be sure to reformat the card before returning it to regular use to remove the firmware software.

launch or, when directed, to copy new firmware from a memory card to the internal memory space where the old firmware is located. Once the new firmware has replaced the old, you can turn your camera off and then on again, and the updated operating system will be loaded.

Because the loader software is small in size and limited in function, there are some restrictions on what it can do. For one thing, it recognizes only memory cards that have been formatted using an organizational system called FAT16 (which again, you might be familiar with if you're comfortable with hard disk technology). To ensure that the memory card is formatted using FAT16, you must upgrade using a memory card at least 8MB in size and no larger than 2GB, and then format the card in your camera. Memory cards that are smaller or larger might be formatted using a different FAT system (FAT12 or FAT32, respectively).

In addition, the loader software isn't set up to go hunting through your memory card for the firmware file. It looks only in the top or root directory of your card, so that's where you must copy the firmware you download. Once you've determined that a new firmware update is available for your camera and that you want to install it, just follow the steps listed on the previous page. (If you chicken out, any Canon Service Center can install the firmware upgrade for you.)

Protect Your LCD

The three-inch color LCD on the back of your Rebel XS almost seems like a target for banging, scratching, and other abuse. Fortunately, it's quite rugged, and a few errant knocks are unlikely to shatter the protective cover over the LCD, and scratches won't easily mar its surface. However, if you want to be on the safe side, there are a number of protective products you can purchase to keep your LCD safe—and, in some cases, make it a little easier to view. Here's a quick overview of your options.

- **Plastic overlays.** The simplest solution (although not always the cheapest) is to apply a plastic overlay sheet or "skin" cut to fit your LCD. These adhere either by static electricity or through a light adhesive coating that's even less clingy than stick-it notes. You can cut down overlays made for PDAs (although these can be pricey at up to $19.95 for a set of several sheets), or purchase overlays sold specifically for digital cameras. Vendors such as Hoodman (www.hoodmanusa.com) offer overlays of this type. These products will do a good job of shielding your XS's LCD screen from scratches and minor impacts, but will not offer much protection from a good whack.

- **Acrylic shields.** These scratch-resistant acrylic panels, laser cut to fit your camera perfectly, are my choice as the best protection solution, and what I use on my own XS. At about $6 each, they also happen to be the least expensive option as well. I get mine, shown in Figure 9.2, from a company called 'da Products (www.daproducts.com). They attach using strips of sticky adhesive that hold the panel flush and tight, but which allow the acrylic to be pried off and the adhesive removed easily if you want to remove or replace the shield. They don't attenuate your view of the LCD and are non-reflective enough for use under a variety of lighting conditions.

- **Flip-up hoods.** These protectors slip on using the flanges around your XS's eyepiece, and provide a cover that completely shields the LCD, but unfolds to provide a three-sided hood that allows viewing the LCD while minimizing the extraneous light falling on it and reducing contrast. They're sold for about $40 by Delkin and Hoodman. If you want to completely protect your LCD from hard knocks and need to view the screen outdoors in bright sunlight, there is nothing better. However, I have a couple problems with these devices. First, with the cover closed, you can't peek down after taking a shot to see what your image looks like during picture review. You must open the cap each time you want to look at the LCD. Moreover, with the hood unfolded, it's difficult to look through the viewfinder: Don't count on being able to use the viewfinder *and* the LCD at the same time with one of these hoods in place.

- **Magnifiers.** If you look hard enough, you should be able to find an LCD magnifier that fits over the monitor panel and provides a 2X magnification. These often strap on clumsily, and serve better as a way to get an enlarged view of the LCD than as protection. Hoodman and other suppliers offer these specialized devices.

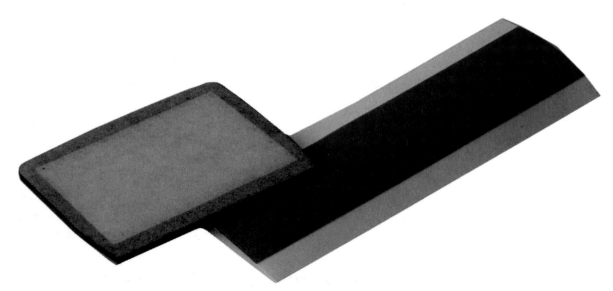

Figure 9.2 A tough acrylic shield, shown here with a piece of plastic containing a set of peel-off sticky strips to help it adhere to the camera, can protect your LCD from scratches.

Troubleshooting Memory Cards

Sometimes good memory cards go bad. Sometimes good photographers can treat their memory cards badly. It's possible that a memory card that works fine in one camera won't be recognized when inserted into another. In the worst case, you can have a card full of important photos and find that the card seems to be corrupted and you can't access any of them. Don't panic! If these scenarios sound horrific to you, there are lots of things you can do to prevent them from happening, and a variety of remedies available if they do occur. You'll want to take some time—before disaster strikes—to consider your options.

All Your Eggs in One Basket?

The debate about whether it's better to use one large memory card or several smaller ones has been going on since even before there were memory cards. I can remember when computer users wondered whether it was smarter to install a pair of 200MB (not *gigabyte*) hard drives in their computer, or if they should go for one of those new-fangled 500MB models. By the same token, a few years ago the user groups were full of proponents who insisted that you ought to use 128MB memory cards rather than the huge 512MB versions. Today, most of the arguments involve 4GB cards versus 2GB cards or 4GB cards versus 8GB cards, and I expect that as prices for 16GB SDHC memory cards continue to drop, they'll find their way into the debate as well.

Why all the fuss? Are 4GB memory cards more likely to fail than 2GB cards? Are you risking all your photos if you trust your images to a larger card? Isn't it better to use several smaller cards, so that if one fails you lose only half as many photos? Or, isn't it wiser to put all your photos onto one larger card, because the more cards you use, the better your odds of misplacing or damaging one and losing at least some pictures?

In the end, the "eggs in one basket" argument boils down to statistics, and how you happen to use your XS. The rationales can go both ways. If you have multiple smaller cards, you do increase your chances of something happening to one of them, so, arguably, you might be boosting the odds of losing some pictures. If all your images are important, the fact that you've lost 100 rather than 200 pictures isn't very comforting.

Also consider that the eggs/basket scenario assumes that the cards that are lost or damaged are always full. It's actually likely that your 4GB card might suffer a mishap when it's less than half full (indeed, it's more likely that a large card won't be completely filled before it's offloaded to a computer), so you really might not lose any more shots with a single 4GB card than with multiple 2GB cards.

If you shoot photojournalist-type pictures, you probably change memory cards when they're less than completely full in order to avoid the need to do so at a crucial moment. (When I shoot sports, my cards rarely reach 80 to 90 percent of capacity before I change them.) Using multiple smaller cards means you have to change them that more often, which can be a real pain when you're taking a lot of photos. As an example, if you use 1GB memory cards with a Rebel XS and shoot RAW+JPEG FINE, you may get only 43 pictures on the card. That's not much more than the capacity of a 36-exposure roll of film (remember those?). In my book, I prefer keeping all my eggs in one basket, and then making very sure that nothing happens to that basket.

There are only two really good reasons to justify limiting yourself to smaller memory cards when larger ones can be purchased at the same cost per gigabyte. One of them is when every single picture is precious to you, and the loss of any of them would be a disaster. If you're a wedding photographer, for example, and unlikely to be able to restage the nuptials if a memory card goes bad, you'll probably want to shoot no more pictures than you can afford to lose on a single card, and have an assistant ready to copy each card removed from the camera onto a backup hard drive or DVD onsite.

To be even safer, you'd want to alternate cameras or have a second photographer at least partially duplicating your coverage so your shots are distributed over several memory cards simultaneously. (Strictly speaking, the safest route of all is to spend some significant bucks on Canon's Wireless File Transmitter WFT-E3/WFT-E3A and a Canon EOS 50D to use it with, and beam the images over to a computer as you shoot them. Not very practical for a Rebel XS owner!) Gadget freaks might want to check out the Eye-Fi, a reasonably priced (about $129 for a 4GB card) Wi-Fi transmitting device embedded in an SD memory card. (www.eye.fi—yes, that URL is not a typo! The company's website is registered in Finland, even though it is headquartered in Mountain View, California.) It will transmit your images over an 802.11a/b/g wireless network, as you shoot them.

If none of these options are available to you, consider *interleaving* your shots. Say you don't shoot weddings, but you do go on vacation from time to time. Take 50 or so pictures on one card, or whatever number of images might fill about 25 percent of its capacity. Then, replace it with a different card and shoot about 25 percent of that card's available space. Repeat these steps with diligence (you'd have to be determined to go through this inconvenience), and, if you use four or more memory cards, you'll find your pictures from each location scattered among the different memory cards. If you lose or damage one, you'll still have *some* pictures from all the various stops on your trip on the other cards. That's more work than I like to do (I usually tote around a portable hard disk and copy the files to the drive as I go), but it's an option.

What Can Go Wrong?

There are lots of things that can go wrong with your memory card, but the ones that aren't caused by human stupidity are statistically very rare. Yes, a memory card's internal bit bin or controller can suddenly fail due to a manufacturing error or some inexplicable event caused by old age. However, if your memory card works for the first week or two that you own it, it should work forever. There's really not a lot that can wear out.

The typical memory card is rated for a Mean Time Between Failures of 1,000,000 hours of use. That's constant use 24/7 for more than 100 years! According to the manufacturers, they are good for 10,000 insertions in your camera, and should be able to retain their data (and that's without an external power source) for something on the order of 11 years. Of course, with the millions of memory cards in use, there are bound to be a few lemons here or there.

Given the reliability of solid-state memory, compared to magnetic memory, though, it's more likely that your memory card problems will stem from something that you do. Although they're not as tiny as the xD cards a few other digital SLRs use, Secure Digital memory cards are still small and easy to misplace if you're not careful. For that reason, it's a good idea to keep them in their original cases or a "card safe" offered by Gepe (www.gepecardsafe.com), Pelican (www.pelican.com), and others. Always placing your memory card in a case can provide protection from the second-most common mishap that befalls memory cards: the household laundry. If you slip a memory card in a pocket, rather than a case or your camera bag, often enough, sooner or later it's going to end up in the washing machine and probably the clothes dryer, too. There are plenty of reports of relieved digital camera owners who've laundered their memory cards and found they still worked fine, but it's not uncommon for such mistreatment to do some damage.

Memory cards can also be stomped on, accidentally bent, dropped into the ocean, chewed by pets, and otherwise rendered unusable in myriad ways. It's also remotely possible to force a card into your XS's memory card slot incorrectly if you're diligent enough, doing little damage to the card itself, but possibly damaging the camera internally, eliminating its ability to read or write to any memory card. I've never heard of this happening with a camera using SD cards, but don't discount the ingenuity of a determined fumble-fingers.

Or, if the card is formatted in your computer with a memory card reader, your XS may fail to recognize it. Occasionally, I've found that a memory card used in one camera would fail if used in a different camera (until I reformatted it in Windows, and then again in the camera). Every once in awhile, a card goes completely bad and—seemingly—can't be salvaged.

Another way to lose images is to do commonplace things with your memory card at an inopportune time. If you remove the card from the XS while the camera is writing images to the card, you'll lose any photos in the buffer and may damage the file structure of the card, making it difficult or impossible to retrieve the other pictures you've taken. The same thing can happen if you remove the memory card from your computer's card reader while the computer is writing to the card (say, to erase files you've already moved to your computer). You can avoid this by *not* using your computer to erase files on a memory card but, instead, always reformatting the card in your XS before you use it again.

What Can You Do?

Pay attention: If you're having problems, the *first* thing you should do is *stop* using that memory card. Don't take any more pictures. Don't do anything with the card until you've figured out what's wrong. Your second line of defense (your first line is to be sufficiently careful with your cards that you avoid problems in the first place) is to *do no harm* that hasn't already been done. Read the rest of this section and then, if necessary, decide on a course of action (such as using a data recovery service or software described later) before you risk damaging the data on your card further.

Now that you've calmed down, the first thing to check is whether you've actually inserted a card in the camera. If you've set the camera in the Shooting menu so that Shoot w/o card has been turned on, it's entirely possible (although not particularly plausible) that you've been snapping away with no memory card to store the pictures to, which can lead to massive disappointment later on. Of course, the No memory card message appears on the LCD when the camera is powered up, and it is superimposed on the review image after every shot, but maybe you're inattentive, aren't using picture review, or have purchased one of those LCD fold-up hoods mentioned earlier in this chapter. You can avoid all this by turning the Shoot w/o card feature off and leaving it off.

Things get more exciting when the card itself is put in jeopardy. If you lose a card, there's not a lot you can do other than take a picture of a similar card and print up some Have You Seen This Lost Flash Memory? flyers to post on utility poles all around town.

If all you care about is reusing the card, and have resigned yourself to losing the pictures, try reformatting the card in your camera. You may find that reformatting removes the corrupted data and restores your card to health. Sometimes I've had success reformatting a card in my computer using a memory card reader (this is normally a no-no because your operating system doesn't understand the needs of your XS), and *then* reformatting again in the camera.

If your memory card is not behaving properly, and you *do* want to recover your images, things get a little more complicated. If your pictures are very valuable, either to you or to others (for example, a wedding), you can always turn to professional data recovery firms. Be prepared to pay hundreds of dollars to get your pictures back, but these pros often do an amazing job. You wouldn't want them working on your memory card on behalf of the police if you'd tried to erase some incriminating pictures. There are many firms of this type, and I've never used them myself, so I can't offer a recommendation. Use a Google search to turn up a ton of them. I like RescuePro, which came free with one of my SanDisk memory cards. (See Figure 9.3.)

A more reasonable approach is to try special data recovery software you can install on your computer and attempt to resurrect your "lost" images yourself. They may not actually be gone completely. Perhaps your memory card's "table of contents" is jumbled, or only a few pictures are damaged in such a way that your camera and computer can't read some or any of the pictures on the card. Some of the available software was written specifically to reconstruct lost pictures, while other utilities are more general-purpose applications that can be used with any media, including floppy disks and hard disk drives. They have names like OnTrack, Photo Rescue 2, Digital Image Recovery, MediaRecover, Image Recall, and the aptly named Recover My Photos. You'll find a comprehensive list and links, as well as some picture-recovery tips at www.ultimateslr.com/memory-card-recovery.php.

Figure 9.3
Rescue software can salvage images that you think are corrupted beyond repair.

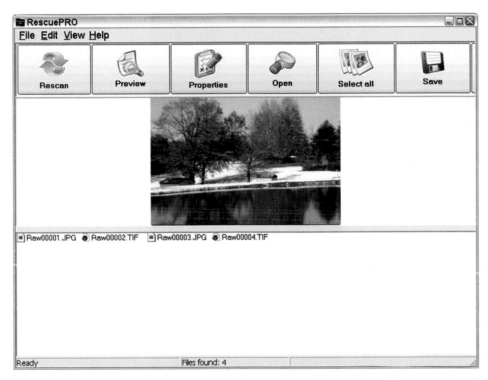

THE ULTIMATE IRONY

I recently purchased an 8GB Kingston memory card that was furnished with some nifty OnTrack data recovery software. The first thing I did was format the card to make sure it was OK. Then I hunted around for the free software, only to discover it was preloaded onto the memory card. I was supposed to copy the software to my computer before using the memory card for the first time.

Fortunately, I had the OnTrack software that would reverse my dumb move, so I could retrieve the software. No, wait. I *didn't* have the software I needed to recover the software I erased. I'd reformatted it to oblivion. Chalk this one up as either the ultimate irony or Stupid Author Trick #523.

> ## DIMINISHING RETURNS
>
> Usually, once you've recovered any images on a memory card, reformatted it, and returned it to service, it will function reliably for the rest of its useful life. However, if you find a particular card going bad more than once, you'll almost certainly want to stop using it forever. See if you can get it replaced by the manufacturer, if you can, but, in the case of memory card failures, the third time is never the charm.

Clean Your Sensor

There's no avoiding dust. No matter how careful you are, some of it is going to settle on your camera and on the mounts of your lenses, eventually making its way inside your camera to settle in the mirror chamber. As you take photos, the mirror flipping up and down causes the dust to become airborne and eventually make its way past the shutter curtain to come to rest on the anti-aliasing filter atop your sensor. There, dust and particles can show up in every single picture you take at a small enough aperture to bring the foreign matter into sharp focus. No matter how careful you are and how cleanly you work, eventually you will get some of this dust on your camera's sensor. Some say that CMOS sensors, like the one found in the Rebel XS, "attract" less dust than CCD sensors found in cameras from other vendors. But even the cleanest-working photographers using Canon cameras are far from immune.

Fortunately, one of the Rebel XS's most useful new features is the automatic sensor cleaning system that reduces or eliminates the need to clean your camera's sensor manually. As I mentioned in Chapter 3, Canon has applied anti-static coatings to the sensor and other portions of the camera body interior to counter charge build-ups that attract dust. A separate filter over the sensor vibrates ultrasonically each time the XS is powered on or off, shaking loose any dust.

Although the automatic sensor cleaning feature operates when you power the camera up or turn it off, you can activate it at any time. Choose Sensor Cleaning from the Set-Up 2 menu, and select Clean now. If you'd rather turn the feature on or off, choose Auto cleaning instead, and then choose either Enable or Disable with the Main dial. Press Set, then press the Menu button to return to the Set-Up 2 menu. (See Figure 9.4.)

If some dust does collect on your sensor, you can often map it out of your images (making it invisible) using software techniques with the Dust Delete Data feature in the Shooting Menu 2. Operation of this feature is described in Chapter 3. Of course, even with the Rebel XS's automatic sensor cleaning/dust resistance features, you may still be required to manually clean your sensor from time to time. This section explains the phenomenon and provides some tips on minimizing dust and eliminating it when it begins to affect your shots. I also cover this subject in my book *Digital SLR Pro Secrets*, with

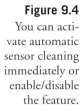

Figure 9.4
You can activate automatic sensor cleaning immediately or enable/disable the feature.

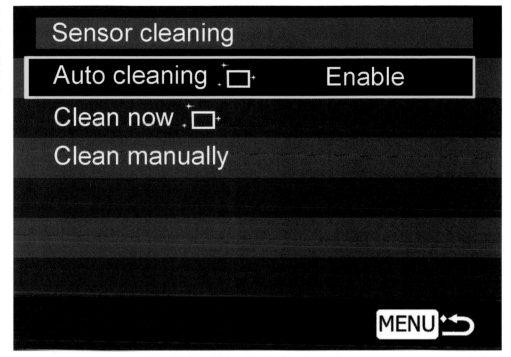

complete instructions for constructing your own sensor cleaning tools. However, I'll provide a condensed version of some of the information in that book, because sensor dust and sensor cleaning are two of the most contentious subjects Canon EOS Rebel XS owners have to deal with.

Dust the FAQs, Ma'am

Here are some of the most frequently asked questions about sensor dust issues.

Q. I see tiny specks in my viewfinder. Do I have dust on my sensor?

A. If you see sharp, well-defined specks, they are clinging to the underside of your focus screen and not on your sensor. They have absolutely no effect on your photographs, and are merely annoying or distracting.

Q. I can see dust on my mirror. How can I remove it?

A. Like focus-screen dust, any artifacts that have settled on your mirror won't affect your photos. You can often remove dust on the mirror or focus screen with a bulb air blower, which will loosen it and whisk it away. Stubborn dust on the focus screen can sometimes be gently flicked away with a soft brush designed for cleaning lenses. I don't recommend brushing the mirror or touching it in any way. The mirror is a special front-surface-silvered optical device (unlike conventional mirrors, which are silvered on the back side of a piece of glass or plastic) and can be easily scratched. If you can't blow off mirror dust, it's best to just forget about it. You can't see it in the viewfinder, anyway.

Q. I see a bright spot in the same place in all of my photos. Is that sensor dust?

A. You've probably got either a "hot" pixel or one that is permanently "stuck" due to a defect in the sensor. A hot pixel is one that shows up as a bright spot only during long exposures as the sensor warms. A pixel stuck in the "on" position always appears in the image. Both show up as bright red, green, or blue pixels, usually surrounded by a small cluster of other improperly illuminated pixels, caused by the camera's interpolating the hot or stuck pixel into its surroundings, as shown in Figure 9.5. A stuck pixel can also be permanently dark. Either kind is likely to show up when they contrast with plain, evenly colored areas of your image.

Finding one or two hot or stuck pixels in your sensor is unfortunately fairly common. They can be "removed" by telling the XS to ignore them through a simple process called *pixel mapping*. If the bad pixels become bothersome, Canon can remap your sensor's pixels with a quick trip to a service center.

Bad pixels can also show up on your camera's color LCD panel, but, unless they are abundant, the wisest course is to just ignore them.

Figure 9.5
A stuck pixel is surrounded by improperly interpolated pixels created by the XS's demosaicing algorithm.

Q. I see an irregular out-of-focus blob in the same place in my photos. Is that sensor dust?

A. Yes. Sensor contaminants can take the form of tiny spots, larger blobs, or even curvy lines if they are caused by minuscule fibers that have settled on the sensor. They'll appear out of focus because they aren't actually on the sensor surface but, rather, a fraction of a millimeter above it on the filter that covers the sensor. The smaller the f/stop used, the more in-focus the dust becomes. At large apertures, it may not be visible at all.

Q. I never see any dust on my sensor. What's all the fuss about?

A. Those who never have dust problems with their Rebel XS fall into one of four categories: those for whom the camera's automatic dust removal features are working well; those who seldom change their lenses and have clean working habits that minimize the amount of dust that invades their cameras in the first place; those who simply don't notice the dust (often because they don't shoot many macro photos or other pictures using the small f/stops that makes dust evident in their images); and those who are very, very lucky.

Identifying and Dealing with Dust

Sensor dust is less of a problem than it might be because it shows up only under certain circumstances. Indeed, you might have dust on your sensor right now and not be aware of it. The dust doesn't actually settle on the sensor itself, but, rather, on a protective filter a very tiny distance above the sensor, subjecting it to the phenomenon of *depth-of-focus*. Depth-of-focus is the distance the focal plane can be moved and still render an object in sharp focus. At f/2.8 to f/5.6 or even smaller, sensor dust, particularly if small, is likely to be outside the range of depth-of-focus and blur into an unnoticeable dot.

However, if you're shooting at f/16 to f/22 or smaller, those dust motes suddenly pop into focus. Forget about trying to spot them by peering directly at your sensor with the shutter open and the lens removed. The period at the end of this sentence, about .33mm in diameter, could block a group of pixels measuring 40 × 40 pixels (160 pixels in all!). Dust spots that are even smaller than that can easily show up in your images if you're shooting large, empty areas that are light colored. Dust motes are most likely to show up in the sky, as in Figure 9.6, or in white backgrounds of your seamless product shots and are less likely to be a problem in images that contain lots of dark areas and detail.

Figure 9.6
Only the dust spots in the sky are apparent in this shot.

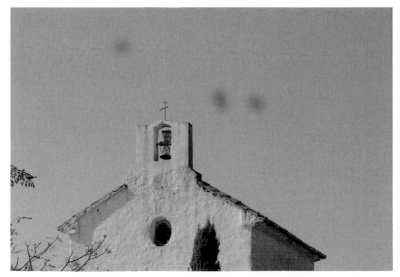

To see if you have dust on your sensor, take a few test shots of a plain, blank surface (such as a piece of paper or a cloudless sky) at small f/stops, such as f/22, and a few wide open. Open Photoshop, copy several shots into a single document in separate layers, then flip back and forth between layers to see if any spots you see are present in all layers. You may have to boost contrast and sharpness to make the dust easier to spot.

Avoiding Dust

Of course, the easiest way to protect your sensor from dust is to prevent it from settling on the sensor in the first place. Some Canon lenses come with rubberized seals around the lens mounts that help keep dust from infiltrating, but you'll find that dust will still find a way to get inside. Here are my stock tips for eliminating the problem before it begins.

- **Clean environment.** Avoid working in dusty areas if you can do so. Hah! Serious photographers will take this one with a grain of salt, because it usually makes sense to go where the pictures are. Only a few of us are so paranoid about sensor dust (considering that it is so easily removed) that we'll avoid moderately grimy locations just to protect something that is, when you get down to it, just a tool. If you find a great picture opportunity at a raging fire, during a sandstorm, or while surrounded by dust clouds, you might hesitate to take the picture, but, with a little caution (don't remove your lens in these situations, and clean the camera afterwards!) you can still shoot. However, it still makes sense to store your camera in a clean environment. One place cameras and lenses pick up a lot of dust is inside a camera bag. Clean your bag from time to time, and you can avoid problems.

- **Clean lenses.** There are a few paranoid types that avoid swapping lenses in order to minimize the chance of dust getting inside their cameras. It makes more sense just to use a blower or brush to dust off the rear lens mount of the replacement lens first, so you won't be introducing dust into your camera simply by attaching a new, dusty lens. Do this before you remove the lens from your camera, and then avoid stirring up dust before making the exchange.

- **Work fast.** Minimize the time your camera is lens-less and exposed to dust. That means having your replacement lens ready and dusted off, and a place to set down the old lens as soon as it is removed, so you can quickly attach the new lens.

- **Let gravity help you.** Face the camera downward when the lens is detached so any dust in the mirror box will tend to fall away from the sensor. Turn your back to any breezes, indoor forced air vents, fans, or other sources of dust to minimize infiltration.

- **Protect the lens you just removed.** Once you've attached the new lens, quickly put the end cap on the one you just removed to reduce the dust that might fall on it.

- **Clean out the vestibule.** From time to time, remove the lens while in a relatively dust-free environment and use a blower bulb like the one shown in Figure 9.7 (*not*

Figure 9.7

Use a robust air bulb like the Giottos Rockets for cleaning your sensor.

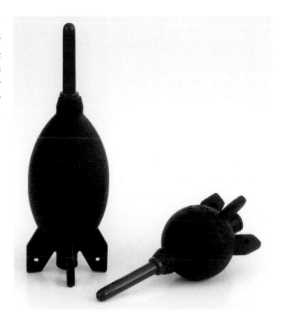

compressed air or a vacuum hose) to clean out the mirror box area. A blower bulb is generally safer than a can of compressed air, or a strong positive/negative airflow, which can tend to drive dust farther into nooks and crannies.

■ **Be prepared.** If you're embarking on an important shooting session, it's a good idea to clean your sensor *now*, rather than coming home with hundreds or thousands of images with dust spots caused by flecks that were sitting on your sensor before you even started. Before I left on my recent trip to Spain, I put both cameras I was taking through a rigid cleaning regimen, figuring they could remain dust-free for a measly 10 days. I even left my bulky blower bulb at home. It was a big mistake, but my intentions were good. I now have a smaller version of the Giottos Rocket Blower, and *that* goes with me everywhere.

■ **Clone out existing spots in your image editor.** Photoshop and other editors have a Clone tool or Healing Brush you can use to copy pixels from surrounding areas over the dust spot or dead pixel. This process can be tedious, especially if you have lots of dust spots and/or lots of images to be corrected. The advantage is that this sort of manual fix-it probably will do the least damage to the rest of your photo. Only the cloned pixels will be affected.

■ **Use filtration in your image editor.** A semi-smart filter like Photoshop's Dust & Scratches filter can remove dust and other artifacts by selectively blurring areas that the plug-in decides represent dust spots. This method can work well if you have many dust spots because you won't need to patch them manually. However, any automated method like this has the possibility of blurring areas of your image that you didn't intend to soften.

Sensor Cleaning

Those new to the concept of sensor dust actually hesitate before deciding to clean their cameras themselves. Isn't it a better idea to pack up your XS and send it to a Canon service center so their crack technical staff can do the job for you? Or, at the very least, shouldn't you let the friendly folks at your local camera store do it?

Of course, if you choose to let someone else clean your sensor, they will be using methods that are more or less identical to the techniques you would use yourself. None of these techniques are difficult, and the only difference between their cleaning and your cleaning is that they might have done it dozens or hundreds of times. If you're careful, you can do just as good a job.

Of course vendors like Canon won't tell you this, but it's not because they don't trust you. It's not that difficult for a real goofball to mess up his camera by hurrying or taking a shortcut. Perhaps the person uses the "Bulb" method of holding the shutter open and a finger slips, allowing the shutter curtain to close on top of a sensor cleaning brush. Or, someone tries to clean the sensor using masking tape, and ends up with goo all over its surface. If Canon recommended *any* method that's mildly risky, someone would do it wrong, and then the company would face lawsuits from those who'd contend they did it exactly in the way the vendor suggested, so the ruined camera is not their fault. If you visit Canon's website, you'll find this recommendation: "If the image sensor needs cleaning, we recommend having it cleaned at a Canon service center, as it is a very delicate component."

You can see that vendors like Canon tend to be conservative in their recommendations, and, in doing so, make it seem as if sensor cleaning is more daunting and dangerous than it really is. Some vendors recommend only dust-off cleaning, through the use of reasonably gentle blasts of air, while condemning more serious scrubbing with swabs and cleaning fluids. However, these cleaning kits for the exact types of cleaning they recommended against are for sale in Japan only, where, apparently, your average photographer is more dexterous than those of us in the rest of the world. These kits are similar to those used by official repair staff to clean your sensor if you decide to send your camera in for a dust-up.

As I noted, sensors can be affected by dust particles that are much smaller than you might be able to spot visually on the surface of your lens. The filters that cover sensors tend to be fairly hard compared to optical glass. Cleaning the 22.2mm × 14.8mm sensor in your Canon XS within the tight confines of the mirror box can call for a steady hand and careful touch. If your sensor's filter becomes scratched through inept cleaning, you can't simply remove it yourself and replace it with a new one.

There are four basic kinds of cleaning processes that can be used to remove dusty and sticky stuff that settles on your dSLR's sensor. All of these must be performed with the shutter locked open. I'll describe these methods and provide instructions for locking the shutter later in this section.

- **Air cleaning.** This process involves squirting blasts of air inside your camera with the shutter locked open. This works well for dust that's not clinging stubbornly to your sensor.

- **Brushing.** A soft, very fine brush is passed across the surface of the sensor's filter, dislodging mildly persistent dust particles and sweeping them off the imager.

- **Liquid cleaning.** A soft swab dipped in a cleaning solution such as ethanol is used to wipe the sensor filter, removing more obstinate particles.

- **Tape cleaning.** There are some who get good results by applying a special form of tape to the surface of their sensor. When the tape is peeled off, all the dust goes with it. Supposedly. I'd be remiss if I didn't point out right now that this form of cleaning is somewhat controversial; the other three methods are much more widely accepted. Now that Canon has equipped the front-sensor filter with a special anti-dust coating, I wouldn't chance damaging that coating by using any kind of adhesive tape.

Placing the Shutter in the Locked and Fully Upright Position for Landing

Make sure you're using a fully charged battery or the optional AC Adapter Kit ACK-E5.

1. Remove the lens from the camera and then turn the camera on.

2. Set the Rebel XS to any one of the Creative Zone exposure modes. The shutter cannot be locked open in any of the Basic Zone modes.

3. You'll find the Clean Manually menu choice in the Set-Up 2 menu under Sensor Cleaning. Press the Set button.

4. Select OK and press Set again. The mirror will flip up and the shutter will open.

5. Use one of the methods described below to remove dust and grime from your sensor. Be careful not to accidentally switch the power off or open the memory card or battery compartment doors as you work. If that happens, the shutter may be damaged if it closes on your cleaning tool.

6. When you're finished, turn the power off, replace your lens, and switch your camera back on.

Air Cleaning

Your first attempts at cleaning your sensor should always involve gentle blasts of air. Many times, you'll be able to dislodge dust spots, which will fall off the sensor and, with luck, out of the mirror box. Attempt one of the other methods only when you've already tried air cleaning and it didn't remove all the dust.

Here are some tips for doing air cleaning:

- **Use a clean, powerful air bulb.** Your best bet is bulb cleaners designed for the job, like the Giottos Rocket shown in Figure 9.7. Smaller bulbs, like those air bulbs with a brush attached sometimes sold for lens cleaning or weak nasal aspirators may not provide sufficient air or a strong enough blast to do much good.

- **Hold the Rebel XS upside down.** Then look up into the mirror box as you squirt your air blasts, increasing the odds that gravity will help pull the expelled dust downward, away from the sensor. You may have to use some imagination in positioning yourself. (And don't let dust fall into your eye!)

- **Never use air canisters.** The propellant inside these cans can permanently coat your sensor if you tilt the can while spraying. It's not worth taking a chance.

- **Avoid air compressors.** Super-strong blasts of air are likely to force dust under the sensor filter.

Brush Cleaning

If your dust is a little more stubborn and can't be dislodged by air alone, you may want to try a brush, charged with static electricity, which can pick off dust spots by electrical attraction. One good, but expensive, option is the Sensor Brush sold at www.visible-dust.com. A cheaper version can be purchased at www.copperhillimages.com. Whichever brand you choose, get a 16mm version, like the one shown in Figure 9.8, which can be stroked across the long dimension of your XS's sensor.

Ordinary artist's brushes are much too coarse and stiff and have fibers that are tangled or can come loose and settle on your sensor. A good sensor brush's fibers are resilient and described as "thinner than a human hair." Moreover, the brush has a wooden handle that reduces the risk of static sparks. Check out my *Digital SLR Pro Secrets* book if you want to make a sensor brush (or sensor swabs) yourself.

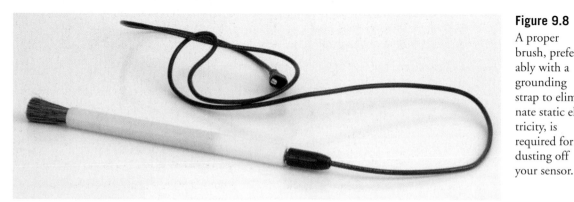

Figure 9.8
A proper brush, preferably with a grounding strap to eliminate static electricity, is required for dusting off your sensor.

Brush cleaning is done with a dry brush by gently swiping the surface of the sensor filter with the tip. The dust particles are attracted to the brush particles and cling to them. You should clean the brush with compressed air before and after each use, and store it in an appropriate air-tight container between applications to keep it clean and dust-free. Although these special brushes are expensive, one should last you a long time.

Liquid Cleaning

Unfortunately, you'll often encounter really stubborn dust spots that can't be removed with a blast of air or flick of a brush. These spots may be combined with some grease or a liquid that causes them to stick to the sensor filter's surface. In such cases, liquid cleaning with a swab may be necessary. During my first clumsy attempts to clean my own sensor, I accidentally got my blower bulb tip too close to the sensor, and some sort of deposit from the tip of the bulb ended up on the sensor. I panicked until I discovered that liquid cleaning did a good job of removing whatever it was that took up residence on my sensor.

You can make your own swabs out of pieces of plastic (some use fast food restaurant knives, with the tip cut at an angle to the proper size) covered with a soft cloth or Pec-Pad, as shown in Figures 9.9 and 9.10. However, if you've got the bucks to spend, you can't go wrong with good-quality commercial sensor cleaning swabs, such as those sold by Photographic Solutions, Inc. (www.photosol.com/swabproduct.htm).

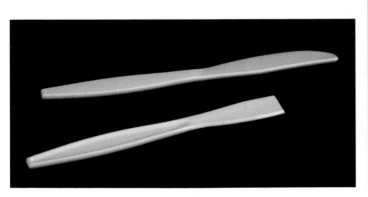

Figure 9.9 You can make your own sensor swab from a plastic knife that's been truncated.

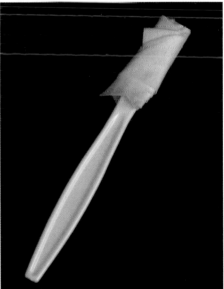

Figure 9.10 Carefully wrap a Pec-Pad around the swab.

You want a sturdy swab that won't bend or break so you can apply gentle pressure to the swab as you wipe the sensor surface. Use the swab with methanol (as pure as you can get it, particularly medical grade; other ingredients can leave a residue), or the Eclipse solution also sold by Photographic Solutions. Eclipse 2 (see Figure 9.11) is actually quite a bit purer than even medical-grade methanol. A couple drops of solution should be enough, unless you have a spot that's extremely difficult to remove. In that case, you may need to use extra solution on the swab to help "soak" the dirt off.

Once you overcome your nervousness at touching your XS's sensor, the process is easy. You'll wipe continuously with the swab in one direction, then flip it over and wipe in the other direction. Figure 9.12 shows a swab being lowered past the lens mount down to the sensor. You need to completely wipe the entire surface; otherwise, you may end up depositing the dust you collect at the far end of your stroke. Wipe; don't rub.

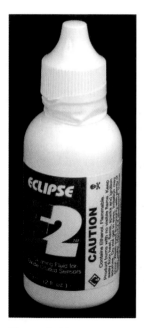

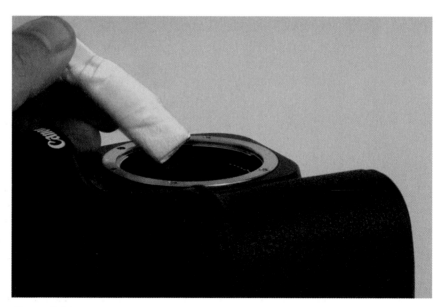

Figure 9.11 Pure Eclipse solution makes the best sensor cleaning liquid.

Figure 9.12 Carefully swab off the dust.

If you want a close-up look at your sensor to make sure the dust has been removed, you can pay $50-$100 for a special sensor "microscope" with an illuminator. Or, you can do like I do and work with a plain old Carson MiniBrite PO-25 illuminated 3X magnifier, as seen in Figure 9.13. (Older packaging and ads may call this a 2X magnifier, but it's actually a 3X unit.) It has a built-in LED and, held a few inches from the lens mount with the lens removed from your XS, provides a sharp, close-up view of the sensor, with enough contrast to reveal any dust that remains.

Figure 9.13

An illuminated magnifier like this Carson MiniBrite PO-25 can be used as a 'scope to view your sensor.

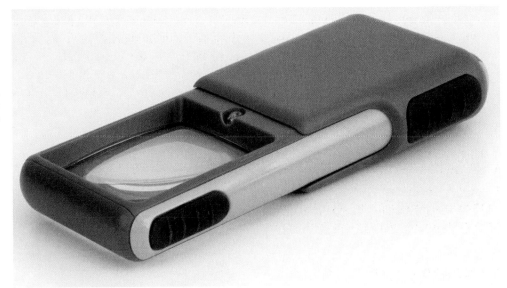

Tape Cleaning

There are people who absolutely swear by the tape method of sensor cleaning. The concept seems totally wacky, and I have never tried it personally, so I can't say with certainty that it either does or does not work. In the interest of completeness, I'm including it here. I can't give you a recommendation, so if you have problems, please don't blame me. The Rebel XS is still too new to have generated any reports of users accidentally damaging the anti-dust coating on the sensor filter using this method.

Tape cleaning works by applying a layer of Scotch Brand Magic Tape to the sensor. This is a minimally sticky tape that some of the tape-cleaning proponents claim contains no adhesive. I did check this out with 3M, and can say that Magic Tape certainly *does* contain an adhesive. The question is whether the adhesive comes off when you peel back the tape, taking any dust spots on your sensor with it. The folks who love this method claim there is no residue. There have been reports from those who don't like the method that residue is left behind. This is all anecdotal evidence, so you're pretty much on your own in making the decision whether to try out the tape cleaning method.

Glossary

Here are some terms you might encounter while reading this book or working with your Canon EOS Rebel XS.

additive primary colors The red, green, and blue hues that are used alone or in combinations to create all other colors that you capture with a digital camera, view on a computer monitor, or work with in an image-editing program, such as Photoshop. *See also* CMYK color model.

A-DEP A Creative Zone mode that analyzes your scene and attempts to choose an f/stop and focus distance that will allow all the important subjects to be in sharp focus.

Adobe RGB One of two color space choices offered by the Canon EOS Rebel XS. Adobe RGB is an expanded color space useful for commercial and professional printing, and it can reproduce a larger number of colors. Canon recommends against using this color space if your images will be displayed primarily on your computer screen or output by your personal printer. *See also* sRGB.

AEB Automatic exposure bracketing takes a series of pictures at different exposure increments to improve the chances of producing one picture that is perfectly exposed.

ambient lighting Diffuse, non-directional lighting that doesn't appear to come from a specific source but, rather, bounces off walls, ceilings, and other objects in the scene when a picture is taken.

analog/digital converter The electronics built into a camera that convert the analog information captured by the XS's sensor into digital bits that can be stored as an image bitmap.

angle of view The area of a scene that a lens can capture, determined by the focal length of the lens. Lenses with a shorter focal length have a wider angle of view than lenses with a longer focal length.

anti-alias A process that smoothes the look of rough edges in images (called *jaggies* or *staircasing*) by adding partially transparent pixels along the boundaries of diagonal lines that are merged into a smoother line by our eyes. *See also* jaggies.

Aperture Preferred A camera setting that allows you to specify the lens opening or f/stop that you want to use, with the camera selecting the required shutter speed automatically based on its light-meter reading. This setting is represented by the abbreviation Av on the XS's Mode dial. *See also* Shutter Preferred.

artifact A type of noise in an image, or an unintentional image component produced in error by a digital camera during processing, usually caused by the JPEG compression process in digital cameras.

aspect ratio The proportions of an image as printed, displayed on a monitor, or captured by a digital camera.

autofocus A camera setting that allows the Canon EOS Rebel XS to choose the correct focus distance for you, based on the contrast of an image (the image will be at maximum contrast when in sharp focus). The camera can be set for One-Shot (generically known as *Single Autofocus,* in which the lens is not focused until the shutter release is partially depressed), AI Servo (known as *Continuous Autofocus,* in which the lens refocuses constantly as you frame and reframe the image), or AI AF, which allows the camera to switch back and forth between One-Shot and AI Servo based on subject movement.

backlighting A lighting effect produced when the main light source is located behind the subject. Backlighting can be used to create a silhouette effect, or to illuminate translucent objects. *See also* front lighting and sidelighting.

barrel distortion A lens defect that causes straight lines at the top or side edges of an image to bow outward into a barrel shape. *See also* pincushion distortion.

Basic Zone modes The EOS XS's automated shooting modes, such as Landscape and Sports, that select lens opening, shutter speed, exposure, and other parameters for you.

blooming An image distortion caused when a photosite in an image sensor has absorbed all the photons it can handle so that additional photons reaching that pixel overflow to affect surrounding pixels, producing unwanted brightness and overexposure around the edges of objects.

blur To soften an image or part of an image by throwing it out of focus, or by allowing it to become soft due to subject or camera motion. Blur can also be applied in an image-editing program.

bokeh A term derived from the Japanese word for blur, which describes the aesthetic qualities of the out-of-focus parts of an image. Some lenses produce "good" bokeh and others offer "bad" bokeh. Some lenses produce uniformly illuminated out-of-focus discs. Others produce a disc that has a bright edge and a dark center, producing a "doughnut" effect, which is the worst from a bokeh standpoint. Lenses that generate a bright center that fades to a darker edge are favored, because their bokeh allows the circle of confusion to blend more smoothly with the surroundings. The bokeh characteristics of a lens are most important when you're using selective focus (say, when shooting a portrait) to deemphasize the background, or when shallow depth-of-field is a given because you're working with a macro lens, with a long telephoto, or with a wide-open aperture. *See also* circle of confusion.

bounce lighting Light bounced off a reflector, including ceiling and walls, to provide a soft, natural-looking light.

bracketing Taking a series of photographs of the same subject at different settings, including exposure and white balance, to help ensure that one setting will be the correct one. The Canon EOS Rebel XS allows you to choose the order in which bracketed settings are applied, or bracket sequence.

buffer The digital camera's internal memory where an image is stored immediately after it is taken until it can be written to the camera's non-volatile (semi-permanent) memory or a memory card.

burst mode The digital camera's equivalent of the film camera's motor drive, used to take multiple shots within a short period of time, with each shot stored in a memory buffer temporarily before writing it to the media.

calibration A process used to correct for the differences in the output of a printer or monitor when compared to the original image. Once you've calibrated your scanner, monitor, and/or your image editor, the images you see on the screen more closely represent what you'll get from your printer, even though calibration is never perfect.

Camera Raw A plug in included with Photoshop and Photoshop Elements that can manipulate the unprocessed images captured by digital cameras, such as the Canon EOS Rebel XS's .CR2 files. The latest versions of this module can also work with JPEG and TIFF images.

camera shake Movement of the camera, aggravated by slower shutter speeds, which produces a blurred image. You can minimize camera shake by using a lens with built-in image stabilization.

CCD *See* charge-coupled device (CCD).

center-weighted meter A light-measuring device that emphasizes the area in the middle of the frame when calculating the correct exposure for an image. *See also* spot meter.

charge-coupled device (CCD) A type of solid-state sensor that captures the image used in scanners and digital cameras. *See also* complementary metal oxide semiconductor (CMOS).

chromatic aberration An image defect, often seen as green or purple fringing around the edges of an object, caused by a lens failing to focus all colors of a light source at the same point. *See also* fringing.

circle of confusion A term applied to the fuzzy discs produced when a point of light is out of focus. The circle of confusion is not a fixed size. The viewing distance and amount of enlargement of the image determine whether we see a particular spot on the image as a point or as a disc.

close-up lens A lens add-on that allows you to take pictures at a distance that is less than the closest-focusing distance of the lens alone.

CMOS *See* complementary metal-oxide semiconductor (CMOS).

CMYK color model A way of defining all possible colors in percentages of cyan, magenta, yellow, and frequently, black. (K represents black, to differentiate it from blue in the RGB color model.) Black is added to improve rendition of shadow detail. CMYK is commonly used for printing (both on press and with your inkjet or laser color printer).

color correction Changing the relative amounts of color in an image to produce a desired effect, typically a more accurate representation of those colors. Color correction can fix faulty color balance in the original image, or compensate for the deficiencies of the inks used to reproduce the image.

complementary metal-oxide semiconductor (CMOS) A method for manufacturing a type of solid-state sensor that captures an image; used in scanners and digital cameras such as those from Canon.

compression Reducing the size of a file by encoding using fewer bits of information to represent the original. Some compression schemes, such as JPEG, operate by discarding some image information, while others, such as RAW, preserve all the detail in the original, discarding only redundant data.

Continuous Autofocus An automatic focusing setting (AI Servo) in which the camera constantly refocuses the image as you frame the picture. This setting is often the best choice for moving subjects. *See also* Single Autofocus.

contrast The range between the lightest and darkest tones in an image. A high-contrast image is one in which the shades fall at the extremes of the range between white and black. In a low-contrast image, the tones are closer together.

Creative Zone modes The EOS XS's semi-automated and manual shooting modes, including A-DEP, Program, Aperture Priority, Shutter Priority, and Manual, that allow you to select shutter speed and/or aperture yourself, with the camera calculating the proper exposure based on those parameters.

Custom Functions A group of 13 different settings you can make to specify how the EOS XS behaves, such as the function of certain controls, electronic flash features, and other customizable attributes.

dedicated flash An electronic flash unit, such as the Canon 580EX II Speedlight, designed to work with the automatic exposure features of a specific camera.

depth-of-field A distance range in a photograph in which all included portions of an image are at least acceptably sharp. With the Canon EOS Rebel XS, you can see the available depth-of-field at the taking aperture by pressing the Depth-of-Field Preview button, or estimate the range by viewing the depth-of-field scale found on many lenses.

diaphragm An adjustable component, similar to the iris in the human eye, that can open and close to provide specific-sized lens openings, or f/stops, and thus control the amount of light reaching the sensor or film.

diffuse lighting Soft, low-contrast lighting.

digital processing chip A solid-state device found in digital cameras (such as the EOS XS's DIGIC III module) that's in charge of applying the image algorithms to the raw picture data prior to storage on the memory card.

diopter A value used to represent the magnification power of a lens, calculated as the reciprocal of a lens's focal length (in meters). Diopters are most often used to represent the optical correction used in a viewfinder to adjust for limitations of the photographer's eyesight, and to describe the magnification of a close-up lens attachment.

equivalent focal length A digital camera's focal length translated into the corresponding values for a 35mm film camera. This value can be calculated for lenses used with the Canon EOS Rebel XS by multiplying by 1.6.

Evaluative metering One system of exposure calculation used by the EOS XS that looks at many different segments of an image to determine the brightest and darkest portions.

exchangeable image file format (Exif) Developed to standardize the exchange of image data between hardware devices and software. A variation on JPEG, Exif is used by most digital cameras, and includes information such as the date and time a photo was taken, the camera settings, resolution, amount of compression, and other data.

Exif *See* exchangeable image file format (Exif).

exposure The amount of light allowed to reach the film or sensor, determined by the intensity of the light, the amount admitted by the iris of the lens, the length of time determined by the shutter speed, and the ISO sensitivity setting for the sensor.

exposure values (EV) EV settings are a way of adding or decreasing exposure without the need to reference f/stops or shutter speeds. For example, if you tell your camera to add +1EV, it will provide twice as much exposure by using a larger f/stop, slower shutter speed, or both.

fill lighting In photography, lighting is used to illuminate shadows. Reflectors or additional incandescent lighting or electronic flash can be used to brighten shadows. One common technique for outdoors is to use the camera's flash as a fill.

filter In photography, a device that fits over the lens, changing the light in some way. In image editing, a feature that changes the pixels in an image to produce blurring, sharpening, and other special effects. Photoshop includes several interesting filter effects, including Lens Blur and Photo Filters.

flash sync The timing mechanism that ensures that an internal or external electronic flash fires at the correct time during the exposure cycle. A digital SLR's flash sync speed is the highest shutter speed that can be used with flash, ordinarily 1/200th of a second with the Canon EOS Rebel XS. *See also* front-curtain sync and rear-curtain sync.

focal length The distance between the film and the optical center of the lens when the lens is focused on infinity, usually measured in millimeters.

focal plane An imaginary line, perpendicular to the optical access, that passes through the focal point forming a plane of sharp focus when the lens is set at infinity. A focal plane indicator is etched into the Canon EOS Rebel XS at the left side of the pentaprism.

focus tracking The ability of the automatic focus feature of a camera to change focus as the distance between the subject and the camera changes. One type of focus tracking is *predictive,* in which the mechanism anticipates the motion of the object being focused on, and adjusts the focus to suit.

format To erase a memory card and prepare it to accept files.

fringing A chromatic aberration that produces fringes of color around the edges of subjects, caused by a lens's inability to focus the various wavelengths of light onto the same spot. Purple fringing is especially troublesome with backlit images.

front-curtain sync (first-curtain sync) The default kind of electronic flash synchronization technique, originally associated with focal plane shutters, which consists of a traveling set of curtains, including a *front curtain* (1st Curtain in the XS's menus), which opens to reveal the film or sensor, and a *rear curtain* (2nd Curtain in the XS's menus), which follows at a distance determined by shutter speed to conceal the film or sensor at the conclusion of the exposure. For a flash picture to be taken, the entire sensor must be exposed at one time to the brief flash exposure, so the image is exposed after the front curtain has reached the other side of the focal plane, but before the rear curtain begins to move. Front-curtain sync causes the flash to fire at the beginning of this period when the shutter is completely open, in the instant that the first curtain of the focal plane shutter finishes its movement across the film or sensor plane. With slow shutter speeds, this feature can create a blur effect from the ambient light, showing as patterns that follow a moving subject, with the subject shown sharply frozen at the beginning of the blur trail. *See also* rear-curtain sync.

front lighting Illumination that comes from the direction of the camera. *See also* backlighting and sidelighting.

f/stop The relative size of the lens aperture, which helps determine both exposure and depth-of-field. The larger the f/stop number, the smaller the f/stop itself.

graduated filter A lens attachment with variable density or color from one edge to another. A graduated neutral density filter, for example, can be oriented so the neutral density portion is concentrated at the top of the lens's view with the less dense or clear portion at the bottom, thus reducing the amount of light from a very bright sky while not interfering with the exposure of the landscape in the foreground. Graduated filters can also be split into several color sections to provide a color gradient between portions of the image.

gray card A piece of cardboard or other material with a standardized 18-percent reflectance. Gray cards can be used as a reference for determining correct exposure or for setting white balance.

high contrast A wide range of density in a print, negative, or other image.

highlights The brightest parts of an image containing detail.

histogram A kind of chart showing the relationship of tones in an image using a series of 256 vertical bars, one for each brightness level. A histogram chart, such as the one the Canon EOS Rebel XS can display during picture review, typically looks like a curve with one or more slopes and peaks, depending on how many highlight, midtone, and shadow tones are present in the image. The XS can also display separate histograms for the red, green, and blue channels of an image.

hot shoe A mount on top of a camera used to hold an electronic flash, while providing an electrical connection between the flash and the camera.

hyperfocal distance A point of focus where everything from half that distance to infinity appears to be acceptably sharp. For example, if your lens has a hyperfocal distance of four feet, everything from two feet to infinity would be sharp. The hyperfocal distance varies by the lens and the aperture in use. If you know you'll be making a grab shot without warning, sometimes it is useful to turn off your camera's automatic focus, and set the lens to infinity, or, better yet, the hyperfocal distance. Then, you can snap off a quick picture without having to wait for the lag that occurs with most digital cameras as their autofocus locks in.

image rotation A feature that senses whether a picture was taken in horizontal or vertical orientation. That information is embedded in the picture file so that the camera and compatible software applications can automatically display the image in the correct orientation.

image stabilization A technology that compensates for camera shake, usually by adjusting the position of the camera sensor or lens elements in response to movements of the camera.

incident light Light falling on a surface.

International Organization for Standardization (ISO) A governing body that provides standards used to represent film speed, or the equivalent sensitivity of a digital camera's sensor. Digital camera sensitivity is expressed in ISO settings.

interpolation A technique digital cameras, scanners, and image editors use to create new pixels required whenever you resize or change the resolution of an image based on the values of surrounding pixels. Devices such as scanners and digital cameras can use interpolation to create pixels in addition to those actually captured, thereby increasing the apparent resolution or color information in an image.

ISO *See* International Organization for Standardization (ISO).

jaggies Staircasing effect of lines, most easily seen at large magnifications, that are not perfectly horizontal or vertical, caused by pixels that are too large to represent the line accurately. *See also* anti-alias.

JPEG A file "lossy" format (short for Joint Photographic Experts Group) that supports 24-bit color and reduces file sizes by selectively discarding image data. Digital cameras generally use JPEG compression to pack more images onto memory cards. You can select how much compression is used (and, therefore, how much information is thrown away) by selecting from among the Standard, Fine, Super Fine, or other quality settings offered by your camera. *See also* RAW.

Kelvin (K) A unit of measure based on the absolute temperature scale in which absolute zero is zero; it's used to describe the color of continuous-spectrum light sources and applied when setting white balance. For example, daylight has a color temperature of about 5,500K, and a tungsten lamp has a temperature of about 3,400K.

lag time The interval between when the shutter is pressed and when the picture is actually taken. During that span, the camera may be automatically focusing and calculating exposure. With digital SLRs like the Canon EOS Rebel XS, lag time is generally very short; with non-dSLRs, the elapsed time easily can be one second or more.

latitude The range of camera exposure that produces acceptable images with a particular digital sensor or film.

lens flare A feature of conventional photography that is both a bane and a creative outlet. It is an effect produced by the reflection of light internally among elements of an optical lens. Bright light sources within or just outside the field of view cause lens flare. Flare can be reduced by the use of coatings on the lens elements or with the use of lens hoods. Photographers sometimes use the effect as a creative technique, and Photoshop includes a filter that lets you add lens flare at your whim.

lighting ratio The proportional relationship between the amount of light falling on the subject from the main light and other lights, expressed in a ratio, such as 3:1.

Live View The ability of some Canon cameras, including the Rebel XS, to provide a real-time preview image, as seen by the sensor, on the rear-panel color LCD, achieved by flipping up the mirror and opening the shutter.

lossless compression An image-compression scheme, such as TIFF, that preserves all image detail. When the image is decompressed, it is identical to the original version.

lossy compression An image-compression scheme, such as JPEG, that creates smaller files by discarding image information, which can affect image quality.

macro lens A lens that provides continuous focusing from infinity to extreme close-ups, often to a reproduction ratio of 1:2 (half life-size) or 1:1 (life-size).

maximum burst The number of frames that can be exposed at the current settings until the buffer fills.

midtones Parts of an image with tones of an intermediate value, usually in the 25 to 75 percent brightness range. Many image-editing features allow you to manipulate midtones independently from the highlights and shadows.

mirror lock-up The ability of the XS to flip up its mirror to reduce vibration prior to taking the photo and to allow access to the sensor for cleaning.

neutral color A color in which red, green, and blue are present in equal amounts, producing a gray.

neutral density filter A gray camera filter that reduces the amount of light entering the camera without affecting the colors.

noise In an image, pixels with randomly distributed color values. Noise in digital photographs tends to be the product of low-light conditions and long exposures, particularly when you've set your camera to an ISO rating higher than ISO 800.

noise reduction A technology used to cut down on the amount of random information in a digital picture, usually caused by long exposures at increased sensitivity ratings. In the Canon EOS Rebel XS, noise reduction is automatically applied for long exposures, and it involves the camera automatically taking a second blank/dark exposure at the same settings that contain only noise, and then using the blank photo's information to cancel out the noise in the original picture. Although the process is very quick, it does double the amount of time required to take the photo.

normal lens A lens that makes the image in a photograph appear in a perspective that is like that of the original scene, typically with a field of view of roughly 45 degrees.

overexposure A condition in which too much light reaches the film or sensor, producing a dense negative or a very bright/light print, slide, or digital image.

pincushion distortion A type of lens distortion in which lines at the top and side edges of an image are bent inward, producing an effect that looks like a pincushion. *See also* barrel distortion.

polarizing filter A filter that forces light, which normally vibrates in all directions, to vibrate only in a single plane, reducing or removing the specular reflections from the surface of objects.

RAW An image file format, such as the CR2 format in the Canon EOS Rebel XS, which includes all the unprocessed information captured by the camera after conversion to digital form. RAW files are very large compared to JPEG files and must be processed by a special program such as Canon Digital Photo Pro or Adobe's Camera Raw filter after being downloaded from the camera.

rear-curtain sync (second-curtain sync) An optional kind of electronic flash synchronization technique, originally associated with focal plane shutters, which consists of a traveling set of curtains, including a *front (first) curtain* (which opens to reveal the film or sensor) and a *rear (second) curtain* (which follows at a distance determined by shutter speed to conceal the film or sensor at the conclusion of the exposure). For a flash picture to be taken, the entire sensor must be exposed at one time to the brief flash exposure, so the image is exposed after the front curtain has reached the other side of the focal plane, but before the rear curtain begins to move. Rear-curtain sync causes the flash to fire at the end of the exposure, a fraction of an instant before the second or rear curtain of the focal plane shutter begins to move. With slow shutter speeds, this feature can create a blur effect from the ambient light, showing as patterns that follow a moving subject with the subject shown sharply frozen at the end of the blur trail. If you were shooting a photo of The Flash, the superhero would appear sharp, with a ghostly trail behind him. *See also* front-curtain sync (first-curtain sync).

red-eye An effect from flash photography that appears to make a person's eyes glow red, or an animal's yellow or green. It's caused by light bouncing from the retina of the eye and is most pronounced in dim illumination (when the irises are wide open) and when the electronic flash is close to the lens and, therefore, prone to reflect directly back. Image editors can fix red-eye through cloning other pixels over the offending red or orange ones.

RGB color A color model that represents the three colors—red, green, and blue—used by devices such as scanners or monitors to reproduce color. Photoshop works in RGB mode by default, and even displays CMYK images by converting them to RGB.

saturation The purity of color; the amount by which a pure color is diluted with white or gray.

selective focus Choosing a lens opening that produces a shallow depth-of-field. Usually this is used to isolate a subject in portraits, close-ups, and other types of images, by causing most other elements in the scene to be blurred.

self-timer A mechanism that delays the opening of the shutter for some seconds after the release has been operated.

sensitivity A measure of the degree of response of a film or sensor to light, measured using the ISO setting.

shadow The darkest part of an image, represented on a digital image by pixels with low numeric values.

sharpening Increasing the apparent sharpness of an image by boosting the contrast between adjacent pixels that form an edge.

shutter In a conventional film camera, the shutter is a mechanism consisting of blades, a curtain, a plate, or some other movable cover that controls the time during which light reaches the film. Digital cameras may use actual mechanical shutters for the slower shutter speeds (less than 1/200th second) and an electronic shutter for higher speeds.

Shutter Preferred An exposure mode, represented by the letters Tv (Time Value) on the XS's Mode dial, in which you set the shutter speed and the camera determines the appropriate f/stop. *See also* Aperture Preferred.

sidelighting Applying illumination from the left or right sides of the camera. *See also* backlighting and front lighting.

slave unit An accessory flash unit that supplements the main flash, usually triggered electronically when the slave senses the light output by the main unit, through radio waves, or through a pre-burst emitted by the camera's main flash unit.

slow sync An electronic flash synchronizing method that uses a slow shutter speed so that ambient light is recorded by the camera in addition to the electronic flash illumination. This allows the background to receive more exposure for a more realistic effect.

specular highlight Bright spots in an image caused by reflection of light sources.

spot meter An exposure system that concentrates on a small area in the image, represented by the circle in the center of the EOS XS's viewfinder. *See also* center-weighted meter.

sRGB One of two color space choices available with the Canon EOS Rebel XS. The sRGB setting is recommended for images that will be output locally on the user's own printer, as this color space matches that of the typical inkjet printer and a properly calibrated monitor fairly closely. *See also* Adobe RGB.

subtractive primary colors Cyan, magenta, and yellow, which are the printing inks that theoretically absorb all color and produce black. In practice, however, they generate a muddy brown, so black is added to preserve detail (especially in shadows). The combination of the three colors and black is referred to as CMYK. (K represents black, to differentiate it from blue in the RGB model.)

time exposure A picture taken by leaving the shutter open for a long period, usually more than one second. The camera is generally locked down with a tripod to prevent blur during the long exposure.

through-the-lens (TTL) A system of providing viewing and exposure calculation through the actual lens taking the picture.

tungsten light Light from ordinary room lamps and ceiling fixtures, as opposed to fluorescent illumination.

underexposure A condition in which too little light reaches the film or sensor, producing a thin negative, a dark slide, a muddy-looking print, or a dark digital image.

unsharp masking The process for increasing the contrast between adjacent pixels in an image, increasing sharpness, especially around edges.

vignetting Dark corners of an image, often produced by using a lens hood that is too small for the field of view, a lens that does not completely fill the image frame, or generated artificially using image-editing techniques.

white balance The adjustment of a digital camera to the color temperature of the light source. Interior illumination is relatively red; outdoor light is relatively blue. Digital cameras like the EOS XS set correct white balance automatically or let you do it through menus. Image editors can often do some color correction of images that were exposed using the wrong white balance setting, especially when working with RAW files that contain the information originally captured by the camera before white balance was applied.

Index